Howard Marchitello's study of narrative techniques in Renaissance discourse analyzes imaginative conjunctions of literary texts, such as those
by Shakespeare and Thomas Browne, with developments in scientific and
technical writing. In *Narrative and meaning in early modern England* he
explores the relationship between a range of early modern discourses, such
as cartography, anatomy, and travel writing, and the developing sense of
the importance of narrative in producing meaning. Narrative was used in
the Renaissance as both a mode of discourse and an epistemology; it produced knowledge, but also dictated how that knowledge should be understood. Marchitello uses a wide range of cultural documents to illustrate
the importance of narrative in constructing the Renaissance understanding of time and identity. By highlighting the inherent textual element in
imaginative and scientific discourses, his study also evaluates a range of
contemporary critical practices and explores their relation to narrative
and the production of meaning.

Cambridge Studies in Renaissance Literature and Culture 20

Narrative and meaning in early modern England

Cambridge Studies in Renaissance Literature and Culture

General editor
STEPHEN ORGEL
Jackson Eli Reynolds Professor of Humanities, Stanford University

Editorial board
Anne Barton, *University of Cambridge*
Jonathan Dollimore, *University of Sussex*
Marjorie Garber, *Harvard University*
Jonathan Goldberg, *Duke University*
Nancy Vickers, *University of Southern California*

Since the 1970s there has been a broad and vital reinterpretation of the nature of literary texts, a move away from formalism to a sense of literature as an aspect of social, economic, political and cultural history. While the earliest New Historicist work was criticized for a narrow and anecdotal view of history, it also served as an important stimulus for poststructuralist, feminist, Marxist and psychoanalytical work, which in turn has increasingly informed and redirected it. Recent writing on the nature of representation, the historical construction of gender and of the concept of identity itself, on theatre as a political and economic phenomenon and on the ideologies of art generally, reveals the breadth of the field. Cambridge Studies in Renaissance Literature and Culture is designed to offer historically oriented studies of Renaissance literature and theatre which make use of the insights afforded by theoretical perspectives. The view of history envisioned is above all a view of our own history, a reading of the Renaissance for and from our own time.

Recent titles include

Knowledge, discovery and imagination in early modern Europe: from trivium to quadrivium.
TIMOTHY J. REISS, New York University

The project of prose in early modern Europe and the New World
edited by ELIZABETH FOWLER, Yale University, and ROLAND GREENE, University of Oregon

The marketplace of print: pamphlets and the public sphere in early modern England
ALEXANDRA HALASZ, Dartmouth College

Courtly letters in the age of Henry VIII: literary culture and the arts of deceit
SETH LERER, Stanford University

A complete list of books in the series is given at the end of the volume

Narrative and meaning in early modern England

Browne's skull and other histories

Howard Marchitello

Texas A&M University

PUBLISHED BY THE PRESS SYNDICATE OF THE UNIVERSITY OF CAMBRIDGE
The Pitt Building, Trumpington Street, Cambridge CB2 1RP, United Kingdom

CAMBRIDGE UNIVERSITY PRESS
The Edinburgh Building, Cambridge CB2 2RU, United Kingdom
40 West 20th Street, New York, NY 10011–4211, USA
10 Stamford Road, Oakleigh, Melbourne 3166, Australia

First published 1997

Printed in the United Kingdom at the University Press, Cambridge

Typeset in 10/12 Monotype Times [SE]

A catalogue record for this book is available from the British Library

Library of Congress cataloguing in publication data

Marchitello, Howard.
    Narrative and meaning in early modern England: Browne's skull and
other histories / Howard Marchitello.
        p.   cm. – (Cambridge studies in Renaissance literature and
culture; 20)
    Includes bibliographical references and index.
    ISBN 0 521 58025 0 (hardback)
    1. English literature – Early modern, 1500–1700 – History and
criticism.   2. Literature and science – England – History – 17th
century.   3. Literature and science – England – History – 16th century.
4. Shakespeare, William, 1564–1616 – Technique.   5. Browne, Thomas,
Sir, 1605–1682 – Technique.   6. Meaning (Philosophy) in literature.
7. Narration (Rhetoric)   8. Renaissance – England.   I. Title.
II. Series.
PR438.S35M37   1997
820.9'23–dc21   96–49143   CIP

ISBN 0 521 58025 0 hardback

PR438
.S35
M37
1997

For Lynne

When the bones of King *Arthur* were digged up, the old *Race* might think, they beheld therein some Originals of themselves; Unto these of our Urnes none here can pretend relation, and can only behold the Reliques of those persons, who in their life giving the Laws unto their predecessors, after long obscurity, now lye at their mercies. But remembring the early civility they brought upon these Countreys, and forgetting long passed mischiefs; We mercifully preserve their bones, and pisse not upon their ashes.

(Sir Thomas Browne, *Hydriotaphia, Urne-Buriall*)

Contents

Illustrations

Acknowledgments

I wish to thank the following publishers for permission to use revised material from previously published articles: "Vesalius's *Fabrica* and Shakespeare's *Othello*: Anatomy, Gender and the Narrative Production of Meaning," *Criticism* 35 (Fall 1993), pp. 529–58. Used by permission of Wayne State University Press. "Political Maps: The Production of Chorography and Cartography in Early Modern England," in *Cultural Artifacts and the Production of Meaning: The Page, the Image, and the Body*, ed. Margaret J.M. Ezell and Katherine O'Brien O'Keeffe (University of Michigan Press, 1994), pp. 13–40. Used by permission of the University of Michigan Press (with special thanks to LeAnn Fields). "(Dis)embodied Letters in *The Merchant of Venice*: Writing, Editing, History," *English Literary History* 62 (1995), pp. 237–65. Used by permission of the Johns Hopkins University Press.

In the writing of this book I have benefited from the generosity and expertise of many people. I would like to acknowledge their kindness and support and thank them for their invaluable help. To begin, some of my debts are historical: thanks to my parents, Howard and Jane Marchitell, for support and sacrifices on my behalf too numerous to calculate; thanks to James Seibel, for his patience and understanding early on; to Leslie A. Fiedler, whose ideas create whole worlds of possibilities. Thanks also to Barbara J. Bono and Jim Swan.

In recent years I have been most fortunate in my friends and colleagues, many of whom read early versions of the following chapters and offered insightful criticisms and helpful advice: David E. Johnson has been constant in his friendship and I – and this book – have benefited from his careful reading and suggestions. Jeffrey N. Cox has helped this book throughout the various stages of its development; with his intelligent and sensitive reading – and friendly conversation – he has greatly enriched this project. My thanks also to Larry J. Reynolds, whose prudent – and sometimes skeptical – readings have helped me avoid a sometimes embarrassing excess.

I have also benefited from institutional support at Texas A&M

University. The head of my department, J. Lawrence Mitchell, has been generous in his support of my work – particularly regarding various reductions in my teaching load over the past several years. I would also like to thank the Dean of the College of Liberal Arts at Texas A&M, Woodrow Jones, Jr., for the receipt of a Faculty Enhancement Grant which allowed me free time to work on this book.

I am also indebted to the Interdisciplinary Group for Historical Literary Study (IGHLS) at Texas A&M. This group of scholars and friends has engendered an exciting intellectual community in which I have been very fortunate to work – and to play – throughout the time I worked on this book. I can scarcely imagine having undertaken this project without the IGHLS colloquia, lectures, conferences, and day-to-day interactions with this outstanding group of people; I especially thank Larry J. Reynolds, Jeffrey N. Cox, Margaret Ezell, Katherine O'Brien O'Keeffe, Lynne Vallone, James Rosenheim, and Mary Ann O'Farrell. I have also received generous support from IGHLS in the form of research grants between 1991 and 1995 that helped generate release time for research and writing.

I would also like to offer my thanks to my editor at Cambridge, Josie Dixon, for her many kindnesses to me throughout this entire process. And my sincere thanks to Stephen Orgel who, in addition to being one of our preeminent critics of early modern England, happens also to be a wonderfully warm and generous man.

I have reserved for last my most profound thanks – that which I owe to my family. To my wonderful children, Max and Rosalie Vallone Marchitello, I owe the great thanks due to children who for years have agreed to share me – and some of our precious time – with a writing project they have been kind enough to tolerate good-naturedly. From them I have learned much about generosity, selflessness, and the nature of unconditional love. Finally, to my wife, Lynne Vallone: critic, scholar, friend, and my most valued reader. Her unselfish assistance and astute insights have benefited me and this book immeasurably. Without her loving and learned participation this book would be a poorer thing indeed: *i miei più sentiti ringraziamenti*.

Introduction: narrationalities

I am dead, Horatio.   (*Hamlet*)

I will begin with an ending (even though now I *end* this book – the process of its writing – with a *beginning*: this introduction; but I will come back to this): Hamlet's "I am dead, Horatio."[1] Here, near the end of the play, as he speaks what sound like (but are not, of course) his final words, Hamlet has never been more like his father. Or, he has never been more like the *ghost* of his father ("I am thy father's spirit"), announcing and professing his own death: "I am dead." This is precisely Hamlet's point: he wants both to be his father and to be his own ghost. On the one hand, we can consider this dilemma of "self" to be Hamlet's critical problem. His is a divided identity, Jonathan Goldberg argues, "divided by the doubling of his 'own' text and the ghost's. Hamlet's being is the fold in that single cloth . . . The depth of his interiority is his foldedness within a text that enfolds him and which cannot be unfolded."[2] On the other hand, we can see that Hamlet's dilemma has equally to do with temporality. Or, his notion of identity is itself understood in relation to temporality: in desiring to be his father *and* to be his own ghost, Hamlet desires to be both that which *precedes* and that which *follows* himself. To be *and* not to be: Hamlet's desire to negotiate a particular temporalization that in *Specters of Marx*[3] Jacques Derrida calls "anachrony" or "untimeliness" – perhaps the central problematic of Hamlet/*Hamlet*: "The time is out of joint. O cursed spite,/ That ever I was born to set it right" (1.5.196–97).

I nearly wrote "Hamlet's *desperate* desire –" just now. But in fact Hamlet's desire to negotiate anachrony cannot be considered desperate any more than can his prophecy ("O my prophetic soul!") – "I am dead" – be called impossible. It surprises, to be sure, but perhaps it should not. Not only because by declaring "I am dead" Hamlet reproduces the father (the Ghost commands Hamlet, "Remember me," even as Hamlet requires Horatio to retell *his* story: "If thou didst ever hold me in thy heart,/ Absent thee from felicity awhile,/ And in this harsh world draw thy breath in pain/ To tell my story" [5.2.351–54]), but also because, as Derrida has argued of

1

Poe's story, "The Facts in the Case of M. Valdemar," being able to say "I am dead" may well be "the condition for a true act of language."[4] Derrida's argument concerning the foundational nature of "I am dead" has explicitly to do with the matter of temporalization and its relation to writing: the decisive absence of the "*present* of discursive time" serves to render the "time of the *énonciation*" the result of "a movement of temporalization which . . . makes the present something complicated, the product of an original synthesis which also means that the present cannot be produced except in the movement which retains and effaces it."[5] In *Specters of Marx*, the figure for such a simultaneous temporal retention and effacement of the present is the specter, the ghost – and the ghost of Hamlet's father, in particular, is of special importance to Derrida's discussion.

In a moment I am going to suggest that another way to think of such temporal retention and effacement of the present *for which the object is knowledge or meaning* is a certain deployment of narrative: what I call in this book *narrationality*. But first, I would like briefly to trace Derrida's discussion of the ghost or specter or (the term I prefer) the *revenant*: *that which comes back*. I wish to do so first because *Specters of Marx* offers powerful ways in which to think the ghost and to think temporalization. But also because *Hamlet* stands both as a kind of pre-text for my book and – at the same time – as its ghost. In order, then – under the sign of anachrony, of untimeliness – properly to preface here at the beginning (*as if* prophetically) the pages that follow, it is necessary that *Hamlet* should come (back) to us once again.

As Derrida rightly observes, *Hamlet* commences with the anticipation of the apparition – or, more precisely, with the "imminence of a *re*-apparition, but a reapparition of the specter as apparition *for the first time in the play*. The spirit of the father is going to come back . . . but here, at the beginning of the play, he comes back, so to speak, for the first time" (*Specters* 4). This double nature of the apparition – repetition *and* first time – is the critical (and defining) characteristic of the "hauntology" Derrida seeks to theorize.[6] At the same time, the figure of the *revenant* is itself characterized by two unique (and enabling) "properties."[7] The first of these has to do with its "paradoxical incorporation"; the specter (like Poe's Valdemar) is positioned precisely between life and death – or, better yet, between body and no body: "a certain phenomenal and carnal form of the spirit" (*Specters* 6).[8]

The second "property" of the *revenant* concerns temporality (which the specter disrupts or disjoins) and arises specifically from the "nothing visible" of the specter: it is a "Thing" (Derrida will later call it "the Thing or the Athing called ghost" [*Specters* 138]) that is "invisible between its apparitions, when it reappears" but that nevertheless "looks at us and sees us not see it even when it is there." This is crucial: the "spectral asymmetry" that results from our relentless visibility and the specter's equally insistent invisible visibility "interrupts all specularity. It de-synchronizes, it recalls us to anachrony."[9] For Derrida, this disjuncture of time – the "non-contemporaneity of the present time with itself" (*Specters* 24–25) – is not to be lamented, but rather recognized – along with its correlative injunction "to set it right" – as the very ground for our *ethical* action in the world.[10]

By virtue of his birth into a world subsequently corrupted (Hamlet laments having been *destined* to set time right – "that ever I was born to set it right"), Hamlet exists in a world in which justice, if it comes at all, comes – as a consequence of the "spectral anteriority of the crime" – only as an *effect* of vengeance. But even in the face of this, Derrida asks, is it not yet possible "[to] yearn for a justice . . . removed from the fatality of vengeance? Better than removed: infinitely foreign, heterogeneous at its source?" (*Specters* 21). It is disjuncture, then, that "opens up the infinite asymmetry of the relation to the other" (*Specters* 22):

> Beyond right, and still more beyond juridicism, beyond morality, and still more beyond moralism, does not justice as relation to the other suppose on the contrary the irreducible excess of a disjointure or an anachrony . . . some "out of joint" dislocation in Being and in time itself, a disjointure that, in always risking the evil, expropriation, and injustice (*adikia*) against which there is no calculable insurance, would alone be able to *do justice* or to *render justice* to the other as other?
>
> (*Specters* 27)

In this "interpretation" (as Derrida calls it) of disjuncture or disjointure "would be played out the relation of deconstruction to the possibility of justice," and, what is the same thing, "the relation of deconstruction . . . to what must (without debt and without duty) be rendered to the singularity of the other, to his or her absolute *precedence* or to his or her absolute *previousness*, to the heterogeneity of a *pre-*" (*Specters* 27–28).

For Derrida, what I have tried to mark here as the ways in which *Specters of Marx* stages a thinking of the ghost/*revenant*, of temporality, and of justice, serves as a point of departure for a discussion of Marx and the specters of Marx in this moment of the "new international" – a discussion in which *Hamlet* is less at stake, less strictly in focus, though nevertheless "present" (as always) spectrally: Derrida confesses, "I cannot hear 'since Marx,' since Marx, without hearing, like Marx, 'since Shakespeare'" (*Specters* 17). But for me – and for the book I am (after the fact, of course) *beginning* – this thinking of the *revenant* and of temporality (untimeliness) that depends, on the one hand, upon the retention and effacement of the present, and leads, on the other hand, to "the heterogeneity of a *pre-*," and of justice, marks an approximation of the concerns of this book. In a manner of speaking, this study shares a similar interest in what Derrida characterizes as the attempt to think history:

a certain deconstructive procedure . . . consisted from the outset in putting into question the onto-theo- but also archeo-teleological concept of history – in Hegel, Marx, or even in the epochal thinking of Heidegger. Not in order to oppose it with an end of history or an anhistoricity, but, on the contrary, in order to show that this onto-theo-archeo-teleology locks up, neutralizes, and finally cancels historicity. It was then a matter of thinking another historicity – not a new history or still less a "new historicism," but another opening of event-ness as historicity that permitted one not to renounce, but on the contrary to open up access to an affirmative thinking of the messianic and emancipatory promise as promise: as *promise* and not as onto-theological or teleo-eschatological program or design. (*Specters* 74–75)

Where for Derrida the retention and effacement of the present serve ultimately for a staging of the inadequacy of ontology, I address what I will call *narrationality* – the retention and effacement of the present *for which the object is knowledge or meaning* – in a variety of early modern cultural practices. Narrationality is, in effect, narrative gone wrong. While narrationality (or, the narrational) shares certain characteristics with narrative – narrationality proceeds, for example, on the model of chronology; its production of meaning depends upon the identification (or creation) of plot; and it tends to *moralize* meaning – it is nevertheless distinct from narrative (as a rhetorical model or strategy) not only in its ambition, but also in its uses, its effects, its methodologies, and in its essential relation to its discursive objects: narrationality takes the "products" of narrative as the primary *objects* of its epistemology. It is in this way that narrationality manifests effects of "non-contemporaneity of the present time with itself." In other words, I intend the term "narrationality" to access the ideational and, simultaneously, the ideological significance of narrative not merely as a mode of discourse but as an epistemology. To speak of narrationality is, then, to invoke a set of issues that arises within given attempts to construct meaning out of non-meaning. This non-meaning may take any of a number of forms, such as the appearance of chaos in a given discursive field or the observation of so-called raw data (or the appearance of the dead bodies that litter the stage at the conclusion of *Hamlet*). Meaning, for its part, can therefore also take a variety of forms: the sudden emergence of order out of chaos, the organization of data into useful information (or the promissory offering of the conventional plot of a revenge tragedy to explain Hamlet's death). But this system of meaning I have just described itself arises narrationally, and its terms are always implicitly bracketed by a pair of quotation marks so that, for instance, "chaos" is understood not so much as a state of nature but rather as a discursive field whose narrative of meaning has yet to be explicitly articulated. This narrative, however, is already in place and is thereby able to construct the very concept of "order" against which "chaos" is subsequently defined. Or: "data" and "information" become terms applied to the objects of investigation (whether historical or scientific) though their status is not a matter of their nature but instead a function of the very "meaning" toward which the inquiry is tending. No object in the world – not Hamlet's corpse, nor the body more generally – can stand phenomenologically as "data" or "information" until that object has already been appropriated by a meaning that then *anachronistically* produces the object as "datum" or "information." Following Roland Barthes, we can say that there are no such things as facts; it is always necessary that there should first be a "meaning" in order that there can be "facts."[11]

Narrationality's founding act is this presupposition of meaning; it declares the world to be saturated with meaning that is in every instance narrative in nature: Hamlet's death simply cannot be "chance" (as he calls it) but must have a specific and, most importantly, *knowable* meaning; it is this "meaning" that is then used to produce substantiating evidence. This is the essential process of the narrational – the narrative production of meaning. Narrationality seeks a renegotiation of temporality: by way of the narrative – which is always by definition *historiographical* in nature, its object always lost, and its method, therefore, always allegedly reconstructive of absence – the narrational would secure meaning even (or, especially) in the face of loss, absence and death. At its core, narrationality – like historiographical discourses such as literary and cultural criticism – is inevitably about death for it is against death that narrative seeks to effect its temporal work. Derrida refers to this as the work of *mourning*: "It consists always in attempting to ontologize remains, to make them present, in the first place by *identifying* the bodily remains and by *localizing* the dead" (*Specters* 9).[12] So Hamlet writes his narrative – first, "I am dead," and then the corresponding and supposedly compensatory production of Horatio as (his) historiographer. And critics write narrative, just as I have written mine. *In the end* (to invoke that most terrifying of narrative's linguistic formulations), we write because we (otherwise) die.

In this book I take up several important instances of the deployment of the narrational across a wide range of cultural practices in early modern English culture: medical anatomy, textual production, cartography, New World discourse, and the emergent processes of artifaction in seventeenth-century natural science. In each of these practices we can detect the operations of the narrational and trace the stages in the narrative production of meaning. In each instance the particular strategies of investigation are determined, in part, by the objects of the investigation; the anatomical body, say, or the curiosities of the New World seem to demand

or even create their own methodologies, but in every instance the informing epistemological model is the same: the analytical, technological and
systematic inquiry into natural facts – dissected human bodies, textual
detail, topographical space, New World discoveries, the objects of natural
science – leads to an immediate apprehension of the "real." In this regard,
the cultural and discursive practices I examine in this book all *appear* to
eschew narrative: Vesalius, for example, in his great work the *Fabrica*,
explicitly repudiates the inherited anatomical teachings of classical medical
theory – including Galen's revered texts – precisely for their fanciful narrative understanding of human and comparative anatomy and replaces
Galenic theory with what he refers to as a practice of the hands – the
systematic dissection of human bodies by the teachers and students of
anatomy. Vesalius claims to redeem anatomy from its fallen state in which
it has come to be regarded more as a doctrine than as a science, and he does
so by clearing away superstition, conventional wisdom and inherited
dogma. In their place he will offer to the eyes of students of anatomy the
body "itself." But this idea is also a fanciful one. Or, to be more precise, this
idea, too, proceeds along lines articulated by narrative – in this case the narrative of intellectual revolution cast as an epic generational change.
Moreover, faith in a transparent meaningfulness of the body constitutes a
mark of the narrational.

That Vesalius should imagine himself to be engaged in the revolutionary
work of stripping away layers of accumulated narrative in his pursuit of
knowledge while all along merely replacing new narratives for old is not
surprising. Together with the programmatic presupposition of meaning,
narrationality is also, and immediately, dedicated to the staging of its own
apparent disappearance. Any claim to unmediated access to the thing-itself
– the textual, the topographical, the curious, etc. – is specious: no object can
be accessed except through a process of artifaction that places the thing-in-
itself within a signifying narrative. We may think we have the thing-itself
when we identify a textual error (chapter 2), for example, or when we quantify characteristics of the land in cartography (chapter 3), of the New World
in travel narratives (chapter 4), of the body (chapters 1 and 5) within
various technologies and sciences, but all that we can be said to possess is
another narrative. This is the tyranny of narrationality.

The following chapters, then, examine the narrative production of
meaning in these early modern cultural practices. At the same time, their
objective is also to examine our own critical and theoretical practices that
are brought to bear on these discourses, and examine their own relation to
the narrational. In our own historical moment, which Lyotard describes as
characterized by an "incredulity toward metanarrative,"[13] we indeed have
become suspicious of theories and critical practices that are underwritten

by an epistemology of transcendence, and as writers and critics we have begun to turn to various theoretical strategies that promise to discard narrative (and metanarrative) – practices such as textual materialism, Foucauldian archaeology, body criticism, and new historicism. Part of the work of the chapters that follow will be to offer some discussion of the success of these claims – the degree to which new historicism, for instance, escapes the liabilities of the *grands récits* of narrative historiography it justifiably finds so problematic.

Chapter 1 begins by exploring the significance of skepticism in two types of early modern theater – the anatomical theater of Vesalius and the public theater of Shakespeare – and the crucial issue for both posed by skepticism occasioned by a human body seemingly reluctant to yield readily its semiological meaning. *Othello* and the *Fabrica* offer similar and related responses to moments of profound skepticism that center on the figure of the female body, as each turns to the narrationality of scientific visualism (ocularity) to produce epistemological certainty.

The narrational theory of visualism critiqued in chapter 1 is underwritten by the notion of immanence – that meaning is itself immanent in the body and that texts can demonstrate and make this textual immanence manifest. The second chapter continues the inquiry into this discourse of immanence and textuality as represented in the complex relation between letters and informing notions of textual embodiment in *The Merchant of Venice* – Shylock's belief, for example, in the pound of flesh embodied in his bond, or Portia's fate (and the expression of her dead father's will) embodied in the texts and icons that the three caskets hold. This chapter offers a discussion of the philosophy and practices of traditional textual criticism by which we *narrationally* produce such notions as authorial intent and the eclectic text – a set of practices, I argue, that is itself determined by the same sort of narrationality as governs the faith in textual embodiment deployed in *Merchant*.

Textual immanence takes a related form in early modern cartography. Chapter 3 investigates the production of early modern cartography and the ways in which the maps that it produces participate fully within the narrational. Although these maps claim to function as neutral observations of natural topographical space, they are in fact highly artificial textual constructs. Maps – like the historical topography of chorography that they attempt to displace (works such as Camden's famous *Britannia*) – are always narratives and as such are always both the effects and the tools of power – including monarchical, state, and (eventually) colonialist desires.

Chapter 4 focuses on New World discourse – made possible, at least in part, by the discourse of early modern cartography. I examine specifically the *anecdotal* nature of New World and new historicist discourse. In both, the anecdote is imagined as creating a space within which history can happen. In discussions of Ralegh's *Discovery of Guiana* and two critical texts on the European contact with and conquest of America – Tzvetan Todorov's *The Conquest of America: The Question of the Other* and Stephen Greenblatt's *Marvelous Possessions: The Wonder of the New World* – I argue, however, that the anecdote itself is entirely embedded within the narrational. Consequently, the "history" that the anecdote produces articulates and enacts the narrationalism of possession. As such, the anecdote and its narrative of possession work to deny the "heterogeneity of a *pre-*" identified by Derrida as the very grounds for the possibility of the encounter with the other.

The fifth and final chapter returns to the discourse of early modern science to consider the practices of what I will call artifaction first codified in their modern sense in seventeenth-century natural science, as articulated in the scientific (and devotional) writings of Sir Thomas Browne. The processes are then traced within pseudo-medical science – first in phrenology in the nineteenth century and then (in the 1920s) in racial craniology – two narrational practices that in their respective moments adopted as the object of their inquiries Browne's accidentally disinterred skull. Both phrenology and racial craniology posit the immediacy of the skull and the immanence of human identity within it, and both forms of pseudo-science lead to and participate in the production of narrationality of racism.

Finally – to return what the opening sentence of this introduction held out as a promised "reapparition": a consideration of what we can perhaps now call my own implication in this book in anachrony and narrationality; to conclude, that is, with a beginning – I end with a brief consideration of *Narrative and Meaning* itself, of the ways in which I hope to have situated the book and its various arguments in relation to narrative and narrationality. As I want to make clear before the conclusion, there is a difference between narrative as a structuring device – or, after Hayden White, as a tropological strategy[14] – and narrative as a fundamental epistemology structured upon a prior narrativization of the world and that is, as a consequence, narrational in nature. To sketch this distinction too hastily: while the former (narrative) self-consciously participates in certain teleologies (those of chronology, for example) in the service of the production of *interpretation*, it resists the tendency of narrationality that unselfconsciously posits *pure meaning* imagined to exist "naturally" in what is in fact a thoroughly narrativized world. Unlike narrationality, narrative – including this book – (ideally) attends to the "heterogeneity of a *pre –* " discussed above. So, while the following chapters are, to be sure, organized sequentially (both internally and relationally), and while I intend there to be something of a cumulative effect – that is to say, a *narratively satisfying* effect – of the organization, structure, and, even, the progression of this book, I nevertheless want to confess here at the end/beginning – beginning/end that this book is of course *untimely*. Written under the sway of anachrony, we could say that it was written by a ghost.

1 Shakespeare's *Othello* and Vesalius's *Fabrica*: anatomy, gender, and the narrative production of meaning

> Villain, be sure thou prove my love a whore,
>   Be sure of it, give me the ocular proof . . .   (*Othello*)

> When as usual I had cut everything off the bones very quickly without delaying for the examination of each organ, I dissected the uterus solely for the sake of the hymen.   (Vesalius, *Epitome*)

If the early modern period is that moment in the history of the west in which science in its distinctly modern form begins to emerge from complex pre-modern assemblages of mystical, hermetic, folkloric, metaphysical, and religious beliefs and practices, it is also the moment in which meaning *in general* begins a gradual transformation into the privileged domain of the discourses of science. This is the imperialism of what comes to be called the empirical sciences: not only are those divergent practices from which it in some manner emerged consolidated and at the same time vilified by their identification as "pre-" or "ir-rational" superstition – as "un-scientific" – but decisively, "meaning" is detached from "belief," with the former elevated to the status of objective and absolute "truth" and the latter relegated to the growing list of history's errors in knowledge. This project is manifest, for example, in one of the great (new) scientific texts of the seventeenth century, Sir Thomas Browne's *Pseudodoxia Epidemica* or *Vulgar Errors*. In Browne (as in emergent empirical science more generally) observation of natural fact replaces speculation on it with one especially significant result being that what before had required interpretation in order to reveal meaning in the natural world (the conventional lore, for example, of the chameleon) came instead to require only careful and studious observation. If anything was thought to require creative interpretation it was no longer primarily the phenomenal world or its objects construed simply as signs (of God's providential will, say) but rather the methods, techniques and tools it was necessary to devise in order better and more accurately to see, to measure, to quantify. In the *Pseudodoxia*, as an example, Browne considers the chameleon and the conventional claim that (as Hamlet reminds Claudius) the chameleon eats only air:[1]

10

Concerning the Chameleon there generally passeth an opinion that it liveth onely upon ayre, and is sustained by no other aliment; Thus much is in plaine terms affirmed by Solinus, Pliny, and others, and by this periphrasis is the same described by Ovid; All which notwithstanding, upon enquiry I finde the assertion mainly controvertible, and very much to faile in the three inducements of beliefe.[2]

Browne sets against the authorities mustered in defense of this extraordinary claim certain other writers: Aristotle, who does not actually refute the claim, but fails to mention it at all; Scaliger, who reported seeing a chameleon "lick up a flye from his breast"; and, most importantly, Bellonius, who "hath beene more satisfactorily experimentall," and whose work confirms

not onely [that] they feede on Flyes, Caterpillers, Beetles, and other insects, but upon exenteration he found these animals in their bellies: whereto we might also add the experimental decisions of the worthy *Peireschius* and learned *Emanuel Vizzanius* in that Chameleon which had been often observed to drink water, and delight to feed on Meal-Worms. And although we have not had the advantage of our owne observation, yet have we received the like confirmation from many ocular spectators. (*PE* 242)

While there is, then, no shortage of counter-authorities to refute the notion of the chameleon's diet, Browne's *scientific* case (like Bellonius's) depends upon a discourse of the visible that characterizes science in general. We cannot all dissect chameleons, but we can all read the texts of those who have. Browne goes on to cite the specific "ocular" facts that serve together to refute the conventional wisdom: the chameleon has the organs of digestion ("where we find such Instruments, we may with strictnesse expect their actions" [*PE* 243]), teeth, a tongue, lungs, and excrements. It is this turn to the ocularly available, to the forms of visual knowledge *made* available by the various discourses of science – including dissection and anatomy – that engenders Browne's epistemological certitude.

As this brief discussion of Browne's science of the chameleon suggests, in this period of the emergence of science as a counter-discourse to inherited and conventional wisdom, concern with (sometimes fanciful) interpretations was supplemented – if not largely supplanted – by a greater concern with method and methodology. But of course this description is itself the *product* of science rather than its pure description: part of the project of science is to naturalize the very terms of science and scientific discourse. In this way science secures both its radical distinction from "prerationalism" and its essentially exclusive proprietary claim to "truth." Science, in other words, is by its own definition chauvinist and always carries within itself the specter of scientism of the sort critiqued by Tzvetan Todorov in later (though nevertheless congruent) forms. In *On Human Diversity* Todorov argues that once it has succeeded in articulating its two related and fundamental postulates – determinism and the subordination of ethics to its own pronouncements – science becomes available and is all-too-frequently invoked to establish a particular ideology. Though for Todorov the particular ideologies in defense of which science is strategically deployed (he is particularly interested in nineteenth-century France) are those of ethnocentrism, racialism, and exoticism, one could as well say that the "meta-" ideology for which science (and scientism) are deployed is the discourse of science itself.[3]

The fundamental articulation of the ambitions of this new discourse was cast in the language of vision; science, we are told time and again, will reveal the secrets of nature to our sight. The trope of illumination was not new to early modern science – one finds it, for example, in the ancient Greek philosophical tradition – but it is only with early modern science that this visualism (as I will call it) becomes systematically and (over time) institutionally applied; this is the first characteristic of scientific visualism. The second is that the metaphor of illumination is no longer understood only metaphorically. Visualism, in other words, begins to be taken quite literally so that the quest for knowledge becomes at the same time the quest for the *seen*. There are of course famous emblems of this literalism that comes to characterize the discourse of science: Galileo with his celestial telescope, for example, and Leeuwenhoek and the microscope – the tools and technologies of science applied to the human eye vastly to improve its powers of resolution on both the cosmic and microcosmic levels. But this visualism was indeed everywhere apparent and the methods of this epistemology came to valorize the *demonstration* over the meditation or (philosophical) speculation. It is this celebration of and growing dependence upon an epistemology of visual knowledge that one can detect – in parallel – in the striking cultural emphasis of the early modern period upon various notions and practices of display and spectacle.

And yet, spectacle is so significant in these contexts not for the fact that it ritualistically fetishizes the visible, but because the visible is both recognized *in itself* as inadequate to establish power (though perhaps adequate as its reflection, as its *representation*) and because spectacle immediately fills the gap in the ideology of display by way of a supplement: what I have identified as narrationality. We can see this in public execution: that exemplary cultural practice of the early modern period so deeply implicated in the very issues of visualism – power, display, and visual knowledge (and one which bears a particularly close relation to science and the discourses of both theater and medical anatomy to which I will turn later in this chapter). In *Discipline and Punish*, Michel Foucault describes in harrowing detail the systematic reduction of the body of the convicted regicide, Damiens. The image – first the broken, then finally the annihilated body of the regicide –

can access meaning only to the extent that it is linked to the word (the voice of the king) and it becomes the special province of power to make such linkage explicit.[4] The image, then (like other artifacts addressed later in this book: the text, the map, the urn, the skull), can only ever *embody* meaning; it cannot *on its own* possess it. Indeed, it is one of the major arguments of this book that meaning can only exist within a given system of representation: like the disinterred skull to which Hamlet will lay his own proprietary claim, the image outside of representation cannot be said to have any meaning at all. But what, one might well ask, if the image – or, to use the more general term, the *artifact* – is a naturally occurring object such as the body? Does the body exist *as an image* outside representation? Do we have immediate access to the body? These are fundamental questions of long standing, the answer to which – or, at least, *our* (modern) answer to which – is "No." The body always exists for us – as an image or as an object of reflection and knowledge – *only* through representation. If this is the case, then it is also the case that the body is always a domain – perhaps the most contested domain – of a certain kind of epistemology. In *Disowning Knowledge in Six Plays by Shakespeare*, Stanley Cavell offers a definition of tragedy as "a kind of epistemological problem, or as the outcome of the problem of knowledge."[5] While I will turn to Cavell's discussion of *Othello* in a moment, I would like here to revise the foregoing definition thus: it is possible (and, in fact, it is historical) to think of the *body* as "a kind of epistemological problem." It is only quite recently that we rediscovered this historical truth.[6]

To think of the body as "the outcome of the problem of knowledge" is, to an extent, to follow a certain trajectory we can call Cartesian. But at the same time it is to follow certain other (and no doubt related) trajectories manifest in two important early modern practices I will take up in this chapter: theater and medical anatomy. Both of these cultural practices themselves participate in the discourses of visualism and spectacle remarked above. At the same time, each in the end demonstrates the complex ways that spectacle and visualism are fundamentally narrational in nature.

I

In her essay "*Othello* and *Hamlet*: Dilation, Spying, and the 'Secret Place' of Women," Patricia Parker returns to the scene of a famous textual crux in the third act of *Othello*, arguing for the "close dilations" of the Folio over the "close denotements" of Q1. For Parker, "dilations" and its alternate, "delations," deploy the related meanings of "either amplifications or delays" (dilation) and – following Dr. Johnson – "secret and occult accusations" (delation). All of these meanings, Parker argues, are vital to *Othello* (and *Hamlet*) and are, moreover, implicated in a larger network of cultural practices in which "that which accuses and that which opens and amplifies" simultaneously are brought to bear: the apparatus of judicial power, state spying, and, finally, gynecological and anatomical writing.[7] Parker argues that the model of dilation as "opening" – meaning "both to 'make large' and to speak 'at large,' expanding or discursively spreading out something originally smaller or more constricted" (*"Othello* and *Hamlet"* 112) – was afforded by rhetorical theory (she cites Erasmus's notion in *De Copia* of rhetorical opening as "an enlarging or unfolding through which the eye is enabled to see things previously 'folded' or closed" [*"Othello* and *Hamlet"* 112]). But such a notion was at the same time not only available but perhaps prone "to suggest an eroticized, voyeuristic, or even prurient looking," as is intimated in a definition of rhetorical opening offered by Henry Peacham as a way "to open the bosom of nature and to *shew* her branches, to that end they may be *viewed and looked upon, discerned and knowen"* (*The Garden of Eloqence*, quoted by Parker, *"Othello* and *Hamlet"* 112). By way, then, of a reading of the word "close" (in "close dilations") as a reference to "'private' and 'secret' in a sexual sense, a hidden place which only through opening can be displayed or 'shown,'" Parker notes that such "language of the 'close' or 'secrete' – of a hidden 'matter' or 'matrix' that might be dilated, opened, and displayed – pervades the literature on the 'privities' of woman in contrast to the exteriorized sexual parts of man" (*"Othello* and *Hamlet"* 113). Citing the work of early modern English anatomical writers such as Thomas Vicary (*The Anatomie of the Bodie of Man*, 1548), John Banister (*Historie of Man*, 1578) and Helkiah Crooke (*Microcosmographia: A Description of the Body of Man*, 1615), Parker argues that anatomical writing in the period participated in the discourse of dilation/delation:

As with rhetorical dilation as an unwrapping or unfolding to the eye, the female "lap" or privity was thus something folded or closed as well as something secret or "close." And here, in the impulse of anatomical discourse to open up to "show," the links are even clearer between the language of the informer exposing something secret to the eye and the discourses surrounding a woman's "secrete" place, not only brought to light but indicted and judged. (*"Othello* and *Hamlet"* 115)

It is part of the profound irony of the masculinist discourse of (medical) anatomy – and its theatrical/spectacular counterpart – that perhaps the most serious consequences of the "dilational" nature of bringing a woman's "privity" to view and judgment that it is exactly such visibility that itself demands indictment and judgment. In other words, it is the very "visibility" of female (reproductive) anatomy caused by the anatomical – or dilational – urge that then immediately requires a retributive punishment. This is Desdemona's fate: she falls victim to what is conventionally considered Othello's problem of knowledge. For Cavell, this problem of knowledge consists of Othello's refusal to accept the unacceptable: not that Desdemona is faithless, but that she is faithful (Cavell 133). Desdemona's faithfulness, Cavell argues, determines Othello's own failing; her "finitude" (her bodily separateness which she would erase by offering her virginity) marks Othello's own separateness, his own dependence. Othello's skepticism comes finally to reside in the inadmissible fact of his own finitude: "What this man lacked was not certainty. He knew everything, but he could not yield to what he knew, be commanded by it. He found out too much for his mind, not too little. Their differences from one another – the one everything the other is not – form an emblem of human separation, which can be accepted, and granted, or not" (Cavell 141–42).

Cavell suggests that sexuality lies at the center of Othello's crisis to the extent that sexuality is that "field" wherein human bodily separateness is inexorably manifested. Othello's crisis, then, is a crisis inextricable from sexuality, and sexuality is understood as fundamentally epistemological. Othello is entirely willing to accept the horrible "truth" of Iago's claims because that truth serves as the occasion for Othello to deny "something yet more terrible to his mind" (Cavell 133): his own finite existence rendered apparent by conjugal love.[8] And yet, Cavell's notion of Othello's interpretive focus on the epistemological hazards of conjugal love depends upon a series of assumptions on Cavell's part – assumptions about sexuality, Othello and Desdemona's wedding night, and about narrative and ocularity – assumptions, in fact, that are very nearly identical to Othello's. Cavell suggests that Othello is driven to the murder by his horror over this understanding of sexuality as epistemological:

If such a man as Othello is rendered impotent and murderous by aroused, or by having aroused, female sexuality – or let us say, if this man is horrified by human sexuality, in himself and in others – then no human being is free of this possibility. What I have wished to bring out is the nature of this possibility, or the possibility of this nature, the way human sexuality is the field in which the fantasy of finitude, of its acceptance and its repetitious overcoming, is worked out; the way human separateness is turned equally toward splendor and toward horror, mixing beauty and ugliness; turned toward before and after; toward flesh and blood. (Cavell 137)

In his interpretation, Cavell obscures female sexuality, or more exactly, the female body. On the one hand, Othello's anxiety over female sexuality is expanded into a general anxiety of human sexuality. On the other hand, the "horror," "ugliness," and "blood" of the last part of the passage for Othello come clearly to be identified with Desdemona, with her body as signifier. In fact, it is this belief in the female body as signifier that underwrites and guarantees Cavell's reading of the play. It is this concern with Desdemona's body as signifier that serves to link Cavell's discussion of Othello's murder to the play's obsessive concern with "ocular proof." While

Cavell asserts that Othello both does and does not believe in Desdemona's virginity (there is "reason to believe that Othello does not know whether it [their marriage] has [been consummated]" [Cavell 131]), and that the matter of their consummation remains indeterminate, he nevertheless participates in an interpretive logic that, like Othello's, "reads" Desdemona's body as a signifier, and that believes in both a logic of virginity and in an absolute equation of sexuality and epistemology. Moreover, these assumptions coincide in a curious privileging of the ocular. While Othello demands the "ocular proof" of Desdemona's sexual purity or impurity, Cavell believes in a *theatrical* ocularity:

My guiding hypothesis about the structure of the play is that the thing *denied our sight* throughout the opening scene – the thing, the scene, that Iago takes Othello back to again and again, retouching it for Othello's enchafed imagination – is what we are shown in the final scene, the scene of murder. This becomes our ocular proof of Othello's understanding of his two nights of married love. (Cavell 132)

Cavell's entire reading of *Othello*, I suggest, depends first upon Othello's call for the ocular becoming *our* identical call, and secondly upon an Othello-like concern with Desdemona's body as a signifier, even as Othello's epistemology does. To "read" Desdemona's body is to construct an understanding of the play, or of the world. This interpretive strategy, however, fails to take into account Desdemona's own knowledge (if nothing else in the play is certain, Desdemona's knowledge of her status *vis-à-vis* virginity certainly is), the dangers of an exclusively semiotic understanding of Desdemona's body, and the costs of (theatrical) ocularity.[9]

At stake in these issues is the desire to decide meaning by virtue of a constructed semiotics of the female body. The problem for Othello has been the problem for criticism. Or, more accurately, Othello has predicted what criticism has posited for him: a (largely masculinist) semiotics of the female body based upon a conflation of sexuality and epistemology.[10] From this perspective, the "problem" with Desdemona is that she refuses to display her semiotic meaning, or the semiotic meaning she does display – innocence and love of Othello – is wholly rejected by Othello. What Desdemona's body signifies, then, ironically, is an apparent illegibility, a refusal to make manifest its own knowledge. It is this notion, I want to suggest, that precipitates Othello's crisis of knowledge. Othello imagines Desdemona's body itself to contain its truth, the truth about her status as his wife and possession. It is from this belief that Othello issues his infamous call for "ocular proof" – a gesture that Iago has perhaps anticipated and fully exploits:

> how satisfied, my lord?
> Would you, the supervisor, grossly gape on?
> Behold her topp'd?[11]

Iago's response is to conjure the image of Desdemona's illicit intercourse with Cassio. While this ultimately will prove effective, it satisfies only part of Othello's demand: it is, in a sense, ocular, but does not itself constitute proof. What allows this image – as well as the fabrications of Cassio's dream and the story of the exchange of the handkerchief – to be accepted by Othello as proof is Othello's own willingness to construe it as such. The success of Iago's dubious evidence marks in the play the transformation of the ocular into the narrational: the image is meaningful for the story (fiction) it is made to tell. This is the form that Iago's seduction of Othello takes. As Stephen Greenblatt has argued, Iago's profound power to affect Othello depends upon his (Iago's) ability to improvise.[12] Through this improvisation Iago is able to insinuate himself – and with him, his fiction of Desdemona's infidelity – into Othello's imagination. It is precisely this vulnerability in Othello, his willingness to be seduced by narrative, that characterizes his profound privileging of narrative and which subsequently asserts itself in his fantasy of Desdemona's punishment.[13] Othello's responses, "I'll tear her all to pieces" (3.3.438) and "I will chop her into messes" (4.1.196) can be read as manifestations of a violence embedded within a reactive fantasy of dismemberment.[14] But they can also be understood within the context of the epistemological crisis remarked above. Othello's desire for violent revenge against Desdemona takes a specific form: he fantasizes not only her punishment, but the radical physical reduction of her body – something closely akin to the practice of both public execution and (public) anatomy. This demand partakes, moreover, of a desire to rectify an epistemology that has been proven inadequate (though only apparently so).[15] Othello's epistemology has proceeded on that which has been apparent, that which he has literally seen. But the prospect of Desdemona's infidelity suggests phenomena that go unseen – at least by him. That which remains unseen proves destructive to Othello's epistemology, but only once it has been narrationally inaugurated.[16] In response, Othello's demand for "ocular proof" is aimed at repairing the epistemological damage he believes he has sustained: he will recover certitude through enacting a violence upon Desdemona's body – a violence that will seek to bridge what Kathleen McLuskie has called "the gap which opens up between what is seen and what can be known about women."[17]

For Othello, anatomization first represents a metaphoric visualization that will guarantee certainty. But almost immediately upon the very demand for visual proof, the epistemology afforded by the science of anatomy releases a rage and fantasy of violence that elsewhere manifests itself in the patriarchal system of enclosure as it is brought to bear on the body of women: the restriction of movement and public exposure.[18] This enclosure seeks a disbarment which, on the one hand, is purely physical (locking women within doors, for example), but which, on the other hand, aspires to be epistemological: the restriction of the knowability of women, the desire to keep women (in) private. The anatomy of Desdemona that Othello imagines exists as an inversion of the misogynist philosophy of enclosure and marks its impossibility: Othello's violence is the mad attempt to punish Desdemona by subjecting her to an anatomization that would make radically open and public the very body over which he desires sole dominion.[19]

This issue of public vs. private – particularly as it is situated along the axis of gender – is central to the world of early modern theater, its transvestite staging conventions, and its very "place" in early modern culture. In "Scripts and/versus Playhouses: Ideological Production and the Renaissance Public Stage," Jean Howard discusses the conventional anti-theatrical polemics (of figures such as Stephen Gosson) and the ways in which antitheatricalism was in a significant way motivated by a profound anxiety associated with women spectators of early modern theater:

> The threat the theatre seems to hold for Gosson in regard to ordinary gentlewomen is that, in that public space, such women have become unanchored from the structures of surveillance and control "normal" to the culture and useful in securing the boundary between "good women" and "whores." Not literally passed, like Cressida, from hand to hand, lip to lip, the female spectator passes instead from eye to eye, her value as the exclusive possession of one man cheapened, put at risk, by the gazing of many eyes.[20]

But, as Howard suggests, this very formulation – i.e., that women spectators existed in the theater as objects of desire – conforms too closely to the patriarchal order an analysis such as hers means to criticize. Another – and a far more radical – observation of the gender dynamics of this theater would note the possibility of these women spectators not only as objects of desire (for this was clearly the case), but also as the active *agents* of desire:

> Is it possible that in the theatre women were licensed to look – and in a larger sense to judge what they saw and to exercise autonomy – in ways that problematised women's status as object within patriarchy?. . . At the theatre door, money changed hands in a way which gave women access to the pleasure and privilege of gazing, certainly at the stage, and probably at the audience as well . . . women at the theatre were not "at home," but in public, where they could become objects of desire, certainly, but also desiring subjects, stimulated to want what was on display.
>
> (Howard 225)

It is precisely the very possibility of Desdemona as a desiring subject that triggers Othello's madness, though, of course, the play makes quite clear that it is just this status as (errantly) desiring subject that enabled

Desdemona's relation to Othello in the first place. This is the reverse side of what Greenblatt identifies as Othello's (unsuccessfully repressed) belief that *he* has been too familiar with his wife (*Renaissance Self-Fashioning* 233). At the same time, it is the largely submerged and occluded notion that helps generate the many attempts one sees staged in the drama to access a woman's "interiority."[21]

In *Volpone*, Corvino's invocation of anatomization as punishment for an equally false accusation of infidelity remarks the publicness of Celia's action ("Death of mine honor, with the city's fool?/ A juggling, tooth-drawing, prating mountebank?/ And at a public window?" [2.5.1–3]), and the sexual betrayal he imagines it to signal: "Well, you shall have him, yes./ He shall come home, and minister unto you/ The fricace for the mother" (2.5.15–17).[22] For Corvino there is an intimate connection between public exposure and sexuality, and he believes that Celia's public display of interest in the mountebank demands an equally public and sexual retribution:

> Nay, since you force
> My honest nature, know it is your own
> Being too open makes me use thee thus.
> Since you will not contain your subtle nostrils
> In a sweet room, but they must snuff the air
> Of rank and sweaty passengers . . .
> Away, and be not seen, pain of thy life;
> Not look toward the window: if thou dost –
> Nay, stay, hear this, let me not prosper, whore,
> But I will make thee an anatomy,
> Dissect thee mine own self, and read a lecture
> Upon thee to the city, and in public.   (2.5.61–72)[23]

We should pause to consider a number of issues at stake in these fantasies of retributive violent anatomization. That these fantasies promise corporeal punishment for an imagined corporeal offense is self-evident. What may perhaps be less evident, although no less significant, is the sexual and public nature of this punishment. Othello would search the anatomized female body for the ocular proof of chastity: Desdemona's intact hymen.[24] And yet, Desdemona's hymen is not entirely Othello's interest. His interest, rather, lies in the significance he can ascribe to it. Her hymen loses, then, its actual corporeality as it becomes a narrational signifier: the sign that marks Desdemona's sexual privacy and Othello's proprietary claims to exclusive possession, the sign that tells the story of Othello's sexual ownership. Here the female body is understood as a semiotic guarantee of male privacy and property which, once threatened, require public verification. Anatomy functions narrationally, then, as a system of politically motivated reading which offers justification for domination. The anatomy reveals not anatomical evidence as phenomenological fact, but rather as narrational proof; what Othello hopes to see (the ocular proof which has become so fetishized) is not physical and natural, but narrational and discursive. The story of his own power.

In "Proof and Consequences: Inwardness and its Exposure in the English Renaissance," Katharine Eisaman Maus discusses early modern conceptions of interiority and "examines some of the important epistemological problems that arise from English Renaissance assumptions about psychological interiority, not in order to reject but rather to refine and advance a historically self-conscious discussion of subjectivity in the early modern period."[25] Her discussion of judicial trials (for treason and for witchcraft), and "the quasijudicial discovery of inwardness in Shakespeare's *Othello*" ("Proof and Consequences" 31) offer a brilliant intervention in contemporary critical discussions of the early modern period and the contemporary ideas of the subject.[26] It is not, Maus contends, that we can speak of early modern (psychological) interiority only as "anachronistic," but that we can see its outlines in the courtroom and the theater – two arenas dedicated to performance and spectatorship.[27] The anatomical theater – as well as texts such as Vesalius's *Fabrica* dedicated to anatomical representation and learning – allows for yet another staging of the quest for interiority.

Criticism of *Othello* (and a wide range of other Renaissance theatrical texts similarly dedicated to the discourse of the skeptical husband) has essentially followed Othello's lead both in determining what the play is about (sexual jealousy) and passing judgment on the viability of epistemological understandings of sexuality. Moreover, Othello decides further that parallel to the epistemology of sexuality (his own, perhaps; Desdemona's, certainly) there exists a corresponding ontology. Othello decides not only that Desdemona deserves punishment (whether for his sin or for hers), but that her (their) sexuality literally determines her being. Desdemona's faithlessness, let us say, is not only a "fact" Othello "discovers," but it is also understood in the play as an ontological state: Desdemona is either an innocent victim or a whore. This is to say that criticism has largely taken Othello's word for it that sexuality is an epistemological field wherein ontological status can be both negotiated and observed. As noted above, the play takes no notice of Desdemona's certainty, but instead focuses on questions – some of which are perhaps unanswerable – of her moral and sexual disposition.[28] Again, in light of what we must agree is Desdemona's certainty, any obsessive fixation on her sexuality – her "maidenhead" – is inadmissible. Strictly speaking, Desdemona's "maidenhead" is literally none of our business. But instead, entire readings of the play are indeed predicated precisely upon what Othello, a less than objective commentator, has already determined are to be the terms of the discussion. We see this clearly in Cavell:

Well, were the sheets stained or not? Was she a virgin or not? The answers seem as ambiguous as to our earlier question whether they are fast married. Is the final, fatal reenactment of their wedding night a clear denial of what really happened, so that we can just read off, by negation, what really happened? Or is it a straight reenactment, without negation, and the flower was still on the tree, as far as he knew? In that case, who was reluctant to see it plucked, he or she? On such issues, farce and tragedy are separated by the thickness of a membrane. (Cavell 135)

To ask such questions is to have already accepted a narrational discourse of gender and sexuality that is itself perverse. It is also to refuse to imagine something like a psychological interiority for Desdemona, and to reduce interiority to a vulgar materiality: "Is her hymen intact?"

II

Theatrical fantasies are by no means unique, but rather particularly striking instances of the larger cultural conflict for which the female body becomes the locus. I would like to turn attention now to the medical anatomy and its inquiry into the body as it is displayed in dissection and performed in the science of anatomy; the inquiry, that is, into the body as an object of knowledge. In this sense the Renaissance medical anatomy can be understood as an epistemological endeavor: the attempt to apprehend, to know, a body.

In *The Body Emblazoned: Dissection and the Human Body in Renaissance Culture*, Jonathan Sawday identifies this medical–anatomical inquiry in the early modern period as part of a larger cultural investment in a dissective epistemology one can trace across a wide range of disciplines and practices:

the "scientific revolution" of the European Renaissance encouraged the seemingly endless partitioning of the world and all that it contained . . . partition stretched into all forms of social and intellectual life: logic, rhetoric, painting, architecture, philosophy, medicine, as well as poetry, politics, the family, and the state were all potential subjects for division. The pattern of all these different forms of division was derived from the human body . . . And it is in this urge to particularize that "Renaissance culture" can be termed the "culture of dissection."[29]

Sawday examines the rich and complex practices of dissection and anatomy from their mid-sixteenth-century forms, represented especially in the works of Andreas Vesalius, to their later seventeenth-century versions represented, for example, by the "Cartesian" anatomical works of William Harvey. For Vesalius and other early anatomists, Sawday argues, the particular form that the anatomical inquiry took was modeled on the notion of "discovery"; the body as an object of knowledge was an "America" to be explored, mapped, and eventually tamed and conquered by the explorer–anatomist:

The process was truly colonial, in that it appeared to reproduce the stages of discovery and exploitation which were, at that moment, taking place within the context of the European encounter with the New World. First came the explorers, leaving their mark on the body in the form of features which were mapped and named and inhabitants who were encountered and observed. The second stage mirrored the narrative of conquest and exploitation insofar as these newly found features and peoples were understood as forming part of a complex economy – a system of production, distribution, and consumption – which was itself in perpetual movement. The project, then, was to harness this system to the use of the discoverer.

(*Body Emblazoned* 25–26)

This notion of what Sawday calls the "geographic body" gradually gives way and is replaced *as a matter of course* by the "mechanical body" legislated in the works of Descartes.[30] It is no longer a matter of the body as microcosmic world (which one finds in many sixteenth-century anatomical – and poetic – works), but rather the body as machine:

Forged into a working machine, the mechanical body appeared fundamentally different from the geographic body whose contours expressed a static landscape without dynamic interconnection. More than this, however, the body as machine, as a clock, as an automaton, was understood as having no intellect of its own. Instead, it silently operated according to the laws of mechanics. We move, then, from an interior in which the body seems . . . to speak its own part, to the modern conception of a physiological system no more capable of speech than is an hydraulic pump – the machine with which Harvey himself had sought to explain the operation of cardiac valves. As a machine, the body became objectified; a focus of intense curiosity, but entirely divorced from the world of speaking and thinking subject. The division between Cartesian subject, and corporeal object, between an "I" that thinks, and an "it" in which "we" reside, had become absolute. (*Body Emblazoned* 29)

The material production of this anatomical epistemology was of uncertain moral, religious, and juridical status. The method of obtaining suitable cadavers for early anatomies involved grave-robbing and the stealing or direct receipt of the bodies of executed criminals – what Sawday calls "penal dissection" (*Body Emblazoned* 54). The frequently extra-legal activity of procuring subjects for anatomies indicates an intimate relationship between civic punishment and the general advancement of anatomical learning. By virtue of its morally sanctified ambition, if not its methods, however, anatomy was generally understood as scientific inquiry: the transformation of the ritualized taking apart of a body from an act of violation into a systematic and analytical discourse.[31]

I would suggest further that anatomy's status as epistemology corresponds to an ontological ambition: anatomy asked not only how and what we can know about bodies, but what the *essential* nature of the body is, and how we are to understand the relationship between the body and the identity it in some manner houses. From this perspective anatomy can perhaps *only* be understood as an act of violation in which either the "temple" of the soul is subjected to an inhuman violence, or – and this is certainly more devastating – the temple is opened to reveal its utter emptiness, the lack, that is, of an interior certainty or meaning. In either case, anatomy becomes an act that makes evident its own impossibility: the systematic removal of layers constitutive of the body reveals not its depth – its meaning, its certainty – but merely the successive play of surfaces.

And yet, this formulation would perhaps be appropriate only had these anatomists been strict phenomenologists, had they been able to see structures simply as material phenomena. To the contrary, however, they were inveterate readers of texts. In *The Tremulous Private Body*, Francis Barker analyzes Rembrandt's famous painting *The Anatomy Lesson*, and discusses what he identifies as the movement toward transforming bodies into texts which the painting emblematizes and which characterizes what he calls the newly conceived "bourgeois body."[32] For Barker, the anatomy textualizes bodies. But I would like to suggest that the anatomy understands bodies *a priori* as texts. This is an epistemological distinction between bodies transformed into texts through the act of anatomization, and encountering bodies in anatomy as preexisting texts: not the body *as* text, but, in a grammatical shift which makes evident an epistemological difference, the body *is* text. The distinction between these two formulations is important; the former refers to a textualization of bodies, while the latter insists upon the (*a priori*) embodiment of texts. It is the textualization of bodies that operates in the work of Andreas Vesalius (1514–64), who studied medicine in Paris, Louvain, and Padua, and produced the single most important anatomical text of the early modern period, *De humani corporis fabrica libri septem* (Basle, 1543) – a text noted not only for its scientific rigor, but prized today for its aesthetic and antiquarian value.

Vesalius understood the project of his anatomical investigation to be largely epistemological: the description of the structures or "fabric" of the human body. Vesalius's ambition, then, was ostensibly identical to that of the earliest anatomists, including Aristotle and Galen. But in fact, this identity is only apparent and Vesalius's contribution to the science of anatomy can be understood more generally as the refutation of inherited anatomical wisdom as it was articulated primarily through the works of Galen. Vesalius differed from the powerful Galenic tradition by his insistence on the work "of the hands" – the actual dissection of human bodies by the anatomist himself – rather than depending upon book-learning. This demand arose from a dissatisfaction with Galenic anatomy and, more particularly, a revolution in epistemology – the birth, one could say, of what we consider today the scientific method: direct observation of the phenomena under investigation rather than an uncritical adherence to narratives of meaning contained in the written opinions of ancient authority. In this sense, then, Vesalius's ambitions – like da Vinci's before him and Bacon's after him – is (perhaps like Othello's) for the "ocular proof" of observable, verifiable "natural fact."[33]

However, anatomy both as a science and as epistemology is inexorably discursive and removed from an unmediated observation of "natural fact." Indeed, it can be said that by virtue of its discursive nature the anatomy fails to achieve access to (much less mastery over) natural fact. As I have suggested above, the bodies anatomized by Vesalius were understood *a priori* as texts – as discursive artifacts to which meaning had always already been ascribed and from which Vesalius proceeded to discover this previously posited significance in a thoroughly redundant manner. This discursive nature that characterizes the body-in-anatomy is paralleled by the rigorous *textuality* of the Vesalian anatomical project more generally. Vesalius's masterwork is titled *De humani corporis fabrica libri septem*, and his attempt to recall anatomy "from the region of the dead" takes the form of the *libri septem*.[34] It becomes virtually impossible (both in the title and in the book that follows) to distinguish between the science of anatomy, its pedagogy, and the system of its representation. Vesalius's desire to restore anatomy necessitated the radical involvement of the anatomist in actual dissections of human cadavers, but this desire also mandated the proper teaching of anatomy – both at the universities and to a larger lay audience – through texts. It was this need for public textual documentation that prompted Vesalius to undertake the publication of his anatomical texts. While Vesalius insisted on the absolute necessity of direct personal experience in dissection ("I . . . have encouraged the candidates of medicine in every way to undertake dissection with their own hands" [O'Malley 323]), he nevertheless maintained that in its present degraded state, anatomy as a science requires *books* in order to be wholly restored:

That this may occur under the happy auspices of the muses, in addition to these things I have published elsewhere on this matter . . . to the best of my ability I have organized my fullest knowledge of the parts of the human body into these seven books, just as I should normally discuss it before a group of learned men . . . Also these things will not be without use for those who are denied any opportunity for inspection of the parts since the books present in sufficient detail the number, site, shape, size, substance, connection to other parts, use and function of each part of the human body . . . Furthermore, the books contain illustrations of all the parts, inserted in the text of the discourse in such a way that they place the dissected body before the eyes of the student of nature's works. (O'Malley 322)

Criticism of the traditional dependence on books in the teaching of anatomy suggested that such dependence would only lead to a stagnation of learning rather than its advancement. Vesalius offered his own versions of this critique, but nevertheless defended the publication of his *Fabrica* and, particularly, the use of the "exquisitely executed" illustrations (O'Malley 322):[35]

> how greatly pictures assist the understanding of these matters and place them more exactly before the eyes than even the most precise language . . . Furthermore, the illustrations of the human parts will greatly delight those for whom there is not always a supply of human bodies for dissection; or, if there is, those who have such a fastidious nature, little worthy of a physician, that, even if they are enthusiastic about that most pleasant knowledge of man attesting the wisdom of the Great Creator – if anything does – yet they cannot bring themselves even occasionally to be present at dissection. Whatever the case may be, I have been at my best to this single end, to aid as many as possible in a very recondite as well as laborious matter, and truly and completely to describe the structure of the human body which is formed not of ten or twelve parts – as it may seem to the spectator – but of some thousands of different parts, and, among other monuments to that divine man Galen, to bring to posterity an understanding of those books of his requiring the help of a teacher. I bear to the candidates of medicine fruit not to be scorned.
>
> (O'Malley 323)

In this passage Vesalius pays tribute to the profound efficacy of pictorial illustrations and remarks on the limitations of linguistic representation ("even the most precise language") of anatomical structures. But at the same time he articulates a further *textual* imperative: the illumination of Galen's texts. The *Fabrica* becomes not only an atlas of the human body, but a critical exegesis of Galen's anatomical and medical writing. Vesalius's text makes explicit its double nature: it is both a text that seeks to understand the body as a body of knowledge, and a text that seeks to apprehend a previous, and flawed, body of knowledge – Galen's corpus – which it will simultaneously explicate and perfect. Vesalius's *aesthetic* interest in the production of the *Fabrica* and *Epitome* speaks, on the one hand, to the nature of his anatomical projects in their textual form and, on the other, indicates his general investment in a particular form of scientific visualism, his quest for ocular proof made available through the practices of medicine and science. In a letter to his printer, Joannes Oporinus, Vesalius manifests this aesthetic interest:

> Now I urge and exhort you very earnestly to print everything as handsomely and swiftly as possible so that in my books you will satisfy the expectations all have of your printing shop . . . Special care ought to be taken on the impression of the blocks which are not to be printed like ordinary woodcuts in common textbooks . . . I desire above all that in the printing you copy as closely as possible the proof struck off by the engraver . . . for thus no character, even one concealed in the shading, will lie hidden from the careful and observant reader. Likewise, take care that the thickness of the lines producing gradation in the shadows, which I find artistically pleasing,

is nicely reproduced. In the final analysis everything depends on the smoothness and solidity of the paper and especially on the carefulness of your supervision, so that each illustration . . . be of the same quality as the proofs I am now sending you. (O'Malley 325)

Vesalius thus makes apparent that the artful execution of the *Fabrica* will fashion the book itself as a body – a body which occupies space and has depth ("for thus no character, even one concealed in the shading, will be hidden"), dimension ("the thickness of the lines"), and substance ("everything depends on the smoothness and solidity of the paper"). The book, like the body it figures, is a corporeal fabric: substantial, present, textured.

The scientific and narrational endeavor Vesalius's anatomical texts embody is founded upon a profound *visual* privileging. In her essay, "Science and Women's Bodies: Forms of Anthropological Knowledge," Emily Martin discusses vision as "a primary route to scientific knowledge" in western thought. Martin suggests that "the illumination that vision gives has been associated with the highest faculty of mental reasoning." This cultural privileging of vision has recently come under significant review in critical and theoretical discussions that have "singled out reliance on vision as a key culprit in the scrutiny, surveillance, domination, control and exertion of authority over the body, particularly over the bodies of women."[36] Vesalius's anatomical project – especially his use of illustrations – participates fully in an epistemology founded on what Johannes Fabian has identified as a "cultural, ideological bias toward vision as the 'noblest sense' and toward geometry qua graphic–spatial conceptualization as the most 'exact' way of communicating knowledge."[37] I would like to turn briefly to a number of Vesalius's "graphic–spatial" conceptualizations of the human body in anatomy and suggest that in his anatomical texts visualism is thoroughly teleological; the project of "plac[ing] the dissected body before [our] eyes" is permeated by an ideological bias in favor of the narrational.[38] Vesalius's texts are not objective descriptions of the structures of human bodies, but rather narrational accounts of his encounters with bodies that have already become texts or stories he then narrates.

The male and female nudes that appear in the *Epitome* are rigorously conventional and highly stylized Renaissance representations of idealized man and woman: graphic representations of the dignity and divinity of humankind (plates 1 and 2). These, and the famous "muscle-men" illustrations of the myological book of the *Fabrica*, are the figures Vesalius visualizes when he describes the human as the "most perfectly constructed of all creatures" (O'Malley 324). "Man," in these images, is surely the measure of all things. But what is of particular interest in these nudes of the *Epitome* is the equally conventional gesture by which the female nude covers her genitals. This modesty is uniquely hers (the male nude seems rather to display

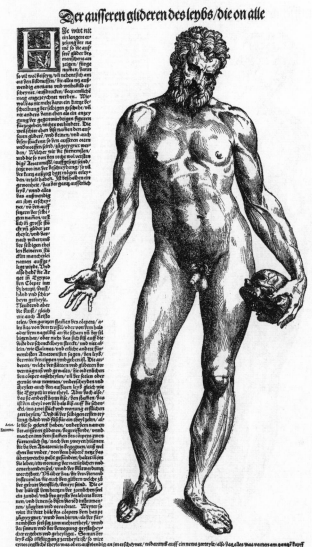

Plate 1 Andreas Vesalius. "Adam," from *Epitome*. German edition, 1543.

aufffchneydung gefeben werden/nammen.

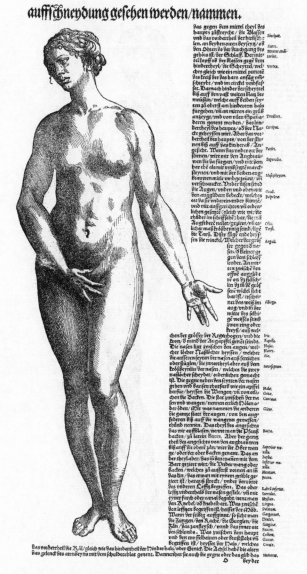

Plate 2 Andreas Vesalius. "Eve," from *Epitome*. German edition, 1543.

his genital nakedness); but this modesty is in enormous contrast to the relentless "immodesty" the female body will be made to display in the anatomy itself. The single illustration from the *Fabrica* that most overtly marks the openness (publicity) of the female anatomical body is that displayed on the title figure (plate 3). In this image the woman's body has been rendered emphatically and publicly open. In his text, Vesalius offers the following description:

The peritoneum and the abdominal muscles have been opened and pulled to the sides . . . Then we have resected all the intestines from the mesentery, but we have left the rectum in the body as well as the whole of the mesentery of which we have to some extent separated the membranes so that its nature is exposed to view. However, the present figure has been drawn for the special purpose of indicating the position of the uterus . . . exactly as [it] occurred in this woman; we have not disturbed the uterus in any way. (O'Malley 143)

Vesalius does not, however, only present the representation of this woman – first the visual representation and then the verbal; in a move that signals the narrational *telos* of his anatomical investigation, he offers the dead woman's story. He tells us that this body was that of a woman who, for fear of being hanged for a convicted crime, claimed to be pregnant. The court ordered an examination of the woman by midwives, who reported her "not at all pregnant" (O'Malley 143). The woman was executed, and her body given to Vesalius for dissection.

Vesalius's interest in the body of this woman lies, I suggest, in its apparent emptiness. Yet, as suggested earlier, the emptiness a body may hold is at the same time a cause of significant anxiety, that anxiety that the body, if it "contains" nothing, *means* nothing. In his anatomization of this woman who had claimed a very specific corporeal content or meaning, Vesalius eludes this anxiety by inverting it back onto (into) the woman. As his anatomy acts as an extension of civil punishment against this woman, it is precisely her un-pregnant state – her demonstrably "empty" uterus – that Vesalius rather savagely attacks. In response to her false claim of pregnancy, Vesalius makes apparent – offers the ocular proof – of not only her un-pregnant status, but her lie (which had now been rendered visible), and her guilt, justifying her execution by the state. Vesalius's account and representation of the anatomy reveal the ideological imperatives regarding gender and procreation at stake both in civic punishment and the advancement of anatomical learning. *De humani corporis fabrica libri septem* promises on its title page that the text is the body itself – the body of a woman whose entirely legible status as non-pregnant locus of the state's power over life and death is materially beyond dispute.

Vesalius's account of this particular anatomy effects a further revelation. Not only is the anatomized figure that of a particular woman ("the present

Plate 3 Andreas Vesalius. Title page, *De humani corporis fabrica libri septem*. Basle, 1543.

figure has been drawn for the special purpose of indicating the position of
the uterus . . . exactly as [it] occurred in this woman"), but Vesalius rhetorically extrapolates the body of the executed woman into a figure for women
in general: "Everything is seen intact just as it appears to the dissector
immediately upon moving the intestines to one side in a moderately fat
woman" (O'Malley 143). It is, moreover, the work of Vesalius as author and
illustrator that has placed the reader of the *Fabrica* in the position of the
dissector who can then view the anatomical material thus displayed. While
he claims to have anatomized this body in order to make apparent its
anatomical structure, I suggest that what Vesalius anatomized was not the
body of this woman, but rather the body already construed as a text, and
that what he then anatomizes is (only) a text and not – as he no doubt
believed – a body at all. The dissected body is made to display not the
natural fact of structure, but rather a narrative: Vesalius incises a body that
turns out in fact to be a text. By this process, the (female) body thus displayed is a text – a *corpus* – that has been made to reveal its (secret) semiotic nature. Vesalius finds in the woman exactly what he believed he would,
since the "ocular proof" had long ago been culturally and ideologically
inscribed. It is this discursivity of the female body that accounts for
Vesalius's unselfconscious and unproblematical interest in seeing the anatomized female body as both particular and emblematic, as private and
public.

Perhaps the most peculiar narrative to appear in the *Fabrica* that has precisely to do with a dispute over the public or private status of a female body
– and (competing) male proprietary claims to it – tells the story of a hastily
removed uterus. Vesalius tells us that the woman had been "the handsome
mistress of a certain monk" and had died from "strangulation of the uterus
or some quickly devastating ailment" (O'Malley 113). Vesalius's Paduan
students (he tells us) then stole the body from its grave for dissection: "By
their remarkable industry they flayed the whole skin from the cadaver lest
it be recognized by the monk who, with the relatives of his mistress, had
complained to the municipal judge that the body had been stolen from its
tomb" (O'Malley 113–14). This episode makes clear the narrational epistemology governing Vesalian anatomy of the female body. It makes clear
that the surface (skin, features) of the body are signs which all may read –
signs by which the monk, for example, would identify his dead mistress;
removing the surface renders her body anonymous, even to the monk. This
action, however, while it serves to obscure the meaning (identity) of the
body for the monk, functions for Vesalius as the first step toward revealing
that body's inner secrets.

One of the illustrations that accompanies this narrative is no less peculiar, as it is virtually unrecognizable as a representation of part of the

female anatomy (plate 4). Vesalius claimed to have had little time to remove the uterus itself, and therefore removed a whole section of the body for a later moment when he and his students could examine it at greater leisure. This is perhaps true of the event, but certainly not of the illustration, which was presumably executed without the fear of the monk and the magistrate interrupting to reclaim the long-lost body. In either case, however, we have in this illustration a material representation of a phallocentrism that, whether consciously or not, seeks to (re-)create the world in its own image.[39]

I have suggested that Vesalius's dissections and descriptions of female bodies are marked by textuality and by the narrational; they have become *loci* of discursive significance: the anatomist's only task was to discover the meaning that lay within. But what is the nature – the significance – of this discursive meaning? In order to answer this it is necessary to investigate ways in which Renaissance anatomies – as represented in the *Fabrica* – can be understood as a gendered discourse.

Public anatomies were subject to legislation:[40] such anatomies could only be performed a certain number of times per year; the cadavers were those of executed criminals; only a certain number of people could attend (in Padua it was stipulated that only twenty could attend anatomies of male cadavers, while the number was set at thirty if the body was that of a woman); attendance was by selection only and admission was charged; and attendance by women was prohibited.[41] Although women were excluded as observers in these anatomies, the female body was of particular interest as the anatomical object. While the female nude of the *Epitome* depicts the Renaissance ideal of woman, I suggest that Vesalius anatomized no such women.[42] The female bodies that were made available (or to which he helped himself) were in fact in striking opposition to the ideal woman articulated in this figure. The female cadavers which both the state and the culture made available to Vesalius for anatomies were those of the executed woman of the title page, pre-pubescent girls, a nun, a "hunchback" girl of seventeen, and prostitutes – bodies, that is, of females distinguished from this conventional ideal in ways entirely determined by sexuality. Indeed, all female cadavers appear to have been the sexual objects of anatomy and the differences between them depend on their apparent sexuality – the varying degrees of their perceived sexual openness: the pre-sexual girls mark a wholly unavailable sexual potential; the nun marks a denial of sexuality, while the "hunchback" girl embodies only rejected (undesirable) sexuality, and the prostitutes figure entirely accessible or open (and therefore devalued) sexuality.

The woman who is conspicuously absent from Vesalian anatomy of the female body is that woman who is married and comfortably middle class –

Plate 4 Andreas Vesalius, from *De humani corporis fabrica libri septem*.
Basle, 1543. 5.27.

the prototypic bourgeois woman whose sexuality is perceived as sanctioned and wholly domesticated. This woman's body holds no secrets; everything about her is clear and legible from the outside. Her place in the family and in society is assured by virtue of her active and responsible sexuality. For patriarchal culture to function as such, her hymen must necessarily be "missing," though the cause of this is in no way doubted. It is only when her sexual fidelity becomes suspect (as does Desdemona's), and therein inaugurates a crisis over her knowability, that her body is imagined as a site of epistemological struggle.

For Vesalius, then, female bodies were fundamentally sexual bodies – but this sexuality is completely discursive. The opening of these female bodies amounts to the opening of the stories they figure. Thus we are told the story of the non-pregnant woman of the title page, or the account of the dissection of the uterus of the "hunchback" girl "for the sake of the hymen" (O'Malley 201). Implicit in Vesalius's masculinist faith in "ocular proof" – much like Othello's – is the conviction that women's bodies contain – or *are* – narratives. And it is by narratives that both Vesalius and Othello are seduced.

In his account of the autopsy of an eighteen-year-old woman "of agreeable appearance," Vesalius decides the cause of death and ascribes responsibility: the woman simply wore her corset too tight in order that "her waist might appear long and willowy," which caused "compression of her torso." Vesalius then offers the following narrative:

After the attendant women had left to shed their corsets as quickly as possible and the rest of the spectators had departed, in company with the physician I dissected the girl's uterus for the sake of the hymen [which] was not entirely whole but had not quite disappeared, as I have found it usually the case in female cadavers in which one can barely find the place where it had been. (O'Malley 63)

Vesalius speculates on the cause of this peculiar state of the hymen and suggests that the girl had "ripped [it] with her fingers either for some frivolous reason or . . . against strangulation of the uterus without the intervention of a man" (O'Malley 63). Vesalius's anatomical investigation here yields not a discussion of structure *qua* phenomenological object, but rather (in dubious fashion, indeed) a narrative (story, fiction) of the woman's private sexuality that purports to account for her anatomical disposition.

The account of this woman's death locates both Vesalius's interest and the woman's fault in her sexuality. In Vesalius's view, the woman's imagined masturbation is clearly "frivolous," though relatively harmless. But her attempt at medical self-help, the attempt to prevent "strangulation of the uterus" by *herself* removing her hymen, constitutes a more significant and dangerous activity. Vesalius's diagnosis depends upon the woman's prior knowledge of sexual matters – particularly her risk of uterine strangulation. Moreover, she must also know that the "proper" preventative treatment is sexual intercourse, which she nevertheless resisted. In Vesalius's phrasing, "the intervention of a man" was necessary, and the woman's resistance an offense against herself. Vesalius's gendered discourse of anatomy suggests that a woman's sexual inactivity is intolerable, not only to the woman herself, but to the (imagined) man who was refused. It suggests, moreover, that the only cure for such a sexual malady is a man's intervention. Vesalius's autopsy speaks to both these concerns. He believes the woman to have been a virgin. His scenario of her solitary autoerotic sexual and medical (mal)practice, though, is perhaps only a fantasy: Vesalius can only *theorize* that there was no man. This attests, I believe, to Vesalius's apparent extreme interest in her virginity – not merely that she was sexually "pure," but that *he*, as a man of science and medicine, was the man whose intervention she needed. Vesalius's proprietary claim to this woman – and her hymen, which he both discovers and destroys – ratifies his sexual claim on her body.

Though Vesalius's intervention comes too late for this particular woman, he offers her story (corrupt sexuality and its anatomical traces) as an emblem, manifest in his lecture upon a corset. This pattern of ideologically motivated medical intervention is by no means exclusively Vesalius's, nor restricted to the sixteenth century. For Freud, masturbation is called "infantile" (rather than "frivolous") sexuality – though equally dangerous – and the intervention of a man in female sexual maladies appears equally essential.[43]

The calculus of the absence and presence of the hymen in the Vesalian body – its occluded presence ("not entirely whole") and present occlusion ("one can barely find the place where it had been") – affords Vesalius the pleasure of Freud's "fort/da": the hymen is gone; the hymen is there. And always, control is in the hands of the captivated manipulator who is caught in the (sometimes morbid) fascination of a repetition-compulsion. Indeed, Vesalius's vigorous attention to the hymen in the feminine body attests to just such a compulsion to repeat the sleight of hand by which both the mere emptiness of the body is inverted and appropriated as a defense against an epistemological collapse, and the politics of the gendered discourse of anatomy is instantiated.

In his "Letter on the china root," Vesalius comments on the recovery (theft) of a body from "the beautiful cemetery of San Pisano." In his account, Vesalius conflates the episode of the recovery of the body of a "hunchback girl of seventeen" with the receipt and dissection of a "cadaver of a nun from some burial vault in Florence [that] was sent on a fast barge":

When the flesh had been removed from the bones of the nun and girl . . . I examined the uterus of the girl since I expected her to be a virgin because very likely nobody had ever wanted her. I found a hymen in her as well as in the nun, at least thirty-six years old . . . I had never dissected a virgin, except a child of perhaps six years. (O'Malley 201)

Vesalius continues the narration with a recollection of the earlier dissection in which, again, he "dissected the uterus solely for the sake of the hymen." Vesalius then makes a curious shift and, in a sentence that is virtually unintelligible for its perplexing syntax, offers as validation his anatomical investigations and his anatomical books – the *Epitome* and the *Fabrica*: "although I found it [the hymen] just as I have seen it recently since the publication of my books, I did not dare make any definite statement about it since I had observed it to be lacking in animals, and furthermore because I am not accustomed to saying anything with certainty after only one or two observations" (O'Malley 201).

The location of the hymen to which Vesalius attached so much significance is in this passage almost unassignable. It seems, however, that the hymen exists finally not in the bodies of the anatomized girls and women, but in the body (*corpus*) of Vesalius's anatomical writing. Anatomy – the "graphic–spatial" science of ocular proof – collapses into a solipsistic self-reflexivity: it realizes its own truth and certainty not in actual bodies, but within its own fabric, body, text.

III

This chapter has attempted to outline in some detail the various desires for and the consequent costs of understanding sexuality and epistemology as inextricable, as well as the ways in which the narrational discourse of ocularity is employed in the service of this interpretive *logos*. The costs to both Othello and Desdemona are both obvious and cataclysmic; the consequences for a particular medical discourse that seeks to discover and articulate an epistemology of the body are nothing less than a blurring (or perversion) of this desire into an embodied epistemology, and the founding of a moralistic and normative discourse of gender and sexuality. The role that gender is imagined to play – particularly the culturally constructed category of the feminine – further complicates scientific inquiry that ideally is phenomenological in nature but which in reality turns out to be highly moral as it negotiates (not entirely successfully) its own skepticism. I have also suggested that criticism has all too often shown a propensity toward accepting the very terms of the debates that themselves ought to be in question – primarily the assumptions that underwrite the notion that one can chart a clear and unproblematical trajectory from sexuality through epistemology to, in the end, ontology: that sexuality does not describe kinds of practices so much as it describes kinds of being – or, that sexuality, finally, is purely a system of representation. Both the early modern anatomical theater and the dramatic theater can be understood as sites for the staging of this system of representation. The crisis I have discussed above that both Shakespeare's *Othello* and Vesalius's *Fabrica* mark is, then, perhaps best understood as a crisis of representation.

I will conclude with a final glance at the early modern English theater, to a play in which punitive anatomization abandons the realm of pure fantasy and "appears" on the stage. In John Ford's *'Tis Pity She's a Whore*, the fantasy of anatomization appears first in the crazed words of Soranzo, ("Not know it [the name of Annabella's lover], strumpet? I'll rip up thy heart,/ And find it there . . . Dost thou laugh?/ Come, whore, tell me your lover, or, by truth,/ I'll hew thy flesh to shreds"),[44] and is later performed by Annabella's lover, her brother Giovanni:

> GIOVANNI: The glory of my deed
>   Darkened the midday sun, made noon as night.
>   You came to feast, my lords, with dainty fare;
>   I came to feast too, but I digged for food
>   In a much richer mine than gold or stone
>   Of any value balanced; 'tis a heart,
>   A heart, my lords, in which is mine entombed:
>   Look well upon't; d'ee know't?
> VASQUES: What strange riddle's this?
> GIOVANNI: 'Tis Annabella's heart, 'tis; why d'ee startle?
>   I vow 'tis hers: this dagger's point ploughed up
>   Her fruitful womb, and left to me the fame
>   Of a most glorious executioner.   (5.6.22–34)

Giovanni's sexual/epistemological desire drives him to the very limits of theatrical representation as he holds before a horrified audience not a metaphor of Annabella's interiority – that private space which Soranzo, for example, finds hopelessly inaccessible – but the thing itself, not the sign of his having possession of her love, but her actual heart. Giovanni, moreover, understands his anatomization of her body as a redemptive act by which he will "dig" from her womb not that unborn child whose future they ponder, but that material fact that acts as guarantor of both their love and his exclusive possession of her. It is, after all, only his sense of possession that allows Giovanni to believe himself entitled to her execution and the fame it creates for him. As Vesalius opens the female body "for the sake of the hymen" and the attendant story its presence/absence can be made to tell, so Giovanni imagines he can open Annabella's "womb" and find in it her heart, that he can open her heart and find in it his own.

In his lover's madness, Giovanni believes this his triumph, his glory. But his victory is of course illusory; Annabella is dead and her heart on his dagger cannot be construed as the fact of their love. By virtue of his deranged attempt to offer the "ocular proof" of love and possession, Giovanni has de-materialized Annabella's heart which exists only semiotically, only as a *sign* of Giovanni's "love." Like Othello and Vesalius, Giovanni never learns the fact of which he is emblematic: that interiority ineffably exceeds the act of representation.

2   (Dis)embodied letters and *The Merchant of Venice*: writing, editing, history

> The concept of the historical progress of mankind cannot be sundered from the concept of its progression through a homogeneous, empty time. A critique of the concept of such progression must be the basis of any criticism of the concept of progress itself.
>
> (Walter Benjamin, "Theses on the Philosophy of History")

The two cultural "sites" dedicated to the narrational discourse of bodily immanence discussed in chapter 1 – the Shakespearean and the anatomical theaters – are both invested in the immediate relation that each supposes exists between the body and presence. For both, the body is imagined as a text whose meaning is available to careful – or sometimes mad – readers. But this act of deciphering can only be secured through the calculated deployment of a particular technology. For Vesalius, that technology is what comes to be called the *science* of medical anatomy, while for Othello it is the technology of the secret police: spies, informers, and, finally, violence. In each instance the particular technology invoked is enabled by a fundamental *visualism* that is believed to secure and to guarantee something like epistemological certainty. As I argued, however, this foundational visualism – just like the specific discourses each unleashes – is thoroughly narrational in nature: the "meanings" they are able to produce are, finally, nothing more than the very effects of prior assumptions about meaning (bodies, texts, truths) upon which each is grounded, and are, strictly speaking, anachronistic.

The body – in dissection, or in "love" – cannot be said to embody presence of the sort imagined by Vesalius and by Othello. Or, in another vocabulary, the body is not, finally, an assembly of characters (letters) to be deciphered. But this is a common enough assumption. In this chapter I would like to turn to the staging of a related set of assumptions concerning the bodies, texts, and immanence: textual production – in *The Merchant of Venice* and in the politics and practices of traditional textual criticism.

39

I

In recent years the practices and ideologies of modern textual criticism have come under extensive review and critique. Our understanding of the linguistic instability of texts, informed by post-structuralism, together with recent retheorizations of modern subjectivity and interpretive innovations offered by such critical practices as new historicism and cultural materialism, have produced a concern for the material or, more to the point, the *textual* nature of culture and its productions – what Jerome McGann recently has called "the textual condition."[1] The practices of this new textual criticism have been theorized in the work of a number of critics, including – most significantly, perhaps – McGann himself, whose project, begun with *Romantic Ideology* (1983) and continued in *A Critique of Modern Textual Criticism* (1983) and *The Textual Condition* (1991), is intended (in part) to heal "the schism between textual and interpretive studies, opened so long ago."[2] McGann's call for a re-imagining of the bibliographical study of texts is predicated upon the identification of texts as "fundamentally social rather than personal" (*Critique* 8). This identification retrieves texts from both the misguided essentialist (and humanist) fiction of the wholly autonomous author and the related discourse of intentionality that are thought to determine the production of texts "outside" or "beyond" both culture and history.

The field of Renaissance studies has proven to be fertile ground for such inquiry. In particular, revisionist work on Shakespearean texts offers us powerful ways to theorize the question, "What is a text?" (even before we can begin to formulate answers to it); new ways of understanding the multiple, often divergent and yet nevertheless equally "authentic" texts we do have; fresh insights into the materiality of texts and textual production (printing house practices, for instance); and increasingly thorough and sophisticated accounts of early modern conceptions of publishing, collaboration, and the complex issues of authorship.[3] These newly articulated critical and theoretical interests and inquiries have served to redefine the nature of textual criticism. This practice of "unediting," as Randall McLeod and Leah Marcus have called it, has "produced" a long list of "recovered" texts – texts (quartos, copies, etc.) that traditional textual theory and criticism have consistently dismissed as "bad," "corrupt," or otherwise inferior to their own texts: the two versions of *King Lear*, or the equally "valid" versions of the much-disputed *Doctor Faustus*, to name two prominent examples.[4]

My use here of the terms "produced" and "recovered" is somewhat ironical: it has been the object of traditional textual criticism to produce "authoritative" texts in the absence of authorial script, which is imagined as recoverable because final authorial intention is believed to reside in the extant texts, even if it becomes visible (present) only in reconstructed texts, or, more frequently, in texts that are more or less hypothetical. "Unediting" *produces* no (new) texts, and can even be said to resist the entire notion of such production. Rather, "unediting" insists upon the integrity of textual productions without recourse to claims for the "authorial" status of these texts, and therein cannot be said either to produce or to recover texts – at least not in the conventional senses of these terms as they come to us through traditional textual criticism.

In discussing the composite nature of the two versions of *Doctor Faustus*, Leah Marcus argues for a sufficiency for both but (greater) proximity to "the absent authorial presence we call Marlowe" for neither:

> It is time to step back from the fantasy of recovering Marlowe as the mighty, controlling source of textual production and consider other elements of the process, particularly ideological elements that the editorial tradition has, by the very nature of its enterprise, suppressed. I would like to second [Michael] Warren's call for a separation of the two texts of *Doctor Faustus*, but carry his argument further by contending that for *Faustus*, and for Renaissance drama more generally, a key element of textual indeterminacy is ideological difference. (Marcus 3)

Marcus argues that "we can learn something about the vagaries of Renaissance authorship and mark out new areas for interpretation if we wean ourselves from the ingrained habit of regarding textual 'accidentals' as insignificant" (Marcus 24), and asks us to reconsider "accidentals" – such as the A text's "Wertenberg" and the B text's "Wittenberg," A's empty stage at the play's end and B's stage littered with the fragments of Faustus's body – as significant in establishing markedly "different configurations of religious experience" in the two plays (Marcus 12).[5] "Accidentals" such as those reflecting divergent religious experience are in fact substantial and consequential elements of both plays, attributable to revisions – Marlovian or post-Marlovian – of the play in history.[6]

As has been suggested above, the case for reconsidering our editorial determinations concerning texts and their (relative) "authority" has gone a long way in helping create the very possibility of this argument: in our relationship to texts we are no longer so strictly bound to the desire to recover – or, for that matter, the very faith in – the lost "original." Indeed, as poststructuralist theory has taught us, the idea of the original is not only misleading, but wholly illusory; "we have no originals," Jonathan Goldberg reminds us, "only copies."[7]

Marcus's discussion of "accidentals" allows us access to non-authorial elements that survive in or help to determine play-texts – evidence, as it were, for textual (and bibliographical) traces of nonauthorial agency. At the same time, however, Marcus's argument – while perhaps controversial in its revisionist claims for the two texts of *Faustus* – is nevertheless dedicated to the discussion of agency within texts, whether that agency is authorial or non-authorial, and as such offers only a restricted critique of textual criticism and traditional practices of editing. This is analogous to what Jonathan Goldberg has identified as "the combination of textual audacity and critical conservatism" to be found even in as bold an intervention in Shakespearean studies as *The Division of the Kingdoms*: "There are two *King Lears*, we are told, but we are assured that the Quarto derives from Shakespeare's manuscript and that the Folio represents an authoritative revision. The kingdom has been divided, but Shakespeare reigns supreme, author now of two sovereign texts" ("Textual Properties" 214).

As audacious as it is, Marcus's argument – perhaps like that of *The Division of the Kingdoms* – returns in the end to texts as instantiations of agency. Perhaps another way to say this is to suggest that in spite of its obvious innovations, unediting of the sort practiced by Marcus still subscribes to traditional textual criticism's identification of the two fundamental components of textuality: accidence (the surface characteristics of the text, such as punctuation and spelling) and substance (the meaning intended). What serves to unite these two forms, of course, is the notion of intention that – however distanced, or non-authorial – nevertheless reigns supreme, a "fact" that allows, then, the validation of such textual accidentals ("Wertenberg," for example) that guarantee the Marlovian character of *Faustus*. But what should happen if we shift our discussion away from the notion of accidence and its place in textualization; if we move instead toward a consideration of *accidents*? What emerges, I suggest, is an interpretive space within which to theorize eruptions not merely of the non-authorial (which unediting can easily accommodate), but of the *non-agential*.

In "Dispatch Quickly: The Mechanical Reproduction of Pages," Elizabeth Pittenger discusses the issue of the accidental in Shakespeare. Pittenger identifies an important moment in *The Merry Wives of Windsor* (*MWW*) that thematizes the disruptive effects of accidents which serves as a marker for a certain gendered and class disruption of and resistance to dominant discourse. The Latin lesson scene, like the educational and pedagogical theories it parodies, is predicated upon the notion of mechanical repetition in the service of a number of cultural imperatives: "Hugh's mission," Pittenger observes, "is not merely to initiate William into the extra-familial world of men; it is also to produce the demarcations of gender, class, and race that would stamp him as a proper English *man*. Social replication is inscribed in the mechanical repetition."[8] But the language lesson does not progress quite so smoothly precisely for the reason of accidence/accidents: the intended study of (Latin) accidence (the stuff, as it were, of formal grammar) is "punctuated by accidents, by accidental similarities between two linguistic codes [the king's and Mistress Quickly's], similarities that are turned into accidents – that is, collisions of sense in the form of malapropisms" (Pittenger 396). In the punning of the scene, which Pittenger argues points to moments of linguistic "looseness" in the lesson – Quickly's confusion of "pulcher" for "powlcats" (whores), for example, and, in response to Hugh's question "What is a Stone," William's slightly obscene response, "A Peeble" – the disruptions of language, translation and pedagogical repetition are clearly evident, yet cannot be identified absolutely with any clear agency. The king's standard language system has been supplemented by Quickly's "substandard" one, whose "multiple dispersals defy the ideal of unmediated transmission, the belief in mechanical reproduction" (Pittenger 401). The effects of the "derailment" of the language lesson are critical:

Although Quickly's disruptions follow a discernible rule and perhaps are completely confined by the limits of the pedagogical lesson, they are still in some sense unpredictable, accidental – or, more precisely, they *represent* the effect of accidents. By foregrounding the capacity of the lesson to go astray, Quickly's malproper speech does not simply overturn, travesty, or burlesque proper speech; rather, the effect is to resituate improper, loose speech in the lag between call and response, to emphasize that there is a lag, a looseness already there. (Pittenger 401–2)

Pittenger's discussion of *MWW* identifies a significant treatment of accident (in relation to accidence) and its ramifications in the play – especially in the domain of gender. But what makes this thematization of accident notable is that it is anything but accidental. In other words, in the language lesson of *MWW*, the accidental is – as a matter of (authorial) intention – entirely *un*accidental; it constitutes, rather, a deliberate *staging* of accident, and is not itself an instance of accident. I would like to extend the radical critique of traditional textual criticism and the traditional practices of text-editing implicit in the project of "unediting" by suggesting that while texts are historically understood as instruments of agentiality *par excellence*, they nevertheless embody traces of *non-agential* writing. Goldberg argues that the "Shakespearean text is a historical phenomenon, produced by ongoing restructurations, revisions, and collaboration; by interventions that are editorial, scribal, theatrical; by conditions that are material, occasional, accidental" ("Textual Properties" 215). New textual theory and practice, such as Marcus's, have indeed revised our notions of these material and occasional conditions. Following Goldberg's extension of the radical instability of the text to include "the typographical character" that stands as "one further sign – literally, a reminder of the compositor – that points to the composite nature of every Shakespearean text," however, and his explicit call ("since it is all that we have") for a "return to the letter"

("Textual Properties" 216), I will focus here on the *accidental* conditions of (Shakespearean) textuality, and suggest that there are ways in which we can understand these significant traces of non-agency, these *accidents* that are precisely *accidental*.

To argue for the value of true textual accidents (misspelled words, compositor's errors, textual obscurities or incoherences) and their availability to critical inquiry is to offer a fundamental revision of the philosophical underpinnings of traditional textual criticism which is founded upon the suspect epistemology of presence, and as such constitutes an elaborate narrational discourse of causality: a complex set of theories and practices dedicated to the description and reconstitution of texts.[9] Traditional textual criticism, then, is nothing less than a form of *historiography*, fundamentally conservative in nature and essentially narrational in form, dedicated to the preservation of presence and historical continuity, and in which the text is construed as the site where historical progress is believed to be materially evident.[10]

In his *Critique*, McGann discusses this notion of the text and/in history, especially as it is reflected in the ideas of the copy-text and the critical edition produced through the practice (I will want to say the *historical* practice) of collation, and the critical apparatus that "displays the 'history' of the text" (*Critique* 24). These practices, it is important to note, are both produced within an entirely historical epistemological framework and at the same time are intended to (re)produce the text in its historical development. And yet, the effect of the critical text that has so thoroughly given itself over to the historical reconstruction of a (hypostatized) "originary" presence, is to evade history, to posit its own existence as transcendental, beyond temporality and outside history: "the critical edition embodies a practical goal which can be (within limits) accomplished, but it equally embodies an illusion about its own historicity (or lack thereof)" (*Critique* 93–94).

McGann finds the terms of this understanding problematical, especially as the long history of modern textual criticism is predicated upon the notion of development or progress: "This view of scholarship and program of general education are based upon a paradigm which sees all human products in processive and diachronic terms. The paradigm has controlled the work of textual criticism from its inception, and it operates to this day" (*Critique* 119).

Like McGann, I want to return the text more fully to history. But unlike McGann, however, I do not understand history to be fully meaningful, or wholly caused. My desire is to renounce the Hegelian philosophy of history that determines historicism in the model of *traditional* bibliographical or textual studies. Textual study has always been informed by an implicit philosophy of history, even when it claimed to be managing an entirely positivistic set of operations and maneuvers. One of the explicit premises of this study is that the textual criticism it advocates is thoroughly historical and resolutely non-Hegelian. I will not argue that any current embodiment of a particular text represents the culmination of its (teleological) evolution, but rather that the text can be said to exist only within history so long as it (the text, our relationship to the text, history itself) is not merely inserted in a narrative that presupposes a paradigm of progress. I hope by this to extricate the following discussion of texts and (textual) embodiment from the appropriative claims of traditional textual criticism that imagines the text as existing *for us*; I want to argue, instead, that texts – like history – exist in spite of us.

I will turn now to *The Merchant of Venice* and its narratives of the scenes of reading and writing – the first of a series of such narratives that extends from Shakespeare to the practitioners of traditional textual criticism. These narratives are predicated upon an implicit science of presence-in-writing and are, moreover, conceived as progressive and wholly inscribed within the world of essential agentiality. The metaphysical notions of writing, editing, and textuality that authorize modern editorial practices, indeed, underlie *Merchant*, a play in which presence (body) is imagined as immanent in the letter. But the actual text (or texts) of *Merchant* and recent critiques of the practices of textual criticism belie these assumptions. Scenes of reading and writing, as Goldberg argues, "do not allegorize a notion of the text itself. Rather, they point to a textuality that is radically unstable, upon which plots move, characters are (de)formed, language and observation is (improperly) staged. They point, that is, to historical and cultural demarcations, to what passes for essences, desires, knowledge, and the like" ("Textual Properties" 217). Presence-in-writing is always merely the dream of writing (even if an enabling dream), and texts do not finally exist in an entirely deterministic universe void of accidents; accidents abound, and they are meaningful precisely because they are uncaused. Accidents are signs forever detached from any system of signification, but the meaning of accidents is specific and absolute: accidents "mean" the absence of meaning. But this is an argument against which *Merchant* offers its considerable resistance.

The particular (textual) accident I will discuss is the "problem" involving the characters Solanio, Salerio, and Salarino in *The Merchant of Venice*, and the editorial decision (suggested by John Dover Wilson in the 1926 Cambridge edition and adopted almost universally by subsequent editors) to consider the name "Salarino" as simply an error, a textual mistake, that should be replaced by "Salerio." Wilson's "evidence" supporting his emendation is, however, problematical, especially as it is generated by the idea of the unitary and authoritative text that depends upon a science of presence that produces both the notion of the "authorial" text and the unmistakable anxiety manifest in certain readers occasioned by its apparent aberrations and incoherences. Wilson's decision to eliminate Salarino offers a striking instance of a willful intervention of non-authorial agency into the Shakespearean text (however we construe that term) precisely at a moment in which the text is marked by an instance of non-agentiality.

I conclude with a discussion of the matter of textual accidents and the imperative evident in traditional textual criticism to over-write them. It is against these practices (of textual criticism and of a certain historicism) that a theory of radical unediting must stand.

II

A letter is brought to Bassanio, a letter from Antonio. In this letter writing is understood as both inscription and incision, as an act of construction and of destruction, as a hopeful act of preservation and at the same time an act of absolute violence:

Sweet Bassanio, my ships have all miscarried, my creditors grow cruel, my estate is very low, my bond to the Jew is forfeit, and (since in paying it, it is impossible I should live), all debts are clear'd between you and I, if I might but see you at my death: notwithstanding, use your pleasure, – if your love do not persuade you to come, let not my letter. (3.2.314–20)[11]

Here is the hope for presence-in-writing, for the body made immanent in the letter – the hope, we could say (in light of the previous chapter) for the "anatomical" body–text. And yet, at the same time – and as Bassanio understands – this is the letter that kills: "Here is a letter lady,/ The paper as the body of my friend,/ And every word in it a gaping wound/ Issuing life-blood" (3.2.262–65). Writing's dream of presence always inscribes its double: erasure. Commenting on the verse line "Your pen-knife as stay in lefthand let rest" that prefaces *A Booke Containing Divers Sortes of Hands*, Jonathan Goldberg discusses this double nature of writing:

"Stay" suggests that the knife is the support of writing (it keeps the place, marks the line, sharpens the quill, smooths the paper: there can be no act of writing without the knife); but "stay" also suggests that the knife impedes the quill (erasure lies within its domain). As Derrida has argued, what is true of the knife is true of the quill: these are the writer's weapons for a scene in which the production of script also effaces such production to produce the writer's hand – to produce the illusory presence of writing. "Stay" re-marks the double structure of the mark, and the scriptive domain that (dis)locates the writer.[12]

Antonio is similarly (dis)located by the letter he has sent to Bassanio. In the letter he identifies his imminent death as embodied in the bond to Shylock; he also both proclaims and rejects Bassanio's debt to him, and uses the letter to request (virtually to command) Bassanio's presence, even as he rejects the notion of such efficacy in a mere "letter": "if your love do not persuade you to come, let not my letter." This is precisely Antonio's predicament in his forfeited bond (the letter) that situates him even as it guarantees his erasure: he stands, as he says, prepared to die.

Antonio's letter manifests both the desire for and the impossibility of presence-in-writing – a tension between a constructive and a destructive notion of writing that is mirrored on a material level in the Hayes Quarto.[13] Dover Wilson recognized that the letters and scrolls in *Merchant* are "bibliographically speaking, textually distinct" from the rest of the play-text.[14] While I disagree with Wilson's argument that such distinctness serves to identify the letters as either scribal or playhouse additions, their bibliographical distinctness does stand as a material manifestation of the very impossibility of the dream of presence-in-writing: these texts that seek to embody or to locate characters are themselves radically dis-embodied and dis-located from the surface of the play-text. Antonio's letter (which we can now see was "mis-quoted" above) actually appears in the 1600 Quarto thus:

[POR.] But let me heare the letter of your friend.

> *Sweet* Bassanio, *my ships have all miscarried, my Creditors growe cruell, my estate is very low, my bond to the Jewe is forfaite, and since in paying it, it is impossible I should live, all debts are cleerd betweene you and I if I might but see you at my death: notwithstanding, use your pleasure, if your love do not perswade you to come, let not my letter.*

POR.: O love! dispatch all busines and be gone.[15]

The text of Antonio's letter is clearly distinct from the rest of the passage: it stands materially apart from the rest of the text most obviously by virtue of its use of italic typeface. At the same time, it separates itself from the rest of the text – and from the rest of the text's normal "grammar" – by virtue of being unassigned: Portia is given a speech tag both before and after the text of the letter, and there is no speech tag for the letter itself.[16]

In his discussion of Hamlet's letter to Claudius, especially the signature that either does (in the Folio) or does not (in the second quarto) accompany it, Jonathan Goldberg discusses a similar instance of a letter and its typographical relationship to the rest of the play-text in which it occurs:

In the Folio [as compared to the second quarto], Hamlet's signature is printed in the same type as the rest of the text of the play and the same type as the names "Horatio," "Rosincrance," and "Guildensterne" that appear in the letter; save for them, the entire body of the letter as well as the subscription is in italics. Do italics therefore mark the letter as *not* part of the play, or not part of the script produced by the hand that wrote the rest of the text? But in that case, to whom does the letter belong when the signature is not in the same hand as the letter, but instead marked the same way as the hand that produces the rest of the text?[17]

Unlike the Folio Hamlet's letter, Antonio's letter is both unassigned and unsigned; it has no voice (that Portia or Bassanio voices the letter on stage is either purely conjectural or merely convenient), and the signature that would "authorize" it exists only under erasure. Though this is the letter that claims to be the body of its author, it is, finally, the letter that inscribes instead the impossibility of presence-in-writing. This is the disembodied letter.

The appearance of Antonio's letter represents a violent eruption of something like tragedy into the scene of romance surrounding Bassanio's choice. But before we see Portia's Belmont as entirely idyllic, it is important to recognize the ways in which Portia's world is in fact organized around a central but unstaged scene of writing/violence: her father's will mandating the test of the three caskets – the very thing that introduces further instances of violence or its implicit threat.

If we can speculate on the nature of this specular scene of writing/violence – as indeed the play invites us to do, particularly in those moments in which Portia herself contemplates her father's mandate (his will and his writing) and its effects on her: "I may neither choose who I would, nor refuse who I dislike, so is the will of a living daughter curb'd by the will of a dead father" (1.2.22–25) – Portia's father's will stands as an exemplary instance of a profound faith in the metaphysics of writing, its supposed ability to figure the presence of the body as immanent in writing itself.[18]

There is little doubt that Portia's father's will has more to do with Portia's father than it does with Portia herself, as is clear in Nerissa's early comment on the test of the three caskets: "who chooses his meaning chooses you" (1.2.30–31). What is at stake, then, in the suitor's choice is the father's meaning – and the father's wealth, all of which Portia gives over to Bassanio, "Myself, and what is mine, to you and yours/ Is now converted" (3.2.166–67). Portia signifies in this economy of male desire merely as the embodiment of wealth and as heir to her father's seemingly limitless fortune, as Bassanio's prioritized list of Portia's characteristics perhaps intimates: "In Belmont is a lady richly left,/ And she is fair" (1.1.161–62). To the materialistic Bassanio (or Morocco, or Arragon), the correct casket holds the license to assume the position of the father, as well as his possessions marked by the representation of its "real-world" signifier: Portia's portrait. The logic of Portia's father's will is predicated upon an informing faith in the myth of presence-in-writing executed across the figure of Portia as its signifier.[19] It is this logic (with which I take exception) that was read so influentially by Freud in his famous essay "The Theme of the Three Caskets."[20]

Freud read well the intentions informing Portia's father; he understood, that is, that the caskets really do *for him* represent Portia herself. But there is no reason that we need to see the same thing in the three caskets. The caskets can be said to hold different versions of the preserved paternal will

– that is, different versions of that will, or, even, of the father "himself."
What is more (and quite unlike the caskets in the source tale of the *Gesta
Romanorum*), these caskets contain *two* sorts of material representations of
the suitors' fates: the death's head, the "portrait of a blinking idiot," and
Portia's portrait constitute the first sort, while *writing* constitutes the
second.

Morocco had earlier announced another writing test by which to determine true from false love, the worthy from the unworthy:

> Mislike me not for my complexion,
> The shadowed livery of the burnish'd sun,
> To whom I am a neighbour, and near bred.
> Bring me the fairest creature northward born,
> Where Phoebus' fire scarce thaws the icicles,
> And let us make incision for your love,
> To prove whose blood is reddest, his or mine.   (2.1.1–7)

Morocco's boast (and it is perhaps more than a mere boast; it may speak
earnestly to the very prejudice of which Portia seems to be a mouthpiece –
"Let all of his complexion choose me so" [2.7.79], she says upon Morocco's
"thus losers part") displays an understanding of the ways in which "truth"
is aligned with writing, or, as he says, inscribing. Much as a writer cuts into
a page with the quill/knife, Morocco imagines the resolution of the racial
obstacles he faces lies in incising his body, in a writing both on and of the
body – a writing that will embody or make present a truth (i.e., his virtue
as equal to and deserving of Portia) symbolized for him in the redness of
his blood.

It is a faith in real bodies, and their persistence even in absence – their
immanence, that is, in the dream of presence-in-writing – that motivates
Portia's father and his will. At the same time, the faith in real bodies motivates Shylock's passionate pursuit of the forfeiture of the bond, under-
writing, as it were, Shylock's much-discussed adherence to "the letter of the
law." Shylock very clearly understands there to be an intimate relationship
between the body and writing, even as he hopes to kill Antonio by inscribing upon his body both the costs of the forfeited bond and the wages of
Antonio's antisemitism. At the same time, Shylock understands that there
is an equally intimate relationship between the body and the state, which
are mutually dependent and discursively figured: Antonio's fate lies in
Shylock's hands to the extent that Venice as a political entity lies embodied
in its laws, hence Shylock's repeated appeals to law and justice. The Duke
necessarily finds this argument compelling and is left no choice but to
endorse what he thinks is the young doctor's sentence against the merchant.
Antonio, for his part, seems to accept the inevitability of his death at
Shylock's hands; in fact, Antonio recognizes that Shylock's execution of the

forfeiture constitutes a writing on his body that will inscribe a specific meaning: "I am a tainted wether of the flock,/ Meetest for death, – the weakest kind of fruit/ Drops earliest to the ground, and so let me;/ You cannot better be employ'd Bassanio,/ Than to live still and write mine epitaph" (4.1.114–18).

For Antonio, the antidote to death is a kind of immortality in writing: his epitaph. He later invokes this imagined presence in his farewell to Bassanio:

> Commend me to your honourable wife,
> Tell her the process of Antonio's end,
> Say how I lov'd you, speak me fair in death:
> And when the tale is told, bid her be judge
> Whether Bassanio had not once a love:
> Repent but you that you shall lose your friend
> And he repents not that he pays your debt.
> For if the Jew do cut but deep enough,
> I'll pay it instantly with all my heart.   (4.1.269–77)

Antonio's narrational faith in presence-in-writing, like Portia's father's and Shylock's, construes the body as the ultimate ground of writing, whether that writing literally occurs on the body (Morocco's incision, Antonio's pound of flesh) or is understood as immanent in writing itself (Portia's father's will, Shylock's bond). In both instances, writing promises presence in absence and articulates its promise on the level of letteral configurations within the play.

Another significant instance of this dream of presence-in-writing is Portia's embodiment as Balthazar, the young doctor of laws. Portia's disguise is of particular interest because, like Jessica's and Nerissa's corresponding changes, it crosses gender: by virtue of the letter (first Portia's letter to Bellario and then, in turn, Bellario's letter to the Duke), Portia and Nerissa will both appear as men ("accomplished/ With what we lack" [3.4.61–62]) before the Venetian court.[21]

In her transformed shape, Portia manifests a profound ability to exploit the hypostatized relationship among the body, writing, and the state by recasting the narrative of embodiment Shylock and the others have imagined. Portia intervenes in Shylock's narrative (and Antonio's, too, as he projects his embodiment in Bassanio's epitaph) by appropriating Shylock's "linguistic" practice: he has insisted upon the letter of the law (the logic, that is, of presence-in-writing) and it is precisely this literalism ("letteralism") that Portia turns upon him:

> This bond doth give thee here no jot of blood,
> The words expressly are "a pound of flesh":
> Take then thy bond, take thou thy pound of flesh,

> But in the cutting it, if thou dost shed
> One drop of Christian blood, thy lands and goods
> Are (by the laws of Venice) confiscate
> Unto the state of Venice.   (4.1.302–08)

While the outcome perhaps startles – it is Shylock and not Antonio who may die by the violence of the letter – the logic of that violence is no surprise as it has in fact underwritten the entire play, even here in the moment of its evident reversal.[22]

Portia draws the play toward its conclusion with a final letter telling Antonio of the safe return of his ships.[23] But if this last letter represents the moment of comic closure in which even the failure of Antonio's merchant venture (by now perhaps a moot issue) is recuperated, it also represents a profound *mystification* of the letter and all that it is held to signify:

> Antonio you are welcome,
> And I have better news in store for you
> Than you expect: unseal this letter soon,
> There you shall find three of your argosies
> Are richly come to harbour suddenly.
> You shall not know by what strange accident
> I chanced on this letter.   (5.1.273–79)

Though this final letter carries a certain signifying and sensational content, like Antonio (and perhaps like Portia) we cannot account for its presence. The play forecloses any such accounting; the letter simply exists as the final sign of comic resolution. While this letter may stand emblematically for the various operations of the letters we have encountered throughout the play – particularly the desire for presence-in-writing upon which they are founded – this letter comes from nowhere and from no one's hand. It serves, then, to destabilize the very philosophy of the letter and its epistemology of presence; it betrays the mystical or, more aptly, the *theological* nature of the letter. In the end, the letter inhabits the realm of the conjectural, and not the contractual, and our confidence in the letter is actually our profound and desperate faith in it. Rather than serving to guarantee desire and anchor it in the material, the mystical letter affords only the vision of such grounding always just beyond reach. And its only pleasures are the pleasures of the narrational dream of immanence that the letter inscribes as the condition of its own ontology.

III

This dream informs *Merchant* in another instance of the conjectural letter – or conjectural letters: Salerio/Salarino/Solanio – and a putative relationship to presence. This critical textual moment – which, I will argue, is also an accident of critical importance – occurs within the play's most important staging of the scene of reading – in 3.2, the moment (discussed above) just after Bassanio has made the correct choice of the lead casket, and a character arrives carrying Antonio's letter. It is the identity of this character that has caused considerable editorial commentary and intervention. The 1987 New Cambridge Shakespeare edition, edited by M.M. Mahood, identifies the three characters in its "List of Characters" thus:

> SOLANIO   ⎫
>   ⎬ *gentlemen of Venice, and companions with Bassanio*
> SALARINO ⎭
>
> · · ·
>
> SALERIO, *a messenger from Venice*

The entry for Salarino is noted at the bottom of the page: "He may very probably be the same character as 'Salerio,'" and we are asked to consult the "Textual Analysis" that supplements the text.[24] In the pages of the "Textual Analysis" devoted to a discussion of these characters, Mahood offers a careful review of the parameters of this textual "problem" and the "solutions" to it offered by various editors:

Earlier editors of the play were reluctant to believe that Shakespeare, after naming two characters "Salarino" and "Solanio" . . . would have made confusion worse confounded by bringing on a third character called "Salerio." To have created so superfluous a character would have violated "dramatic propriety," put the actors to unnecessary expense, and shown a singular lack of inventiveness in the choice of names . . . In the New Shakespeare edition of 1926, [John Dover] Wilson concurred with Capell in making Salarino and Salerio one and the same person but decided that Shakespeare's name for him must be "Salerio" since this occurs five times in the dialogue. He therefore substituted "Salerio" for "Salarino" or its variants in all previous stage directions and speech headings. All subsequent editors have followed Wilson in this, and Salarino has not put in an appearance for the past sixty years. On a number of grounds, I have restored him to the text of this edition.

(Mahood 179)

Mahood argues there is "no *prima facie* case against Shakespeare having had three different personages in mind. On the other hand, the positive evidence in favor of three characters is admittedly slight" (Mahood 179). After a lengthy discussion of the various arguments both for and against the eliding of Salarino and Salerio, Mahood maintains the distinction between these characters within the text, while noting in the textual apparatus the possibility that this decision may be untenable. This decision is underwritten, however, not by an argument for one "character" over the other, but is instead guaranteed by an appeal to a reputed authorial intention or the (lost, conjectural or – at the very least – the specular) authorial script:

It is always open to the director to identify Salarino with Salerio, thereby econom-
ising on minor parts and very probably fulfilling Shakespeare's final intention into
the bargain. But the printed text must, I believe, retain three Venetian gentlemen
with similar names because, whatever his intentions, Salarino, Solanio, and Salerio
all figured in the manuscript that Shakespeare actually gave to his actors as *The
Merchant of Venice*. (Mahood 183)

Embedded within this final comment are a number of crucial issues. To
begin with, Mahood accepts a fundamental distinction between the play as
it is performed and the play as a text: in the first instance, the "textual"
stand taken *vis-à-vis* Salarino/Salerio simply does not signify; in the latter,
the "textual" becomes occasion for taking a stand. In other words, this
textual matter finally doesn't matter if the play is imagined in performance
– as *spoken* language – but matters a good deal more if it is instead imagined as a text, as *written* language. This constitutes a "performative"
version of the logocentrism described by Derrida: spoken language is imagined as prior to and more immediate than the written, with the consequences in this particular instance being that in production the play is
substantially different in such a way as to allow an editorial emendation
that in print may be inadmissible. At the same time, Mahood suggests that
whatever the decision in performance, *in print* the three characters must
nevertheless still appear. The performed play, then, enacts yet another split-
ting, reifies the posited distinction between performed and textual play, as
an actor may be – in performance – Salerio while in print he may (still) be
Salarino.[25]

There is another issue at stake in Mahood's "double vision" of a "single"
version of the play, and it is an issue relevant to our understanding of
Merchant more generally. In the above paragraph Mahood identifies the
three characters as "three Venetian gentlemen," while in the "Textual
Analysis" she suggests that their status as "gentlemen" is perhaps open to
some question, and that, moreover, Salerio may not be a gentleman at all,
as his nomination "a messenger from Venice" may well suggest:

a messenger from Venice (3.2.218 SD) could imply that not only is Salerio not to be
confused with the two men-about-town, but that his social status is rather different.
Gratiano's "My old Venetian friend *Salerio*" (218) need not imply equality; it can
be a condescending form of address and also an explanatory phrase such as the
audience would not need if it had met Salerio four times already. Salerio . . . can be
seen as a kind of state functionary . . . This would accord with his role in the trial,
where he is a kind of gentleman usher. (Mahood 181–82)

But Salerio's social status is not the only one at stake: while the "social
nuances of four hundred years ago are not . . . something on which we can
speak with confidence today," Mahood suggests, "it would be quite easy to
make out a case, in the play's first scene, for a social difference between

Solanio and Salarino on the one hand and Bassanio's more immediate group of friends on the other" (Mahood 182). Mahood clearly brings certain notions of class and class-distinctions to the play, and just as clearly suspects Shakespeare to have done so, as well.

While Mahood's decision to retain Salarino seems to depend in part upon his presumed class-based differences from Salerio, it is in fact underwritten by an unquestioned adherence to the tenets of traditional textual criticism – particularly the faith in authorial intentionality. In this regard, then, Mahood's inclusion of Salarino is effectively no different from Wilson's exclusion of him.

Wilson's discussion of what he calls "the muddle of the three Sallies" (Wilson, *Merchant* 100) is a careful analysis of this textual problem and has stood as the almost universal "resolution" reproduced by every subsequent editor of the play until Mahood. Wilson's argument – that "Salarino" is a repeatedly misrecognized or misprinted version of "Salerio" – is heavily indebted to a complex textual genealogical argument in which the copy-text for the 1600 Hayes Quarto is believed to have been pieced together not from prompt-books or manuscript (the latter is the argument favored by recent editors), but from what Wilson calls "secondary theatrical manuscripts" (Wilson, *Merchant* 105). Wilson finds corroborating evidence for this conclusion in a number of the play's more striking textual characteristics: the evident addition of texts into the play – specifically, the letters read aloud in 3.2 and 4.1 and the three scrolls of the casket scenes – the play's stage directions, the related matter of the "three Sallies," and what Wilson deems the evident playhouse additions to the play.

Wilson notes the curious textual features associated with the letters and the scrolls – that they are bibliographically "marked off" within the Quarto, and that for each a speech heading is missing. This bibliographical distinctness, Wilson claims, is "a textual fact of capital importance":

For the absences of prefixes before the letters and the duplication of prefixes in the speeches afford clear evidence that both letters and scrolls are, bibliographically speaking, textually distinct from the rest of the copy, or in other words, insertions . . . Any text, therefore, in which letters, songs or scrolls are seemingly insertions, is to be suspected of being derived, not from the original "book," but from some secondary theatrical source, composed of players' parts. (Wilson, *Merchant* 97–98)

The "frequent vagueness" of entry directions ("Enter Bassanio with a follower or two" [2.2.109], one of whom later turns out to be Leonardo; the entry for the "man of Portia's" who we later learn is Balthazar, and the "Messenger" [5.1.24] who "is discovered four lines later to be Stephano, one of Portia's household") prove that, as Wilson had argued earlier in the New Shakespeare edition of *The Comedy of Errors*, "the dialogue had been copied out (from the players' parts) by one scribe and the stage-directions supplied by another . . . who 'possessed very vague ideas of the text he was working on'" (Wilson, *Merchant* 100). It is precisely this "scribe responsible for the stage-directions" whom Wilson holds accountable both for the "muddle of the three Sallies" and for the general textual state of the entire Quarto.

In his argument for resolving the Salerio/Salarino crux, Wilson lays the responsibility for the problem entirely at the hands of the scribe, reconstructing, based upon his sense of evidence, what must have happened in the scribe's production of the text:

Whence then came this curious "Salarino"? If we assume, as we have already found ourselves entitled to assume, that the text before us was made up of players' parts strung together, transcribed and then worked over by a scribe who supplied the stage-directions, the reply is not difficult . . . [T]his scribe had before him at the outset, we must suppose, a transcript from the parts containing only the bare dialogue and the abbreviated prefixes, so that he would be obliged to rely upon his memory of the play upon the stage for the full names of those characters which were not mentioned in the dialogue itself. Now the form "Salarino" is found, apart from the stage-directions, nowhere in the dialogue and in only one prefix, which occurs at 1.1.8. The prefix "Salari" (which is of course a variant spelling of "Saleri') is, on the other hand, fairly frequent. The beginning of all the muddle, we suggest, was that the scribe found the prefix "Salari" in his text at 1.1.8, took it as a contraction for "Salarino," added "no" to it, and framed his entry-direction accordingly. It accords with this theory that the only time we get the erroneous "Salanio" in the prefixes is at 1.1.15 . . . Clearly, we think, the meddling scribe made the two changes at the same time. (Wilson, *Merchant* 103–04)

From this description of an imagined scene of scribal intrusion and disruption of the Shakespearean text, Wilson constructs an entire narrative of the scribe's work and his absolute consistency in his erroneous and meddling ways:

"Salarino" (or "Salerino") marches happily along in the stage-directions hand in hand with "Salanio" (or "Solanio") up to the end of 3.1, by which time the former name had become such a habit with the scribe that when he comes upon "Salerio" in the dialogue of 3.2 he quite fails to recognize his identity and puts him down as "a messenger from Venice." (Wilson, *Merchant* 104)

The final evidence for Wilson's theory of the "assembled text" is what he identifies as the playhouse additions to the play itself, arguing that "texts derived from secondary theatrical manuscripts are likely to preserve traces of actors', or at least of playhouse, additions." Wilson identifies an early section of 5.1 as such a trace – a "piece of 'fat,' as the modern actor would call it, [that] has clearly been inserted in the text": the prose lines introduced by Lancelot's repeated "sola's" and concluded with what Wilson conjectured was the misassignment of "sweete soule" (Wilson, *Merchant* 105). In his analysis of the significance of the textual irregularities he finds in this brief passage, Wilson has recourse to the assistance of W.W. Greg, "whose authority on matters of this kind is unrivalled" (Wilson, *Merchant* 106). When asked by Wilson what he made of the "sweete soule" matter, Greg theorized a version of the assembled text argument:

I think it is pretty clear that the preceding passage was an insertion in the margin, or more probably on a slip, ending up, as was usual, with a repetition of the *following* words to show where it was to come. The sense shows that the insertion must have begun with the Messenger's words: "I pray you is my Maister yet returned?" I suppose that the printer finding the words repeated in the MS, omitted the second occurrence. The compositor would not be very likely to do this, but a proof-reader might – or there may have been an intermediate transcript.

(qtd. in Wilson, *Merchant* 106)

"Authorized" by Greg's words, Wilson continues his argument by wondering why there should be this addition at all – especially as "the passage . . . might be omitted without any injury to the context." The answer, Wilson declares, is simple: "to give the clown who played Lancelot an opportunity of making the theatre ring with his 'sola!'" "Evidently," Wilson concludes, "the clown in Shakespeare's company, Will Kempe presumably, was fond of caterwauling tricks" (Wilson, *Merchant* 106–7).

Let us for a moment consider the rhetoric of this derisive passage which manifests a certain ideological bias brought to bear not only on the passages under review, but to the editing of the entire play, and, moreover, to that play's "meaning."[26] In this passage Wilson makes the small but serious mistake of referring to Will Kempe not as the *comedian* of Shakespeare's company, but as its *clown* – an error akin to the misidentification of the effect of narrative as its prior object that characterizes narrationality in general. To confuse or conflate the two is to eradicate any distinction between actor and the part an actor might play upon the stage; the consequences of this confusion are significant. In Wilson's rhetoric, Kempe literally *is* a clown, and as such occupies in the "space" of the social world the same position a clown does in the "space" of the theater. So Kempe's addition here – his "piece of 'fat'" – is pure clowning, but clowning with serious ramifications. For Wilson, Kempe's addition represents nothing less than the eruption of chaos and disorder into the otherwise decorous and high-aesthetic world of the Shakespearean play. Kempe becomes the sign of both social and aesthetic disruption and literal (letteral) textual corruption. Wilson's vision of Kempe as the figure of radical instability does not end here, however, for as Wilson says, "if an addition was made to this 'assembled' prompt-book at one place, why not at others?" (Wilson, *Merchant* 107); the text stands hopelessly vulnerable to the pernicious effects of Kempe as the socially and aesthetically disenfranchised figure of instability and subversion. Wilson identifies a second "prose-patch, this time of a ribald nature," in 3.2: "It is pretty certainly a textual addition, and we suspect that it was made by the same hand as wrote the 'sola' slip. Indeed, we are inclined to go even further and to attribute a whole scene to this unknown scribe" (Wilson, *Merchant* 107).

The passage under review here – the opening 59 lines of prose – includes Lorenzo's famously obscure charge, "the Moor is with child by you Lancelot!" (3.5.35–36), and ends when Lancelot exits to prepare dinner. Wilson argues that not only is this so-called prose-patch an addition, but that the entire scene was (again) instigated by Kempe:

it is the verse with which the scene closes that seems to provide the clue we are seeking. The first five and a half lines of this verse are a tribute to Lancelot, or rather to the actor who played him, while the reference to "A many fools that stand in better place" is obviously intended as a hit at some successful rival. In a word, we suggest that Shakespeare had no hand whatever in the composition of 3.5, which might be omitted altogether without loss to the play; that it was added to the "assembled" prompt-book at the same time as the insertions at 5.1.39–49 and 3.2.214–18; and that while 3.5.60–5 was written by some second-rate poet as a compliment to William Kempe, Kempe himself may have been responsible for the very dull fifty-nine lines of prose with which the scene opens.

(Wilson, *Merchant* 108)

Wilson concludes his discussion of the copy for the Hayes Quarto by offering the suggestion that Kempe's role was not limited merely to his assumption of poetic rival to Shakespeare (Kempe has presumed to write, that is, in Shakespeare's hand), but extended to include his role as the "unknown" and "meddling" scribe Wilson's theory of the text had posited: "To sum up, our contention is that the manuscript used as copy by Roberts' compositors in 1600 contained not a line of Shakespeare's handwriting, but was some kind of prompt-book made up from players' parts, to which a theatrical scribe (maybe Kempe himself) had added stage-directions and additions of his own devising" (Wilson, *Merchant* 108). For Wilson, Kempe's intrusive and radically disruptive acts of destabilizing self-promotion are complete, but at a material cost to the integrity of the Shakespearean hand and text. Wilson's theory of the production of *Merchant* attributes virtually everything that is of uncertain authority and authorship – and therefore everything that is deemed aesthetically bankrupt – fully to the hands of Will Kempe.[27]

These suspicions of Kempe's destabilizing presence in *Merchant* betray Wilson's fundamental distrust – not to say fear – of the lower class of which Kempe is made to stand as the embodiment. Wilson's "aristocratic" position, in turn, stands in steadfast opposition to such a disruption, as it seeks to guarantee the "sovereignty" of the Shakespearean texts against dissent, disruption, or subversion from below. This is precisely the sort of political and critical conservatism Terence Hawkes has so brilliantly analyzed in Dover Wilson's career as a "social" writer on Russia and its revolution, and as a literary critic.[28] Hawkes describes Wilson's conservatism (like Tillyard's) as "a version of what, by the time of the second world war, had become a standard British response to national crisis: the construction of long-past, green, alternative worlds of percipient peasants, organic communities, festivals, folk art, and absolute monarchy to set against present chaos" (Hawkes 324). Such a vision imposes a radical reconstruction of "peasant" and "folk" culture as happily acquiescent to the absolute monarch. This is an Edenic vision of folk culture that fails to see in it any potential source of subversive energy, any potential for misrule. But this vision is not imagined, however, as necessarily *natural*. In fact, it takes the very deliberate and careful intervention on the part of people such as Wilson (and figures such as Shakespeare) to produce it, to identify potentially disruptive people such as Will Kempe, and re-create them as docile (royal) subjects. This is achieved, in Wilson's view, through a well-regulated and maintained aesthetic and nationalistic education. Hawkes discusses Dover Wilson's participation in this pedagogic regime as it was articulated in the famous Newbolt Report of 1921 (*The Teaching of English in England*). Wilson's contribution falls into the category of "Literature and the nation," asserting, Hawkes suggests, that "teaching literature to the working class is a kind of 'missionary work' whose aim is to stem the tide of that class's by then evident disaffection." In this manifestly political vision, "literature is offered as an instrument for promoting social cohesion in place of division":

The specter of a working class, demanding material goods with menaces, losing its national mind, besmirching its national character, clearly had a growing capacity to disturb after the events of 1917, particularly if that class, as Dover Wilson writes in the Newbolt Report, sees education "mainly as something to equip them to fight their capitalistic enemies." . . . To Dover Wilson . . . the solution lay quite clearly in the sort of nourishment that English literature offered: the snap, crackle and pop of its roughage as purgative force of considerable political power. (Hawkes 326–27)

Wilson's political conservatism is like his critical and editorial conservatism – both are dedicated to the preservation of so-called traditional (that is, transcendent) values: nation, high-aesthetic value, and the sovereign individual, whether that individual is Shakespeare or, presumably, Tsar Nicholas II. And these transcendent values are themselves underwritten by a Hegelian philosophy and historiography that understands human activity not merely as diachronic, but as processive and, finally, teleological. It is precisely against such a teleological or exclusively linear model that Hawkes offers "Telmah." For Hawkes, *Hamlet* is structured on the model of recursivity: events, words, and phrases appear and then are replayed again ("action replays"), the most famous perhaps being *The Mousetrap*. Hawkes warns us, however, not to be deceived by this recursivity and its symmetries:

It would be wrong to make too much of "symmetries" of this sort, and I mention them only because, once recognized, they help however slightly to undermine our inherited notion of *Hamlet* as a structure that runs a satisfactorily linear, sequential course from a firmly established beginning, through a clearly placed and signaled middle, to a causally related and logically determined end which, planted in the beginning, develops, or grows out of it.

Like all symmetries, the ones I have pointed to suggest, not linearity, but circularity: a cyclical and recursive movement wholly at odds with the progressive, incremental ordering that a society, dominated by the metaphor of the production line, tends to think of as appropriate to art as to everything else. (Hawkes 312)[29]

The metaphor of the production line bespeaks a deep-rooted notion of (historical) progress and it is this narrationalism that authorizes and determines Wilson's editorial practices and produces his version of *Merchant*. Moreover, this philosophy of progress and the epistemology of presence together have powered traditional textual criticism, regardless of local responses to textual "problems." Mahood's decision, for instance, to retain or restore Salarino to the play is a good one, though I disagree with her traditionally determined reasons for doing so. Our current understandings of (Shakespearean) textuality no longer require or endorse the appeal to authorial intention or authorial script. My argument is more concerned with the untenable nature of traditional editorial practice typified by Wilson than with evidential weight behind retaining Salarino. In fact, it seems to me not much to matter *how* there came to be three characters with such names in the Hayes quarto, but simply *that* there came to be these three letteral (mis)configurations we have decided to call characters. The matter of the three Sallies is important here not because it stands as yet another site for our intervention in the attempt "to solve" a textual crux, but rather precisely because it marks the eruption – inexplicable and yet undeniable – of the accidental.

In the anticipated aftermath of the collapse of traditional textual criticism can we theorize a textual practice and a theory of textuality *not* determined by a Hegelian processive philosophy?

IV

To the interpreter, texts often appear as images of time; to the makers of texts, however, they are the very events of time and history itself.

(Jerome McGann, *The Textual Condition*)

I begin this concluding section with the above quotation in part because it strikes me as an apt characterization of the various ways in which the relationship between texts and history is frequently construed: for some readers and critics, texts often are imagined as fully self-present representations of the past (though this idea is of course increasingly difficult to maintain in these post-modern days), while for their creators texts simply are, one might say, "the stuff of history." In criticism texts are typically implicated in history only to the extent that they either (1) represent (embody) a particular historical moment, or (2) can *themselves* stand as historical fields. The latter is precisely what happens in traditional textual criticism that posits the eclectic text as its interpretive paradigm. The model of the eclectic text (the text produced "historically") construes the text as an historical field, the "place" of history, and, moreover, as the site of historical evolution and progress – that "homogeneous, empty time" Benjamin identified as the "foundational" conceit so much in need of what we might today call deconstruction.

To imagine the text not *in* time but *as* time. This is the tendency of traditional textual criticism, powered, as it is, by an underlying Hegelian conception of history as the gradual exfoliation of a master-narrative. Thus traditional editorial practice emerges as a kind of historiography predicated upon an essentially teleological model of progress. For Dover Wilson it is the progressive narrative of an "aristocratic" or "monarchical" political and class conservatism that seeks in archaic forms of absolutism the "redemption" of traditional aesthetic and national value against the threat of proletarian political struggle and revolution. Wilson's is a redemptive vision of the social place of high literary culture: it is in this high literary culture, Wilson suggests, that we can find transcendent liberation and salvation. The appeal to these putative redemptive and salvational powers has been characteristic of our cultural appropriation of Shakespeare, and literary and aesthetic "genius" more generally. But if it is true that texts do not necessarily embody or imply a politics of redemption or liberation, what, then, can texts be said to embody?

In truth, I have asked an unfair question. Or, to put it another way, I have simply changed the terms of what has ever been a false question. In that embodiment (as a textual "property") depends on the now manifestly suspect, if not untenable theory of presence-in-writing, rather than asking what this or that text might or might not embody, let us instead agree that texts do not embody but rather *occur*; texts are not objects but rather events. As McGann suggests, "Properly understood . . . every text is unique and original to itself when we consider it not as an object but as an action" (*Textual Condition* 183). Texts happen in a way analogous to the "happening" of events (historical, social, political, accidental) outside the anachronistic narrationalities of authorship, textuality, causality, diachronicity, history, nationalism, liberation, and so on. This is a way of reading that goes entirely against the grain of a play such as *Merchant*, which articulates the very faith in and philosophy of presence-in-writing and embodiment I have tried to critique here. In place of this narrational theory of reading predicated upon the metaphysics of presence, let us put in place a non-appropriative theory and practice of reading and historiography that allows the texts to exist more purely in history, rather than as latter-day (re)constructions of our own self-interested narratives.

And what of accidents? To the extraordinary extent that they are routinely subjected to narrative strategies dedicated to the explanation or discovery of meaning (the establishment of chronology, the articulation of significance – in short, the demonstration of absolute causality and accountability), textual and historical accidents (the two seem almost indistinguishable) have always been subjected to a reactive practice of over-writing. "Corrected," "emended," or "redefined" out of existence, accidents have almost universally been construed as sites for the contestation of the subject (the author, or – more likely – the critic) against error, confusion, and meaninglessness, and seldom as mere instances of the *uncaused* – that great bugbear to systems of the narrative production of meaning. Accidents are important precisely because as accidents they mark eruptions of phenomena for which we simply cannot account. It is the accident that gives the very notion of causality the lie, and as such accidents can be said to delimit the domain of agency. Traditional textual criticism (like most other forms of narrationality) is motivated by a relentless desire to articulate – in some instances, to manufacture – causality, and as such is dedicated to the description and, more importantly, the extension of the domain of agency. We can see this in the paradigm of the eclectic text in which every word is entirely caused. And in which nothing is allowed to remain accidental. To "clean up" accidents in a text is to construct a narrativized world of total causality and accountability, a purely rational world in which everything is under control; it is to ignore what Derrida calls "the heterogeneity of a *pre-*."[30] This is Dover Wilson's practice, for example, in his construction of a wholly meaningful text of *Merchant*, or in his meaningful description of Russian absolutism. And there are accidents within the narrative of *Merchant* that the play clearly attempts to over-write: the "accident" of a Jew's domination of a Christian that Portia over-writes, for example, or the accident of the loss of Antonio's merchant ships which is redeemed through the mystification of the letter. And there are legion over-writings of accidents in criticism of the play – whether textual or interpretive in nature.

The three Sallies, then, are certainly part of the play. Or, to be more precise, the multiple Sallies are all of them part of the play: the quartos and Folio present, Wilson remarks, not only Salerio, Solanio, and Salarino, but "Salerino," "Salari," and "Saleri," while Mahood lists the cornucopic variety of textual incarnations of these "characters": Salaryno, Salino, Slarino, Salerino, Sala, Salan, Salanio, Salarino, Salar, Sola, Sal, Solanio, Salari, Saleri, Sol (Mahood 180–81). Mahood's list of the Sallie "characters" is emblematic not only of the radical instability of the text, or the proliferation of accidents in that text, but also of our sheer inability historically to account for these "characters," our inability to construct a narrative (of a story or of a text) in which they all have a truly meaningful place. Unediting, then, of the most radical sort – unediting, that is, opposed to the narrational and dedicated to the domains of both the agential and the non-agential – returns the text more fully to history, and at the same time understands texts as more fully historical. And as such demonstrates the limits of agency. In spite of our collective insatiable desire for meaning, there is, as it happens, a world apart – an *accidental* and heterogeneous world.

3   Political maps: the production of cartography in early modern England

Power comes from the map and it traverses the way maps are made.
(J.B. Harley, "Deconstructing the Map")

The previous chapter discussed some of the ways in which traditional textual criticism (and, frequently, the texts upon which such criticism works) can be understood as a manifestation of the will to narrational meaning in its project of textual embodiment, editing, and history. This same desire for absolute meaning – even in the face of sometimes profound resistance – emerges in the early modern period in a number of related cultural practices. This chapter focuses on the production of cartography in early modern England and the ways in which the narrational desire to produce entirely meaningful texts – based in part upon an unquestioned faith in the logic of immanence – constitutes the principal inheritance for early modern cartographers. Cartography in the sixteenth and seventeenth centuries (and perhaps cartography of the modern world, more generally) is predicated upon a particular notion of embodiment in which the object supposed to be embodied in texts is not (merely) the body, but indeed the entire world, or some special fragment of it. Just as textual embodiment proceeds on the notion that its practices are "natural," so too does cartography. In its various – and increasingly technical, or technological – operations, cartography never abandons the implicit premise by which its products (maps) are constructed: that maps represent the natural world. But, as I will argue in this chapter, maps are indeed texts and can be read as texts that are engaged in a vast array of highly artificial and technical maneuvers that are in fact anything but "natural." Maps, as I will argue, are always narrational in nature.

Historically, the study of cartography has been dedicated almost exclusively to discussions of the technical aspects of maps and their production, the innovations and improvements in the science of cartography, and the aesthetic and antiquarian value of maps and map collecting.[1] Invoking explicitly or depending implicitly upon an essential – and essentializing –

63

evolutionary and narrational model, the study of cartography has sought to tell the story of maps and their gradual and inexorable perfection; from the earliest graphic representations in stone or wood to the most sophisticated LANDSAT satellite images, maps, we are told, march in an inexorable progression toward absolute truth in representation made possible by nothing so much as the supposed messianic nature of science and technology. There are, however, a number of problematical assumptions that inform this argument – that maps are pure descriptions of geographical reality, for example; or, that maps are value-free; that maps represent zero-degree intervention; and that maps are, finally, *true* – each of which follows from the primary belief among not only scholars of cartography but "lay people" (map users) as well, that maps exist outside of discourse.

It is only recently that these cartographic and epistemological assumptions have come under any serious review. The most significant challenge – I should say, the most significant *revision* – has come from the work of J.B. Harley. In July 1985, at the Eleventh International Conference on the History of Cartography, Harley presented a keynote speech (published as an article the following year in *Cartographica*) in which he offered an assessment of the state of affairs within the field of the history of cartography by way of an analysis of the state of what is perhaps that field's flagship annual publication, *Imago Mundi*. In his discussion, "*Imago Mundi*: The First Fifty Years and the Next Ten," Harley offered a clear-eyed evaluation – "organized like the proverbial sermon into three parts, a eulogy, an elegy, and some reflections upon utopias" – of the successes and failures of both the annual and the history of cartography as a discipline, more generally.[2] It is the "elegy" section of the article that offers the most striking challenge to the status quo in the history of cartography. While there have been occasional expressions of "disquiet" – some by such luminaries in the field as Gerald Crone and R.A. Skelton in the 1960s – regarding the "antiquarian and bibliographical bias of the history of cartography and its lack of philosophical and methodological direction," Harley suggests that "historians of cartography have seldom engaged in the excavation of their own intellectual landscape":

As a result, too often, perhaps, research in the history of the map has taken the form of a hunt for cartographic truffles. It has taken the form of an elevation of the rare and the beautiful above the everyday and the ordinary . . . It has taken the form of inventory rather than of synthesis, and of description rather than insight. And it has often been concerned with maps as "detached" and value-free artefacts and images to the exclusion of their historical context, their meanings, and their social significations. ("*Imago Mundi*" 6)

While Harley's elegaic analysis emphasizes a number of important issues for historians of cartography to consider – frequency and timing of publication, professional and "lay" audiences, subscription figures, possible academic affiliations, among others – I will look briefly at just two: his concerns regarding the desired *international* character of the history of cartography (and of *Imago Mundi*), and his call for a more multidisciplinary approach to the history of cartography.

In the first instance, Harley cites the initial intention of *Imago Mundi*'s founding editor, Leo Bagrow, to make the journal foster international cooperation and one day become (in Bagrow's words) "an international centre of information" ("*Imago Mundi*" 5). But against this (utopic?) vision, Harley offers rather grim statistics that reveal a "predominant pattern [of] a predominantly Eurocentric course for the development of the history of cartography": from 1935 to 1978, for example, four-fifths of the articles published in *Imago Mundi* "relate to European cartographers and their products." Moreover, the range of international contributions to the "Chronicle" section of the publication announcing events of potential interest to the international community of historians of cartography is strikingly limited ("at most thirty countries" in the forty years between 1935 and 1975, with those nations with five or more entries all coming from Europe or North America). Additionally, Harley calls *Imago Mundi*'s circulation "extremely patchy" – especially outside English-speaking countries. Harley argues:

It may be concluded that in the past fifty years there has only been a rather uneven movement towards Bagrow's initial aims for *Imago Mundi*. In many countries, even those with active groups of researchers in the history of cartography, the tendency has been, at least insofar as it can be monitored through *Imago Mundi*, not so much to dismantle national and linguistic frontiers but to further strengthen and formalise their existence. ("*Imago Mundi*" 8–9)

This is a danger, Harley warns, that threatens the hoped-for "internationalism" of the history of cartography – particularly in terms of *Imago Mundi* – even within the very mechanisms that might be applied to further the "demoting [of] what may be described as the 'national model of development'":

We have already seen how nationalism has stifled rather than stimulated scholarly exchanges in the past. The question is, therefore, would a greater degree of national representativeness in the councils of *Imago Mundi*, *ipso facto*, result in intellectual growth? My own view is that in the process of strengthening international links for our subject we have to avoid the pitfall of further institutionalising nationalism in our arrangements as indeed in our writings. The future of *Imago Mundi* cannot be carved up as though we were some nineteenth-century European imperialists dividing a continent and saying this part belongs to England, this to Germany, this to France, this to the USA, and so on. Its territory belongs not to individuals nor to nations but to the subject and to ideas. ("*Imago Mundi*" 11–12)

This critique of nationalism and its potentially devastating effects on the history of cartography leads to the second issue mentioned above: multidisciplinarity. As is clear, I believe, from the argument for the demotion of nationalism in the history of cartography, the only possible answer to the question of *how* we move away from nationalism and toward internationalism is to move non-institutionally – to move, that is, by way of a new form of historical and interpretive practice that resides, in some manner, outside the institution of cartography itself. This is precisely what Harley calls for, even if he does not explicitly theorize such an enterprise in this particular article. What he does do, however, is predict the new cartography's multi-disciplinary form:

Particular attention could be paid . . . to recruiting editorial advisors – as indeed authors – from a wider spread of disciplines. The history of cartography lies in a no-man's land. It is situated between a range of subjects and its students need to be especially aware of the idea, methods and techniques which develop in those overlapping provinces. We need to become more of a multi-disciplinary subject before we can hope to develop a valid interdisciplinary position for the history of cartography. ("*Imago Mundi*" 12)

Significant disciplinary and epistemological change within the history of cartography, such as Harley outlined in 1985, has been rather slow in coming and appears in the texts of a relatively small number of writers, including the collaborative semiological writings on cartography by Denis Wood and John Fels. In "Designs on Signs: Myth and Meaning in Maps," Wood and Fels subject maps and the various practices and mechanisms of cartography to a thorough semiological reading prompted quite explicitly by the theoretical writings of Roland Barthes – especially those concerned with the "naturalization of the cultural." Wood and Fels assert their structuralist understanding of cartography and maps:

It is, of course, an illusion: *there is nothing natural about a map*. It is a cultural artifact, a cumulation of choices made among choices every one of which reveals a value: not the world, but a slice of a piece of the world; not nature but a slant on it; not innocent, but loaded with intentions and purposes; not directly, but through a glass; not straight, but mediated by words and other signs; not, in a word, as it is, but in *code*.[3]

Wood and Fels later collaborated on a book, *The Power of Maps*, which likewise argues for the constructedness of maps in distinction to their allegedly "natural" status. In their discussion of the map's supposed ability *to represent* property (of various sorts) as *real* by way of marking boundary lines and property lines by inscribing lines on a plan, for example, Wood and Fels argue that it is only within the traditional understanding of the map as "a window on the world" that these lines can be accepted – and *must* be accepted "as representing things . . . [in the world] with the ontological status of streams and hills":

But no sooner are maps acknowledged as social constructions than their contingent, their conditional, their . . . *arbitrary* character is unveiled. Suddenly the things represented by these lines are opened to discussion and debate, the *interest* in them of owner, state, insurance company is made apparent. Once it is acknowledged that the map *creates* these boundaries, it can no longer be accepted as *representing* these "realities," which alone the map is capable of embodying.[4]

The other major contributor to the new epistemology of cartography predicted by Harley is – perhaps not surprisingly – Harley himself in his post-structuralist writings on cartography, from 1985 until his death in 1991. In a series of articles that can be read as a response to his own call for a more rigorously theoretical model for the history of cartography – beginning with "Silences and Secrecy: The Hidden Agenda of Cartography in Early Modern Europe" (1988), and including (among others) "Maps, Knowledge, and Power" (1988), "Deconstructing the Map" (1989), and "Rereading the Maps of the Columbian Encounter" (1992) – Harley argues for a new understanding of cartography that explicitly places maps within discourse, an understanding that recognizes cartography as a *social* practice embedded in both ideology and the politics of power. In many ways, this new understanding arises as a reaction to Harley's own critical observations regarding the problematical relationship between the traditional practices of the history of cartography and that disruptive and corrupting set of constraints collected under the rubric of "nationalism." If Harley recognized in 1985 that the interests of particular nationalisms indeed determine the very structure and practices of the history of cartography, it is so to no small extent because cartography itself – as Harley's work reveals quite powerfully – has *always* been in the service of nations and national ideologies. In other words, Harley's work enables us to see the ways in which cartography and its maps are produced by specific, local, and historical interests of political and national power.

Harley's late work on cartography is heavily influenced by the writings of Michel Foucault, which enable Harley to propose a *political* reading of maps within their particular historical and nationalist contexts as manifestations of a certain power-knowledge system. In "Silences and Secrecy," Harley asserts that early modern cartography "was primarily a form of political discourse concerned with the acquisition and maintenance of power."[5] With this assertion Harley effectively reinvents the history of cartography and the kinds of question it asks concerning the very maps we have traditionally believed to be entirely objective:

As cartography became more "objective" through the state's patronage, so it was also imprisoned by a different subjectivity, that inherent in its replication of the state's dominant ideology. The old question of whether particular maps are true or false has not been my concern in this paper. On the contrary, this question has to be downgraded if it is accepted . . . that maps are perspectives on the world at the time of their making. My aim in this essay has been to initiate the interrogation of maps as *actions* rather than as impassive descriptions and to persuade historians of cartography to ask the crucial question "What are the 'truth effects'" of the knowledge that is conveyed in maps? ("Silences and Secrecy" 71)[6]

It is within this new cartographic discourse that I would like to situate the following discussion of the complex practices of cartography in early modern England. My aim is twofold: 1) to read cartography both theoretically (What is a map? What can we say about its system of representation?) and practically, especially as it is implicated in an emergent discourse of nationalism and the antithetical discourse I will here call *localism*; and 2), to offer a discussion of early modern cartography's fundamental narrational nature.

I

> Whilst my physicians by their love are grown
>   Cosmographers, and I their map, who lie
> Flat on this bed, that by them may be shown
>   That this is my south-west discovery
> *Per fretum febris*, by these straits to die,
>   I joy, that in these straits, I see my west;
>   For, though their currents yield return to none,
> What shall my west hurt me? As west and east
>   In all flat maps (and I am one) are one,
>   So death doth touch the resurrection.
>
> (John Donne, "Hymn to God my God, in my sickness"[7])

By the time Donne wrote "Hymn to God my God, in my sickness," the idea of man as microcosm was a familiar, though still powerful, conceit. And yet, Donne transforms this conceit through the invocation of maps: Donne does not claim to be the world, but rather its map – not the world, but its representation.[8] In this distinction Donne points to the fundamental act of signification by way of which maps are understood as representations of the world.

The map that Donne has in mind in the "Hymn" is what had been, even into Donne's own historical moment, the fundamentally heretical map representing the earth as a sphere and not, as had been the case for centuries in Christian representations of the world, as a flat disk with Jerusalem at its center, surrounded by water (plate 5).[9] Donne has something like Mercator's famous global map in mind. The innovations Mercator's map would codify for centuries (some of them down to our own moment, in fact) were enabled by the growing belief in a spherical world, made evident by the voyages of Columbus, and then by Magellan's circumnavigation, and

Plate 5 World map: "Fra Mauro Map" (copy of a 1453 original).

represented in the "new" cosmography made available once again (for hadn't ancient Greek natural philosophy determined a spherical earth set in a heliocentric universe?) by the work of Copernicus.[10] While it is difficult to determine precisely the nature of Donne's relationship to the new cosmography, in his satirical attack on the Jesuits, *Ignatius His Conclave*, he does manifest a certain distrust – or resentment – aimed at both Columbus and Copernicus.[11] In that book the narrator experiences an "Extasie" in which he is able to survey the dominions in Hell and the appearance of several claimants to occupy "a secret place" in Hell with Lucifer, including, among others, both Columbus and Copernicus.[12] The narrator of *Ignatius* reserves the hallowed place nearest Lucifer for those "which had so attempted any innovation in this life" (*Ignatius* 9). It is the innovation of the heliocentric universe that constitutes Copernicus's claim:

I am he, which pitying thee who wert thrust into the Center of the world, raysed both thee, and thy prison, the Earth, up into the Heavens; so as by my means *God* doth not enjoy his revenge upon thee. The Sunne, which was an officious spy, and a betrayer of faults, and so thine enemy, I have appointed to go into the lowest part of the world. Shall these gates be open to such as have innovated in small matters? and shall they be shut against me, who have turned the whole frame of the world, and am thereby almost a new Creator? (*Ignatius* 15)

Donne's cosmographical ambiguity – at least at this moment in his writings – is present even in Ignatius's refutations of Copernicus's claims to transcendent evil. Ignatius refutes Copernicus by suggesting that the heliocentric revolution has had little consequence for mankind – and, therefore, for Lucifer – even if it happens to be true:

what new thing have you invented, by which our *Lucifer* gets any thing? What cares hee whether the earth travell, or stand still? Hath your raising up of the earth into heaven, brought men to that confidence, that they build new towers or threaten God againe? Or do they out of this motion of the earth conclude, that there is no hell, or deny the punishment of sin? Do not men beleeve? Do they not live just, as they did before? Besides, this detracts from the dignity of your learning, and derogates from your right and title of comming to this place, that those opinions of yours may very well be true. (*Ignatius* 17)

Columbus is not given the opportunity to speak but is simply presented before Lucifer and then preemptively cried down by Ignatius who lays his own claim to the exalted position. As he did with Copernicus, Ignatius refutes Columbus's innovation. In this instance, interestingly, Ignatius repudiates Columbus by offering the record of the Spanish (Jesuit) genocide of the Amerindians as a far greater instance of man conducting Lucifer's work on earth:

You must remember, sir, that if this kingdome have got anything by the discovery of the *West Indies*, al that must be attributed to our *Order* [the Jesuits]: for if the opinion of the *Dominicans* had prevailed, *That the inhabitants should be reduced, onely by preaching and without violence*, certainly their 200000 of men would scarce in so many ages have beene brought to a 150 which by our meanes was so soone performed. And if the law, made by *Ferdinando*, onely against *Canibals: That all which would not bee Christians should bee bondslaves*, had not beene extended into other Provinces, wee should have lacked men, to digg us out that benefite, which their countries affoord. (*Ignatius* 69)[13]

Donne's satire on the innovations represented by these two figures is all the more curious given what is perhaps his ultimate acceptance (some would even say his celebration) of the new cosmology and cartography and the new worlds they afford.[14] This simultaneous acceptance and rejection is played out in the "Hymn" in which the cosmological vision is simultaneously Ortelian in its progressiveness and medieval in its typological dimensions. In the poem, Donne refers to "cosmographers" and not "cartographers" – a distinction of some significance in this period that witnessed the reemergence of cosmography in a new and revised form evident, for example, in several works by Sebastian Münster and André Thevet intended to update Ptolemy's *Geography*. Unlike the more "localist" discourse of cartography, Renaissance cosmography – or, as it is sometimes called, the New Geography – depended, as Frank Lestringant argues in his study, *Mapping the Renaissance World: The Geographical Imagination in the Age of Discovery*, an over-riding attention to a "full, global world with no other limits than the celestial orb that, projected on to it, formed its poles, regions and zones."[15] Lestringant argues that the cosmographical vision of the totality of the universe ("the cosmographical is synonymous with the small scale, in the cartographical sense of the term") – because it "presupposes that one can assume the ideal gaze of the Creator upon his world, or that one can transport oneself, like Menippus, into the lunar realms" – is made available to the cosmographer by two "privileged means of access to the knowledge he seeks: that opened up by ecstacy, and that opened up by satire" (Lestringant 19). While it is the latter mode – cosmographical ascension via satire – that Donne offers in *Ignatius*, and the former – access to cosmographical totality via ecstacy – in the "Hymn," it is the relation between the ecstatic cosmographical vision and divinity stressed in the "Hymn" that Donne celebrates. It is as if *true* religious devotion alone (which is by definition, then, *protestant* religious devotion) can access the God's-eye-view of the world. In this regard, Donne follows closely the founding principle of Renaissance cosmography that (in Thevet's words in his *Cosmographie universelle*) "after theology there is no science that could have a greater virtue of making us understand the divine grandeur and power, and cause us to admire it, than this one."[16]

In the cosmographical context, one of the curiosities of Donne's poem is his reference to flat maps, and not to globes. While Donne means to draw a parallel between flat maps and his body rendered prone by the ravages of disease, the notion upon which the poem articulates its resolution depends upon the idea of the earth's sphericity, which is figured tropically as types of circularity – both the circularity of the Christian notion of the resurrection (a circularity of time), and upon the notion that "in the world" east does in fact meet – or rather, *become* – west (a circularity of space). If one "projects" this conceit onto graphic representations of the world, the globe would be the most apt choice since on it east and west (as termini, though not as directions) are, finally, unrecognizable. And yet, Donne chooses the metaphor of the flat map. By this Donne admits to having accepted the epistemology of cartography, which is to say he has accepted either the mathematics of projection (the calculus by way of which spherical objects can be approximately imaged on a plane), or he has accepted the fiction of maps. Indeed, that flat maps actually do promise a coterminous east and west depends upon the acceptance of the fictional nature of the frame of the map itself: in this moment, direction (movement through time) evaporates as linearity gives way to circularity. Donne's conceit works, then, because it literalizes the circularity flat maps hold out purely metaphorically: all flat maps figure *straight* lines on the surface of the earth (typically in the form of lines of latitude) even though the earth *as a sphere* does not embody any straight lines at all; even lines of latitude curve so that their "straightness" is purely relative to north and south deviation, and the matter of lines of longitude and straightness is even more vexed since they necessarily curve both toward the poles and toward each other. In other words, straight lines are wholly mythical in both cosmography and cartography.

Donne also accepts that maps are not only representations of the world, but are, moreover, *metaphors* of the world. "Scientific" maps (such as Mercator's) are distinguished from "allegorical" maps in that they suggest they are like the world while they are obviously not the world; their systems of graphic imaging illustrate a metaphorical relationship to the phenomenal world.[17] Allegorical maps, on the other hand, are intended primarily to represent the world's *meaning* from a given (usually religious) perspective, and only secondarily to project how that world might "actually look."

The metaphoricity of maps also demands that the viewer change both the system of signification and the system of reading by which the map is made intelligible. Allegorical maps understand the world as already imbued with meaning. In allegorical maps, the relationship between document (map) and object (phenomenal world) is literally the inverse of scientific understanding: in the traditional "T-and-O" map, for instance, what we would call the phenomenal world already stands – prior to its mapping – not as the signified of the map, but rather as the signifier of God's divine plan. For allegorical maps, the world is not imagined as an essentially chaotic and meaningless field but rather as ordered and significant: divine meaning has already been written into the landscape. The map does not signify the phenomenal world (whether coherent or incoherent), but the fact of God in the world.

Scientific maps, to the contrary, "officially" endorse the view of the landscape, or of the world, as essentially meaningless, without significance; it holds no meaning, signifies nothing. It stands as desacrilized matter, natural phenomena. What the map does, then, is establish itself in relationship to the world in such a way that it becomes the signifier of the now signified world. In a way, this is how the map sanctifies itself. Sacrality resides in the map itself as *it* organizes and generates meaning for the natural world. Quite literally, scientific maps have inverted the traditional order of things: the world inchoately awaits the grand map – like the grand narrative – that will organize it and name it once and for all. As Jean Baudrillard has suggested, the map "precedes . . . [and] engenders the territory."[18]

This transformation in the nature of maps in their imagined relationship to the world initiates a corresponding transformation in the system of reading maps. Allegorical maps tell us to read in their systems of representations traces of theological arguments; scientific maps ask us to read matters of scale, projection, angle, proportion, direction, size, and proximity. Further, scientific maps ask us to accept what are essentially the mathematical properties of projection and cartographic semantics as natural: the desired effect of these kinds of map is our sense as readers that we are in fact not reading at all, merely looking at "pure" representations of the world, representations that are not filtered through any ideological lens whatsoever. Donne's "Hymn" announces that he has mastered these "new" techniques for reading maps and the world to which they refer, though he is still interested in yoking together scientific and allegorical (or Christian) significance he believes the maps to hold. This is what allows Donne to accept the notion of circularity in flat maps as a function of both the sphericity of the earth, and the redemptive powers of Christ's death and resurrection.[19]

In fact, precisely because maps are *texts* and because (in Harley's words) "maps are at least as much an image of the social order as they are a measurement of the phenomenal world of objects" ("Deconstructing the Map" 7), reading maps is a highly technical and artificial activity, not at all simply a matter of recognizing the metaphor that asserts a relationship between map and world. In other words, *reading* maps depends upon the critical activity of denaturalizing the processes of cartography that are themselves dedicated to *naturalizing* their own interpretive and constructive maneuvers. Maps never simply *mean* anything but rather mean something only by virtue of being read. Reading scientific maps, then, is an act of interpretation – an interpretation that takes as its fundamental necessary condition (but is certainly not limited to) a familiarity with the mathematical properties of projection cataloged above. And there are instances, such as the following, in which people have demonstrated a sometimes unfortunate lack of familiarity with the rules of maps and their required reading. One of the early (and historically consistent) state benefits of cartographic representations of the English counties – in fact, this was also one of the prime forces that generated both the interest in and the governmental money supporting their production – was their use in Parliamentary districting, jurisdictional responsibilities for county JPs, and (perhaps most importantly) the levying of appropriate taxes on each county. Victor

Morgan, in his article "The Cartographic Image of 'The Country' in Early Modern England," discusses these governmental uses of county maps and relates a incident involving an appeal to the Privy Council over an alleged instance of over-taxation. The Welsh chorographer George Owen suggested that the culprit in this instance was not malice or bias on the part of the officials, but rather their inability to read maps. Morgan writes:

in George Owen's opinion, one of the reasons why Pembrokeshire was unduly burdened with royal demands compared with its neighbouring counties was that councillors sitting in London were using [Christopher] Saxton's maps, and unfortunately Saxton had devoted a whole sheet to Pembrokeshire, but crowded the other four Welsh counties, with which comparisons were made, on to one. According to Owen, the councillors, not being properly trained in the reading of maps, had failed to consult the different scales on the two maps, and had proceeded in their allocation of burdens according to the superficially similar areas depicted on the two sheets.[20]

This story offers anecdotal evidence that at least on some level maps have for a long time been understood – and misunderstood – as texts, and that they require a system of reading, even if it is a system that seeks to conceal both its presence and its effects. Maps, that is, have always functioned politically, within discourse and within ideology. My first task has been to speak this truth about maps and cartography. What remains is the further articulation of specific political and ideological contexts within which maps and cartographical practices are produced and in turn produce meaning.

III

I would like to turn from Donne's poem to the practices of cartography, bringing along Donne's concerns for temporal and spatial circularity. I will begin with a formulation of what I take to be the central epistemological tenet of the traditional understanding of cartography: maps are expressions of space. Maps are intended as purely descriptive images of the world, the organization of its features in space – both the space of the world (in which objects of certain dimension and location exist in greater or lesser proximity to one another), and the space of the map (the flat paper on which not only objects but space as well are projected). But, as Denis Wood and John Fels remind us, among the various codes they deploy (iconic, linguistic, and tectonic, to name a few), *all* maps are infused by temporal codes, which can be divided into two basic forms: tense ("the direction in which the map points" – past, present, and future) and duration ("which concerns its temporal scale") ("Designs on Signs" 82). While the "tense" of a map enables such past temporal directions as to allow, for example, the mapping of ancient civilizations, or present temporal directions for contemporary road atlases, or such future temporal directions as weather forecasts, the map's durative code "operates on the scalar aspect of time": "As spatial scale is a relation between the space of the map and the space of the world, temporal scale is a relation between the time of the map and the time of the world. To understand this, we have to see the map as having thickness in time" ("Designs on Signs" 83). Wood and Fels offer as an illustration three versions of the same durative map describing a bus ride through the city of Raleigh, North Carolina. The first is virtually a moment-by-moment itinerary recorded by a hypothetical traveler as he gazes out of the window of the bus *en route*. The second – graphic – version is a spatio-temporal map of the trip with the route plotted in three dimensions. The third is a planar projection in which the temporal dimension (of the spatio-temporal model) has been collapsed to "zero thickness." In the third, the route of the bus as it returns to its starting point ends precisely where it began – in space, since time has been collapsed. The result is that the route articulated by the bus has "surrounded and captured" a certain space within its closure so that "time has collapsed into space. It is still present in the map, but *as space*" ("Designs on Signs" 85). Wood and Fels tell us that we can always pretend that maps are not concerned with space – "that the dimensions of the map are entirely synchronic, that it has no diachronic quality except as a specimen of technical or methodological evolution" ("Designs on Signs" 85). But we do so, in a sense, at our own epistemological risk – and at the cost of the radical erasure of the inherent time-function of maps:

Time is always present in the map because it is inseparable from space. They are alternative and complementary distillations, projections of a space/time of a higher dimensional order. We cannot have a map without thickness in time unless we can have a map without extension in space; we cannot squeeze time out of the map, only into it. ("Designs on Signs" 85)

This revision of the traditional – and exclusive – visibility of space within maps to include time stands as a central tenet of a new understanding of cartography, especially as cartography historically has endeavored to appear as if time were none of its concern. This retheorization of the time-function in maps, however, depends upon a mechanism that, while it does enable the graphic collapse of time "into" space as described in the three versions of a local bus circuit, cannot be said to be universally present and operative. Under what conditions, one could ask, does time collapse into space in, say, a map of a county, which one presumably is not touring at the exact cartographic moment? What, then, allows the map – any and all maps – to compress time sufficiently so as to encircle and therein engender space? Wood and Fels, it seems to me, do not theorize this mechanism beyond its immediate occurrence (and usefulness – like a map?). The answer to this problem, I would suggest, resides precisely within the idea of the *narration* they offer as their first version of the bus-route map. While the Wood–Fels model would seem to require a literal traveler whose *movement through time* constructs identifiable space, a cartographer such as Christopher Saxton, for example, need not have walked the shoreline of Cornwall before he could produce his map of its coast. But what does happen and what does enable some movement through time that therein produces (cartographic) space is narration itself. In other words, it is the production of a system – we can call it "narrational" – that moves signs (signifiers) through time that generates the very possibility for cartographic practices such as Saxton's. While Wood and Fels depend (unrealistically and uncritically, I believe) upon a virtual narrator to generate and insure the possibility of a carto-graphics of spatiality, I want to argue that it is a *prior* narrationality that enables not only particular cartographic narrators and their specific narra-tions but that enables spatiality itself. It is in this way that the maps cartog-raphers produce make evident their essential narrational natures. This is the argument, I believe, that informs a point Harley asserts (but fails to pursue) concerning the effects for historians of cartography of the deconstruction of the *textual* map: "Rather than working with a formal science of communication, or even a sequence of loosely related technical processes, our concern is redirected to a history and anthropology of the image, and we learn to recognize the narrative qualities of cartographic representation as well as its claims to provide a synchronous picture of the world" ("Deconstructing the Map" 8). Harley refers to an article by Denis Wood, titled "Pleasure in the Idea: The Atlas as Narrative Form," in which Wood indeed argues that atlases can be and, in fact, are arranged narratively:

But the . . . possibility that the maps [of an atlas] be arranged *narratively*, to make a point, to tell a story, implies a movement from the simple desire to get things into shape to the more complex one of making of that shape some *thing* of its own, of giving it some sort of role and meaning beyond that of the individual maps, of making, in effect, an atlas.[21]

But, I would offer, maps – *even individual maps* – are never "simple" in their desire, nor (as indeed Wood elsewhere argues) is the "shape" into which they wish to get their "things" ever disinterested or natural. All maps make their meaning by way of narrative, whether they are sequenced with other maps or not.[22]

Another important distinction between Wood's theory of the relation between the map and narrative and the one for which I am arguing here has to do with Wood's sense that once freed from the pressures to pass as some-thing it is not – once freed, that is, from having to act *as if* it were not (impli-cated in) narrative – the map is truly liberated and vastly empowered: "The narrative reading is inevitable: *make the most of it*. After all, objectivity does not consist in suppressing an unavoidable subjectivity, but in so acknowledging its intrusion that the reader is relieved of the necessity of ferreting out with difficulty what must sooner or later in any case come to the surface." ("Atlas as Narrative" 32). This strikes me as a rather hopelessly utopian sentiment: the problem is – and this has been a problem with maps just as it has been with other forms of textuality, such as that close relative of the map, the travel narrative – that not all "subjectivities" (as Wood calls them) are either available to the "selves" that might project them (either onto maps of the New World, say, or onto its unlucky inhabitants), nor necessarily as acceptable as Wood's vision of mere and adequate disclosure supposes to be the case. Mercator, to take just one example, probably thought *in good faith* that he was disclosing his "subjectivities" – they just happened to have come in the form of scientific and technical "accuracy," which actually moved Mercator no closer indeed to a realization of the ideologically motivated graphic distortions his map of the world introduced and codified, to the enduring benefit of western Europe. In fact, we can trace the difficulties inherent in the narrational nature of cartography (and its related discourses) to early modern England.

The development in Tudor and Stuart England of what typically is called cartography (but which includes, in fact, a variety of divergent practices) marks a simultaneous double movement. On the one hand, this is a movement toward greater technical accuracy; on the other hand, it is a movement away from "pure" survey and cartography, as represented most famously in Saxton's atlas of Britain (1579), toward the historical topography and chorography of writers such as William Camden (*Britannia*), John Norden (*Speculum Britanniae*), and John Speed (*Theatre of the Empire of Great Britain*), to the chorographical poetics of Michael Drayton's *Poly-Olbion*. These later works make evident a greater overt concern with narrative: they are texts that offer not only representations of topographical characteristics, but also topographically organized historical accounts of local or national identities. But in both instances, I want to maintain, the representations produced (maps and chorographies) are images of the world engendered by a narrativizing of topography and history: both are made to tell historical tales, and these tales, moreover, are deployed in the service of specific political and cultural ideologies. I locate this discussion of cartography within the context of sixteenth- and seventeenth-century English texts – both cartographic and literary – not only because this is the period in which one can identify the beginnings of what we call today modern cartography, but also because it is the period in which we can identify equally well the occlusion of the counter-tradition of chorography: a rival to cartography that is grounded *overtly* in the narrative desire it is covertly the purpose of cartography to repress.

Chorography is the typically narrative and only occasionally graphic practice of delineating topography not exclusively as it exists in the present moment, but as it has existed historically. This means not only describing surface features of the land (rivers, forest, etc.), but also the "place" a given locale has held in history, including the languages spoken there, the customs of its people, material artifacts the land may hold, and so forth. Lestringant describes chorography and cosmography as "diametrically opposed." Chorography, he writes,

recorded from place to place the events of the past, and made the regional map into a genuine "art of memory" in the sense that classical antiquity attached to the term. The topographer's landscape-map was a profuse and indefinitely fragmented receptacle of local legends and traditions that were rooted in vagaries of relief, hidden in folds of terrain, and readable in toponymy and folklore; whereas the reticular and geometrical map of the cosmographer anticipated the conquests and "discoveries" of the modern age. No doubt the marvellous was not absent from it; but it subsisted there only by special dispensation. (Lestringant 3–4)[23]

Chorography as an organized practice – as (in Lesley Cormack's words) the "investigation of the local setting as text"[24] – has its origins for early modern England in the antiquarian work of John Leland. In his letter commemorating the fruits of his antiquarian research to Henry VIII, "The Laboriouse Journey and Serche of Johan Leylande for Englandes Antiquities, Geven of hym as a Newe Yeares Gyfte to King Henry the viii. in the xxxvii Yeare of his Raygne" (1546), Leland discusses his commission from Henry "to peruse and diligently to serche al the libraries of monasteries and collegies of this yowre noble reaulme."[25] In his "New Year's Gift," as it is familiarly known, Leland identifies the nature of his antiquarian project as designed "to the intente that the monumentes of auncient writers as welle of other nations, as of this yowr owne province mighte be brought owte of deadely darkenes to lyvely lighte, and to receyve like thankes of the posterite, as they hoped for at such tyme as they emploied their long and greate studies to the publique wealthe" (Leland xxxvii–xxxviii).

In the same letter, Leland makes evident that for Henry, Leland's antiquarian research is a fundamentally "nationalistic" endeavor; occurring as it did at the time of Henry's dissolution of the monasteries, Leland's commission can be seen as a further attempt to take control of – to mark monarchical claim to – monastic property and possession. While such endeavors were no doubt part of the attempt to expel the influence and confiscate the wealth of the Roman Catholic church in England (Leland asserts that part of his ambition is to insure "that the holy Scripture of God might bothe be sincerely taughte and lernid, al maner of superstition and craftely coloured doctrine of a rowte of the Romaine bishopes expellid oute of this your moste catholique reaulme" [Leland xxxviii]), it also constitutes the concerted maneuvers toward centralized monarchical control over the as-yet not quite controlled English country. The relationship between the state and chorographical (and cartographical) investigation is at least as old as Leland's early work, and, moreover, points to the intersection of monar-chical governance and topographical study. Henry's ambition for Leland was not merely the desire to patronize a new form of study, but also to establish more firmly and overtly the king's claim to something approxi-mating a truly *national* sovereignty.

For Leland, whose official program was so obviously in concert with Henry's, the antiquarian project is primarily *textual*, as is, in fact, the very ambition which generates it. Leland describes his desire to produce what he believes to be a monumental work of history as a direct consequence of his reading of other historiographers:

Wherfore after that I had perpendid the honest and profitable studies of these historiographes, I was totally enflammid with a love to see thoroughly al those partes of this your opulente and ample reaulme, that I had redde of yn the aforesaid writers: yn so muche that al my other occupations intermittid I have so travelid yn yowr dominions booth by the se costes and the midle partes, sparing nother labor nor costes, by the space of these vi. yeres paste, that there is almoste nother cape, nor bay, haven, creke or peere, river or confluence of rivers, breches, waschis, lakes, meres, fenny waters, montaynes, valleis, mores, hethes, forestes, wooddes, cities, burges, castelles, principale manor placis, monasteries, and colleges, but I have seene them; and notid yn so doing a hole worlde of thinges very memorable.

(Leland xl–xli)

Leland established the methodological protocols that would organize chorographical study for generations: the personal accumulation of raw data gathered on personal tours of geographical areas, linguistic investiga-tion, the study of history in the landscape, to name but the most prominent. In the work of subsequent chorographers – particularly William Camden, whose *Britannia*, in its many editions, stands as the greatest expression of the chorographical ambition – the personal gathering of data takes on something of the character of a quasi-religious quest.[26] Camden's famous county perambulations, for instance, inspired imitators for generations.

While Leland seems to have been driven mad beneath the accumulated weight of his empirical data, and his life work thereby left uncompleted at his death, Camden, who was the inheritor of both Leland's chorographic ambition and his mass of notes, achieved greater success. Camden was able to organize the prodigious amount of material he collected in the years he devoted to his antiquarian research. The basic unit Camden chose for his *Britannia* was the county, and the book is divided into fifty-two chapters, each devoted to a single county. The single-county plan had been employed seven years earlier by Christopher Saxton, who also personally surveyed almost all of England and Wales for his atlas.[27]

For chorography, natural fact (the phenomenal world) hides its truth, and therein calls for an investigation of its secrets. The form these secrets take is largely that of history (though for Drayton, it is also more explicitly political – though in a politics not of governments, but of the land itself). To these ends, chorography does not seem to embrace the technological: Camden's first edition of *Britannia* contains none of the graphic-spatial conceptualizations that typify Saxton, and Drayton's maps in *Poly-Olbion* are, in terms of cartographic technology, emphatically regressive (see plate 6).

Drayton's chorographical ambition in *Poly-Olbion* – as Richard Helgerson has demonstrated – is to make "the land speak."[28] On the one hand, this removes Drayton from the realm of the cartographer's "facts" about the land and places him in the realm of allegory; in *Poly-Olbion*, topographical characteristics become poetical "characters": rivers become river nymphs who then tell their own narratives of their historic and topo- graphic courses. And yet, on the other hand, Drayton nevertheless tena- ciously maintains a faith in the poem's "realism." Like the chorographical surveys before him – from Leland to Camden to Norden – Drayton's choro- graphical–poetical enterprise is devoted to the accurate description of Britain. The first part of *Poly-Olbion* takes this desire to the extreme with the inclusion of "Illustrations": notes appended to each of the poem's books (each of which is also devoted to one of Britain's counties), commis- sioned by Drayton and executed by the great jurist and antiquarian, John Selden. In these notes, Selden offers his own documentary survey of authoritative texts relevant to Drayton's historical and topographical con- cerns. With the inclusion of the entirely linguistic (and not graphic) "Illustrations," Drayton's chorographical enterprise becomes even more emphatically a *textual* one. With Drayton it is clear that the ambition of chorography can be understood as the telling of stories, the desire to narrate the land – its topography in history. The success, then, of chorography is measured by its ability to narrate meaningful (historical) stories.[29]

For Camden, in his *Britannia* and the later *Remains Concerning Britain*, the chorographical project is manifestly devoted to the narration of historic and pre-historic Britain. While Camden is concerned with topography – he claims to have surveyed most of Britain on his famous county perambula- tions – he is not as concerned with measurement as he is with history: "I have compendiously settl'd the bounds of each County," Camden asserts, "(but not by measure)."[30] For Camden, his *Britannia* is not so much the measure of the land but the measure of the man.[31] The forms this history takes encompassed not only general topographical descriptions and

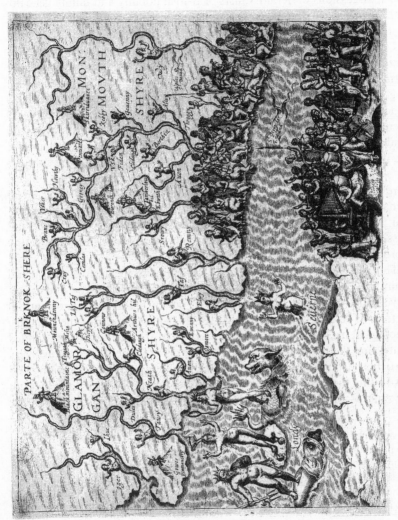

Plate 6 Michael Drayton, map of Monmouthshire, from *Poly-Olbion*, London, 1612.

accounts, but extended studies of place-names, ancient languages (Camden took the then extraordinary measure of learning ancient languages and dialects to understand more fully the personal and place names he encountered in his research), and included the study of ancient (typically Roman) coins, discussions of heraldry, lists of British nobility and family genealogies, as well as catalogs of commonplace adages, anecdotes, proverbs, folk customs, and practices.

For its part, cartography appears almost wholly uninterested in these antiquarian and historiographical matters, and appears instead to be concerned primarily with the topographical characteristics chorography largely subsumes into its historiographical concerns. In its topographical concern, cartography suggests that maps are drawn to represent the world accurately and objectively: maps simply represent the world the way it is. And yet, in one of the central operations of cartography the continuity of the topographical world is systematically violated: maps deny the contiguity of the world by virtue of breaking it into disparate pieces.[32] This process of rendering the world radically discontiguous is an entirely political narrational practice taken up in the service of regional or national identity, political or military power, personal or private property boundaries and possession. Maps, that is, are finally the various and sometimes conflicting stories we wish to tell about the phenomenal world.

This is a way of saying that maps are documents meant to establish and maintain certain social, economic, and political circumstances – and to preserve them, moreover, not as matters of policy, but as matters of natural fact. In "The Land Speaks," Helgerson suggests that one of the principle ideological uses of maps was in the service of the interests of the landed gentry and that this particular use for maps is itself predicated upon a very particular definition of the idea of the nation, or country. Supporting and advocating the rights of landowners (a discourse of localism) is in fact not the same as advocating monarchical rights to an ideal of national identity:

The cartographic representation of England did have an ideological effect. It strengthened the sense of both local and national identity at the expense of an identity based on dynastic loyalty . . . Maps let [sixteenth-century English people] see in a way never before possible the country – both county and nation – to which they belonged and at the same time showed royal authority – or at least its insignia – to be a merely ornamental adjunct to that country. Maps thus opened a conceptual gap between the land and its ruler, a gap that would eventually span battlefields.

("The Land Speaks" 332)

The story of localism is one the sixteenth-century map-maker John Norden tells in his book *Surveiors Dialogue* (first edition, 1618). In this book Norden defines and defends surveying in its various forms and capacities. The book is divided into six parts, each of which addresses a particular function of surveying – including its uses for the landlord, its uses for purchasers of land, as well as its (professional and moral) protocols. The book takes the form of an accomplished surveyor's exchanges with several figures among whom the Farmer emerges as both the most obstinate and the most important. The Farmer begins by claiming surveying to be unnecessary and detrimental to the interests of farmers. The surveyor is that person, the Farmer claims, who will "pry into mens Titles and estates, under the name (forsooth) of Surveyors," to "bring men and matter in question oftentimes, that would (as long time they have) lye without any question."[33] The effect, he says, limits the farmer's ability to make a living from the landlord's land. The surveyor of course defends his function as merely ascertaining the exact truth of the landlord's manor: the size of tenant's farms, the precise amount of yields, the exact rents and fines, etc. The remainder of the book is dedicated to two projects: first, to the "conversion" of the Farmer to the surveyor's (and the landlord's) way of thinking, and secondly, to the Farmer's subsequent education (technical and moral) in the art and practice of surveying. Norden's book, then, which has the appearance of a technical manual, also functions as a kind of conduct book.[34] Norden wants not only to reform the Farmer's initial greed and self-serving attitudes (the correct adjustment of his property lines, he is told, does in fact serve the interests of farmers in that it allows the landlord a more true and therefore profitable overall land-management program, the benefits of which reach everyone), but Norden wants also to offer his surveyor's wisdom for the improvement of parent–child relationships, the establishment of a love of virtue in the peasants, and the refining of their relationship to God. By the book's end, the Farmer has not only converted to the surveyor's philosophy (he becomes, the book tells us, a better person), but he has also himself become knowledgeable and adept in surveying, a surveyor himself.

Norden's text makes clear, however, that the true benefits of proper surveying are almost exclusively the landlord's, that the project of the book is, finally, the disciplining of the tenant farmers to the landlord's clear and proper mastery. The Farmer declares:

This I cannot deny, although indeed some busie fellowes will disswade, and breede a doubt herein, but I see it is to good purpose, and for our better security, to doe all things requisite in this businesse, and that all the Tennants within the Mannor should conjoyne in one, and every one for himselfe, and all for one, and one for all, should looke, examine and declare the uttermost truth of every thing, towards the exact performance of this service, and that the Surveyor should know the quantities, qualities, and indifferent values of every mans Tenement and Lands, their rents, services, custome, works, and whatsoever the Tennant is in Law or conscience bound to yield or performe to his Lord. (*Surveiors Dialogue* 33)

Norden's vision, spoken by the now-converted Farmer, is of a neo-feudalism wherein tenants fulfill their duties, and the landlords know and exercise their privileges:

> therefore happy are those Tennants, that have a gracious Lord, and an honest Surveyor: for then there cannot be but an equall and upright course held betweene them: then cannot the Tennants but be faithfull and loving to their Lords, and their Lords favourable to them, so should the Tennants be defended by their Lords, and the Lords fortified by their Tennants, which were the two principall causes of the originall foundation of Mannors, as I have heard. (*Surveiors Dialogue* 33–34)

Norden's philosophical desire to legislate what he believes to be the appropriate relationship to the land focuses not on the issues of the monarchy (though Norden includes occasional references to the king and his subjects' duties to him), but instead on the local level:

> [landlords] should keepe such an even, and equall hand over their Tennants, as may continue mutuall love, and in them a loving feare: And not to seeke the increase of Revenues so much for vaine-glories, as for vertues maintenance . . . which I must leave to every mans owne fancie, wishing all to fashion their waies in this kinde, to Gods glory, the Kings service, the good of the Common-wealth.
>
> (*Surveiors Dialogue* sig. A6$^\text{v}$)

Norden's text offers one particular instance of the ideological appropriation and use of cartography. Norden's own relationship to the monarchy was a complex and conflicted one; he had earlier embarked upon an ambitious attempt to write individual county chorographies for all of Britain, a text he would title *Speculum Britanniae*.[35] Norden also sought monarchical support for this project, first from Elizabeth and then from James, but was unsuccessful in both his bids.[36] Norden no doubt saw himself as a loyal subject, and his advocacy of the landed interests in all likelihood not an act of overt subversion. And yet, that his texts, and others like them, function in the political ways I have tried to describe speaks to a kind of unintentional character of these cartographic (and chorographic) texts that locates their potentially subversive qualities within the very discursive forms that they take – forms that are (at least in part) determined by their relationship to technology, and time – and that can be understood as narrational in nature.

By the time of Saxton's *Atlas*, cartography was clearly a dedicated technological endeavor against which chorography seemed regressive – or, more appropriately, antitechnological. And yet, in the differences between cartography and chorography we discern not one "advanced" practice and one "primitive" one, but rather two different representational systems at work – and sometimes in conflict. For Saxton, cartography represents a commitment to an epistemology founded on what Johannes Fabian has identified as a "cultural, ideological bias toward vision as the 'noblest sense' and toward geometry *qua* graphic–spatial conceptualization as the most 'exact' way of communicating knowledge."[37] To these ends, Saxton (and "scientific" cartographers after him) turn to technological innovations that afford more "accurate" versions of graphic–spatial conceptualizations (e.g., new surveying techniques, better mathematical models for more sophisticated projections, more sensitive and precise instruments, etc.). In this sense, technical competence becomes the measure of success (see plate 7). Harley argues that scientific cartography, seeking to establish itself as a "mirror of nature," also succeeded in trapping itself into a "mimetic bondage" predicated in large part upon an evolutionary model: "Most striking is the belief in progress: that, by the application of science ever more precise representations of reality can be produced" ("Deconstructing the Map" 4).[38]

Another measure of success for Saxton's cartography is the degree to which it presents itself as natural and not technological at all. That is, Saxton's maps work (succeed) best when they seem not to work (labor) at all, when they seem to present what in fact is the highly intrusive organization of phenomena in the guise of data as if it were *natural*. Saxton's maps work because they seem not to tell stories, because they seem not to narrate, but rather appear to describe objectively the phenomenal world.

Cartography and chorography also differ in their apparent or declared relationships to history, both the historical – or *pre*historical – past, as well as the passage of time. Cartographies attempt to present their texts as a-historical; Saxton's maps of England, for example, represent an eternal present: the land as it *is*, as if in a wholly continuous moment. What escapes explicit representation, but what is nevertheless implicitly represented, is the history that informs the production of not only the map itself (England looked different to cartographers a generation before), but also the production of England itself as political entity. History and politics are both subsumed within the cartographic ideology as matters of natural fact, facts that the map implicitly speaks, but refuses to represent explicitly. In these terms, cartographic representations aim at synchronic representation and the material (that is to say, historical) manner of cartography's production exists largely in excess of its system of representation.

Chorographical representations, on the other hand, reject the notion of synchronic representation, and opt instead for the diachronic. Camden's and Drayton's texts seek to represent Britain *in time*: the land persists, as does its history.[39] For Camden, national identity is not simply a fact, but rather a narrative, and his texts are devoted to its telling. Chorography is interpretation deployed through time; cartography is interpretation ostensibly outside of – or in spite of – time.

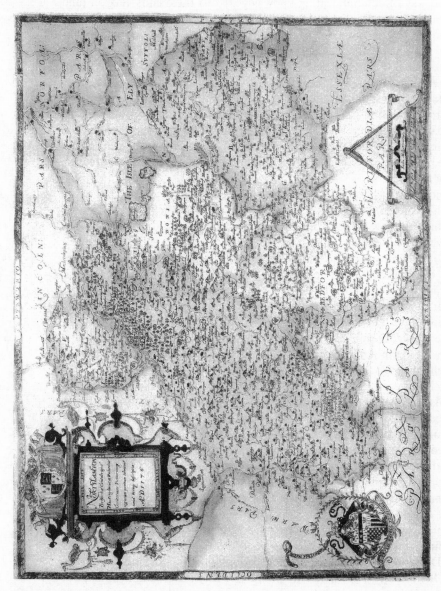

Plate 7 Christopher Saxton's map of Northamptonshire, from *An Atlas of the Counties of England and Wales*, London, 1590.

To understand the world as the movement of time is to have created a narrativized world. It is to this assertion that the projects of chorography are explicitly dedicated. Maps, as I have tried to suggest, attempt to deny this same narrativizing of the world, but this denial does not succeed, not if we re-place the cartographic enterprise into the political world that is its true milieu. Maps are narratives, even though part of the cartographic ideology is the radical denial of this narrational nature of the cartographic practice and its artifacts. Among the oldest maps to survive from antiquity are the Roman itineraries: maps constructed along an axis connecting two distant locations (plate 8). These maps are constructed entirely from calculations of distances between various points that lie along the trajectory from point A to point B. They are constructed with a total disregard for orientation. In these maps the frames correspond not with directions, but simply with the outer edge of concern. The nature of these maps – the *desire* of these maps – is entirely narrational: the movement from A to B to C, until one reaches the pre-determined destination, the foregone conclusion. Within the genres of maps, these itineraries correspond to the most formulaic of literatures: they hold no surprises, afford no digressions.

In these regards, itineraries are very like their contemporary counterparts, the American Automobile Association (AAA) Triptiks (plate 9). This particular image depicts (I will want to say "narrates") the movement from Nashville to Memphis, Tennessee.[40] In this map, narrative reigns supreme. Again, orientation is utterly disregarded; digression (in the form of the sidetrip to, say, anywhere off Interstate 40) is utterly unthinkable; trajectory becomes the equivalent of plot, and the plot alone exists in the very midst of what is evidently blank space – a white noise, of sorts, just out of earshot, just off the map, a void that offers us its own enclosed narrative: "I-40 . . . leads through rolling to hilly, mostly wooded terrain along eastern portion of route; gentle relief and more farmlands along the western portion"; and geographical space is quantified into calculations of drive-time noted parenthetically and along the margins. Harley suggests that we indeed can read the "silences" on maps – those projections of blank space that speak loudly:

the lack of qualitative differentiation in maps structured by the scientific *episteme* serves to dehumanise the landscape. Such maps convey knowledge where the subject is kept at bay. Space becomes more important than place: if places look alike they can be treated alike. Thus, with the progress of scientific mapping, space became all too easily a socially-empty commodity, a geometrical landscape of cold, non-human facts. ("Silences and Secrecy" 66)

It is not difficult to see, then, the Nashville to Memphis narrative operating as an ideologically loaded text in the service of a number of larger ideological and political discourses – including the social–economic–political

Plate 8 "The Peutinger Map: Rome." Codex Vindobonensis 324, segment IV.

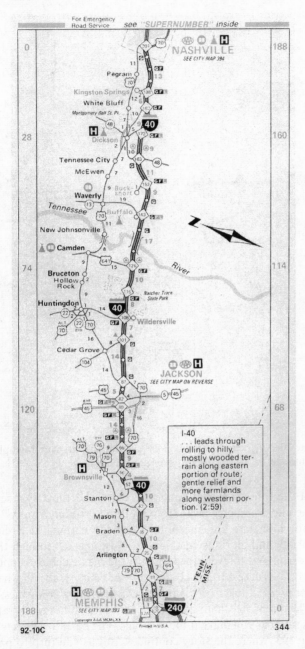

Plate 9 American Automobile Association Triptik map:
Nashville to Memphis, Tennessee.

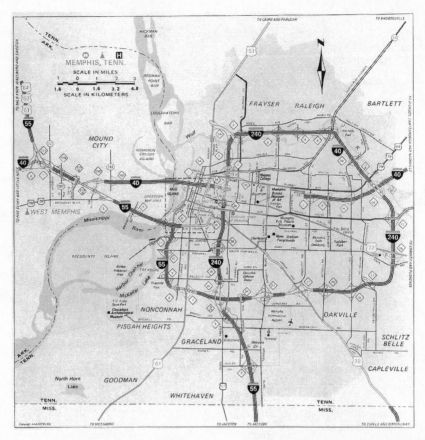

Plate 10 American Automobile Association Triptik map: Memphis,
Tennessee.

discourse of the Interstate, that American cultural artifact that serves to
funnel traffic and commerce away from all those "socially-empty" locales
"just off" the interstate and inexorably into the nationalist circuit that
promises variety and glorious destinations "just ahead," though they are
merely rhetorical and forever receding into the incalculable distance. The
interstate promises access to the country but of course leads no where – to
no particular *place*; it just exposes one to the interminable vastness of the
country.[41] The interstate stands as a materialized metaphor of narrativity.[42]

But let us say that you make it to Memphis. The narrative directs you to
turn to page 393, where the story continues. But as you turn to page 393
you have entered a radically different – and strange – world (plate 10). Here,
the world has evidently and suddenly shifted on its axis sufficiently to return

the vestigial compass rose to its customary north-orientation. Now that we have reached Memphis (or, page 393), we turn the page on a new world so that we can learn how *to avoid* Memphis. Quite apart from the curious phenomenon of a map of a city that exists to help you avoid the city, the radical juxtaposition of these two images invites a kind of geographical vertigo, wherein the top of the frame both is and is not north, where the world is, if only for a moment, turned upside-down. In the west we have been taught, that is, to understand north-oriented maps, and when we see maps that violate this orientation, they are (if only briefly) quite incomprehensible.

Early modern maps, as surely as the Roman itinerary maps, or the AAA maps, tell their own stories of their conception of topography and cartography, of the value of the particular and the unique, and are made to tell various other narratives of the sites of power or of wealth, for example, or the narrationalities of localism or nationalism.[43] Cartography does not exist – and of course never has existed – outside of discourse. The costs of imagining cartography as non-ideological, however, are both insidious and untenable: whether the finally inadmissible Eurocentrism Arno Peters so powerfully identifies in the ubiquitous Mercator's projection, or the class-based prejudice of the cartography of privilege, cartographic narratives simply need reexamination.[44] The revision of these (and other) cartographic narratives may or may not be technological (as Peters predicts), but the necessary first step is to recognize cartography and its productions as explicitly part of history and as manifestly discursive, making available political readings of inevitably political maps. Maps are produced, and tend to be received, as if they were the primary objects of a scientific epistemology when – as is always the case with any narrational discourse – they are in fact (already) its effects.

4 Possessing the New World: historicism and the story of the anecdote

> Possession is preeminently the form in which the other becomes the same, by becoming mine. (Emmanuel Levinas, *Totality and Infinity*)

The status of maps as *political* documents characterizes cartography generally, but this is especially so for the early modern period not only because this was the moment in which cartography becomes (in the modern sense of the term) a "technology," but because this is the moment in which "discovery"/"exploration" on a global scale becomes (also in the modern sense of the term) an "industry." As such, this industry required more of its maps than had ever been the case before. The "discovery" of the New World had as much to do with the advances in the science of cartography as cartography would have in the ensuing discourses and practices of New World possession. In "Rereading the Maps of the Columbian Encounter," J.B. Harley argues for a complex new understanding of the role of cartography in this monumental encounter for *both* the invading Europeans and the Amerindians. For the former, Harley argues, "maps can be shown to operate not only within material and practical processes but also as reified symbols of power . . . Whether we call the process invention or visualization, maps were critical agents in the geographic inscription by which the space of America was filled."[1] For the Amerindians – whose supposed cartographic ignorance Harley powerfully refutes – "maps were part of the intellectual apparatus by which the imposition of colonial rule was resisted" ("Rereading the Maps" 527). In these ways, cartography was deployed quite deliberately in the practices of discovery – and, as Harley notes, "Discovery was possession" ("Rereading the Maps" 529). In this chapter I discuss the various strategies of discovery in the early moments of English contact with the New World and in our own contemporary critical discussions of New World discourse – focusing particular attention on the *anecdotal* nature of both.

The history of the New World – from the moment of its European "discovery" to its lengthy periods of conquest and subsequent emergence from colonialism – has been a history of possession: claiming islands and mainland territories in the names of European monarchs, planting European national flags, constructing forts, founding settlements and towns, extracting and eventually transporting both natural and human resources – all of these stand as manifestations of what emerged as the standard European philosophy and method of responding to the surprise of and contact with the New World. But for all its unfortunate familiarity, *possessing* the New World should not be construed simply as the form discovery (or conquest or colonialism) happened to take; possession is first a particular and calculated *social* – or, more aptly, *antisocial* – strategy conventionally invoked in the face of what Emmanuel Levinas calls the "mystery" of the other. It is this desire to procure the other as the same *in the model of possession* that then serves to structure the New World encounter and the various discourses that arise out of it, including travel narratives, promotional literature, colonialist propaganda (exemplified, for instance, in texts such as Ralegh's *Discovery of Guiana*), and, perhaps, even our own no doubt admirable but potentially appropriative historical and historicist attempts to (re)write the New World or theorize our relation to it.

The European discovery of the New World provoked the implementation of the systematic appropriation of the other on a virtually global scale – an act for which European states brought the full weight and power of their political, legal, and religious systems to bear, as all three worked first to make further encounter possible, and then to allow for the *legal* possessing of New World lands, people, and resources.[2] For Tzvetan Todorov, in his important book *The Conquest of America*, the discovery of the New World occasioned the opportunity for the collective negotiation of a cultural encounter with the other; and yet, as the history of this contact has demonstrated for centuries, this "encounter" literally failed to occur, and in its place was substituted conquest and genocide.[3] Todorov dedicates his book to "the memory of a Mayan woman devoured by dogs," who is condemned to her fate by a Spanish conquistador after the slaughter of her husband, and after her own attempt at defiant resistance, "because she is both an unconsenting woman and an Indian woman. Never was the fate of the other more tragic" (*Conquest* 247). Todorov's entire project stands as a critical analysis of the failure to encounter the other that is emblematized so poignantly in the fate of this woman. He considers both this failure and his own (personal) response to it:

I am writing this book to prevent this story and a thousand others like it from being forgotten. I believe in the necessity of "seeking the truth" and in the obligation of making it known; I know that the function of information exists, and that the effect of information can be powerful. My hope is not that Mayan women will now have European men thrown to the dogs (an absurd supposition, obviously), but that we remember what can happen if we do not succeed in discovering the other.

(*Conquest* 247)

But how does one – whether an explorer, a conquistador, or a critic – avoid the narrative of possession that has effectively structured so much of our philosophical and practical lives? This question, then, poses the challenge before this chapter: to conduct a discussion of New World discourses that at the same time resists the tendency embedded within such discourses – and within even our critical responses to them – to replace the encounter with yet another form of the conquest.

I would like to suggest that the challenge in avoiding the narrative of possession resides, in large part, in the challenge of avoiding the narrational. Let me explain: if one could assign a rhetorical or literary term to the form of the encounter with the other in which (following Levinas) one takes responsibility for the other *from the start*, one could call it *description*. To describe the other without positing any use-function for such a description is to be responsible both for and to the other first. Description – as I will use the term here – resists the appropriative nature of possession that comes to characterize narrationality in which the other always exists secondarily – after the fact, as it were, of the narrator's own primary and privileged existence.[4] Description localizes and particularizes the contingent (or, say, the "event") while the narrational universalizes and totalizes. Description is dedicated (more fully) to difference, to the radically contingent, to alterity, while the narrational is dedicated to the eradication of difference and the (ideological) production of sameness. Hence the extreme danger associated with history, for example, when construed as any of a variety of possible narratives or meta-narratives.

If these definitions hold, then, the agenda of this chapter will be to mark the occlusion of description and the corresponding emergence of narrationality in New World discourses. This formulation is offered provisionally; description, to be sure, cannot be said to hold the line against an imperialist narrative, nor can it, for that matter, avoid the fate of appropriation by narrative – to mark, perhaps, difference but only so as to condemn the other, or to found a pretext for "inferiority" by which to authorize conquest. But narrative can be said to articulate or figure a specific politics of possession, appropriation, and conquest that description by its nature seems to disallow. If there is a domain of the truly heterological (Derrida's "heterogeneity of a *pre* – "), a space for the non-appropriative encounter with the other in any form of New World discourse, I argue that it is the domain of description.

The consequences for New World discourses of what I am suggesting is the non-dialectical relation between description and narrationality are many and their effects significant, especially as the largely antagonistic relation between them serves to structure both historical and contemporary "European" responses to the New World. Travel writing of the early modern period is the literary-historical form *par excellence* for the articulation of European responses to the New World. This writing offers the implicit formulation of its own nature as essentially descriptive: explorers voyage into the unknown lands of the New World and return to write their supposedly objective descriptions of them. Yet we know that this promise of theoretical objectivity in fact breaks down almost immediately and the writing that emerges from its ruins is a more or less explicit narrative of possession. But is noting this breakdown of description the same thing as suggesting that these explorers and writers knew all along that description was a mere pretext – a cover for their appropriative and acquisitive desire to possess? This interpretation may seem reasonable enough: we know as a matter of fact that what Europeans finally desired from their contact with the New World was possession and ownership, even at the cost of genocide. But to suggest that description *even on a theoretical level* was always merely tactical is to rush too quickly through a number of issues that deserve more careful attention. Can we theorize a *primary* reaction to the New World, and to the other more generally, that precedes (if not preempts) the possessive response? In what ways do the very *forms* of New World discourse derive from the contested relation between description and the narrational? Can description be recovered as an antidote to the narrationality of possession?

In the following discussion I will invoke a series of paired terms that arise from the complex and over-determined ideologies and practices of description and the narrational, pairs of terms that maintain across their particular deployments in history and in the arena of New World discourse the essential (if only theoretical) characteristics of description and narrationality: "anecdote and history," "story and novel," and, lastly, "moral and meaning." The last two pairs of terms are borrowed from Walter Benjamin's essay "The Storyteller." While I will offer a more thorough discussion of Benjamin's terms and theoretical consideration of stories and novels, morals and meanings later in this chapter, it is important to announce here that these terms and the place they have in my interpretive framework are integral to my historical account of the anecdote.

One way to characterize the relation between anecdote and history, story and novel, and moral and meaning is to say that the first term precedes the second, or is prior to it within the field of thought (and possibly within history as well) so that, for example, description comes before the narrational. A further characterization would suggest that the second term inverts its own belatedness (sometimes violently) and proceeds to consume its predecessor, so that the narrational – travel writing, say, of the early moments of European contact with the New World – subsumes description, or re-creates description in its own possessive image. Likewise, the anecdote precedes history, but is obliterated – especially in its theoretical relation to description (and story and moral) – by the emergence of history. The story, for its part, precedes the novel, though the novel takes its revenge, as it were, by consuming the story and thereby – in Walter Benjamin's terms – contributing to the decline of storytelling. And finally, the "*moral* of the story" becomes lost in the face of the "*meaning* of life."[5]

To suggest that description precedes a subsequent – and corrupting – appropriation by the narrational (or the anecdote by history, the story by the novel, or the moral by the meaning) is to argue for a primacy of description, but a primacy that may be of extremely short duration. This historical account is offered here in both the macro- and the micro-historical levels. Thus, in terms of early modern travel writing, the occlusion or loss of description at the hands of the narrational can be charted roughly against the historical transformations in the genre from medieval encyclopedic texts (such as Mandeville's *Travels*) that are clearly constructed on a faith (even if such a faith is naive) in "pure" description, to the Renaissance travel texts (such as those of Columbus, for example, or Cortés) that have obviously abandoned or conscripted description in the ideological service of narratives of possession. At the same time, on the micro-historical level, this trajectory from description to the narrational can be enacted by a single individual whose first response to the New World (or, more generally, to the other) can be simply the desire to describe, but whose initial desire can be replaced immediately (within the context of commerce, for example) by the appropriative desire to narrate. For once you begin to calculate value and use, you have begun to narrate.

A similar dynamic obtains regarding the *forms* these texts take, and the rhetorical and literary devices that they employ. The most significant structuring device for travel texts is the anecdote – whether one is speaking of Mandeville or Cortés. But the anecdote for Cortés (and countless other possessive writers like him) is no longer what it had been for Mandeville. For Mandeville, the anecdote is intended as a literary embodiment of description, while for Cortés the anecdote has already lost its posited relation to description and has been subsumed within the larger domains of narrationality and history. Stephen Greenblatt characterizes Mandeville's *Travels* as a text of non-possession – "Mandeville takes possession of nothing" (26) – in direct contrast to what will emerge in travel writing beginning with Columbus as standard European narratives of possession. By the time Europeans begin to write about the New World the anecdote has already lost its relation to description and has already been coopted, as it were, by the narrational discourse of possession. While for Mandeville the anecdote serves as the vehicle for a non-acquisitive description, for later European travel writers the anecdote serves as the very structure upon which appropriation is articulated. In this sense, much of the work of early modern travel writing is dedicated to the production of the anecdote: not the anecdote as the vehicle for description (analogous, as remarked above, to "description," "story," and "moral"), but rather the anecdote as a form of historiography. In these texts, the anecdote is made to bear the coordinated weight (in the sense of "burden") of both narrative and history.

One can detect a striking instance of this newly emergent anecdote within early modern travel writing in Sir Richard Hakluyt's *Principal Navigations*, the primary text of the English tradition. Hakluyt opens his dedicatory epistle to Sir Francis Walsingham that prefaces his first edition (1589) with the following anecdote:

I do remember that being a youth, and one of her Majesties scholars at Westminster that fruitfull nurserie, it was my happe to visit the chamber of M. Richard Hakluyt my cosin, a Gentleman of the Middle Temple, well knowen unto you, at a time when I found lying open upon his boord certeine bookes of Cosmographie, with an universall Mappe: he seeing me somewhat curious in the view therof, began to instruct my ignorance, by shewing me the division of the earth into three parts after the olde account, and then according to the latter, & better distribution, into more: he pointed with his wand to all the knowen Seas, Gulfs, Bayes, Straights, Capes, Rivers, Empires, Kingdomes, Dukedomes, and Territories of ech part, with declaration also of their speciall commodities, & particular wants, which by the benefit of traffike, & entercourse of merchants, are plentifully supplied. From the Mappe he brought me to the Bible, and turning to the 107 Psalme, directed mee to the 23 & 24 verses, where I read, that they which go downe to the sea in ships, and occupy by the great waters, they see the works of the Lord, and his woonders in the deepe, &c. Which words of the Prophet together with my cousins discourse (things of high and rare delight to my yong nature) tooke in me so deepe an impression, that I constantly resolved, if ever I were preferred to the University, where better time, and more convenient place might be ministred for these studies, I would by Gods assistance prosecute that knowledge and kinde of literature, the doores whereof (after a sort) were so happily opened before me.[6]

This passage is particularly important as it articulates – quite apart from Hakluyt's declared objective of introducing his own relation to travel writing – three related aspects of Hakluyt's project: (1) its *textual* nature, (2) its embeddedness within the discourse of nationalism, and (3) its investment in the production of the anecdote. First, one finds here a dramatic illustration of Hakluyt's conception of the *textual* nature of travel: in his essentially historical account of the generation of his own interests, Hakluyt makes explicit that he comes to travel by way of texts – "certain books of Cosmographie," a "universall Mappe," and the Bible. Clearly Hakluyt construes travel as writing.[7] In *Voyages in Print*, Mary C. Fuller discusses Hakluyt's appropriation of the language of travel (especially the rhetoric of hardship): "Travel between England and the New World, no longer irreducibly foreign or actual, reemerges in Hakluyt's appropriations as metaphor and metonymy for what was domestic and textual."[8] Indeed, in the final line of the passage from *Principal Navigations* quoted above – "I would by God's assistance prosecute that knowledge and kinde of literature" – Hakluyt explicitly identifies travel as a form of (textual) knowledge.[9] Travel itself becomes both a form of knowledge and – simultaneously – a form of literature. In *The Conquest of America*, Todorov identifies a similar tendency in Columbus to construe travel as a textual act; Columbus's consistent desire "to discover" – which takes precedence at times over the desire for the objects of discovery and as such is reinvented by Columbus as "an intransitive action" – Todorov argues, is

subject to a goal, which is the narrative of the voyage: one might say that Columbus has undertaken it all in order to be able to tell unheard-of stories, like Ulysses; but is not a travel narrative itself the point of departure, and not only the point of arrival, of a new voyage? Did not Columbus himself set sail because he had read Marco Polo's narrative? (*Conquest* 13)

It seems clear both from Hakluyt's introductory anecdote and from the enormous textual and editorial project he assumes for himself in the production of *Principal Navigations* that travel is understood as a fundamentally discursive cultural practice. To a limited extent this practice may be seen as "intransitive" – Hakluyt's collection (particularly its 1599–1600 edition) claims its interests are encyclopedic and its editorial philosophy by definition inclusive – but a closer look shows us a text and a project that stand quite explicitly as a testament to the *transitive* nature of travel writing. Indeed, compared to Columbus's project, Hakluyt's is positively acquisitive in its desires and motivations.

Secondly, Hakluyt's textual-acquisitive project is explicitly marked by its investment in – and contribution to – the emergence of a new phase in the related enterprises of English global exploration and the literature of travel characterized by, and in some sense dedicated to, the production of travel writing as an overtly nationalistic discourse. Hakluyt is quite clear both in his editorial comments and practices and in his selection and presentation of the travel narratives themselves that his task is nationalistic.[10] Mandeville's *Travels* is clearly *not* motivated by any structuring sense of national pride, or national sentiment. Perhaps this is due in large part to the fact that Mandeville's *Travels* is more heavily invested in its didactic and moralizing discourse on the unkempt state of Christianity than it is in that of any particular nation – something that is simply no longer the case once Columbus writes of his voyages, or by the time that Cortés first envisions the conquest of Mexico. Yet, by the end of the sixteenth century, when Hakluyt assembles his great national monument, there are already significant differences between an exploration in the service of particular *monar-chical* interests – Columbus, for example, or Cortés, in the Spanish tradi-tion – and exploration and its narrational production in the service of a nation. For Hakluyt, as I discussed in chapter 3 in terms of cartography and its nationalistic form, the nation is no longer self-identical with the *kingdom*, and is therefore more removed from the monarch: in Hakluyt, the nation has clearly already become the *people* – particularly its adventurers and its merchants, its editors (including Hakluyt) and their readers. In many ways this new definition comes to signify commerce – a change that is most evident in Hakluyt's addition of the word "traffiques" to the title of the second edition of *Principal Navigations*, but is also made obvious in any number of narratives within the text, especially those that document what Hakluyt in his opening anecdote had characterized as the elder Hakluyt's discussion of the exotic places in the world and "their speciall commodities, & particular wants, which by the benefit of traffike, & entercourse with mer-chants, are plentifully supplied."[11]

Thirdly, Hakluyt's project is fully engaged in the production of the anec-dote – first in terms of the relation he believes his text has with history, and then in terms of the relation his text has with evidence in the form of New World curiosities. Hakluyt is concerned that his readers should understand the nature of *Principal Navigations*, which he calls explicitly a "historie," and to that end devotes a rather lengthy discussion to "the Methode and order" of his book (I.xxiii). Hakluyt chronologically organizes his project's three great divisions – the first part of which will be devoted to discoveries to the east and southeast (the Near and Far East), the second to discover-ies in the northeast (especially Russia), and the third to the western discov-eries (especially, of course, the New World). He will later write in the reader's preface to the first volume of the second edition (1598) that it has been his intention

to gather . . . and as it were to incorporate into one body the torne and scattered limmes of our ancient and late Navigations by Sea, our voyages by land, and traf-fiques of merchandise by both: and having (so much as in me lieth) restored ech par-ticular member, being before displaced, to their true joynts and ligaments; I meane, by the helpe of Geographie and Chronologie (which I may call the Sunne and the Moone, the right eye and the left of all history) referred ech particular relation to the due time and place. (*Principal Navigations* I.xxxix)

For Hakluyt, history itself can only see – and, presumably, *be seen* – through the lenses of geography and chronology. His own project, then, is dedicated to the more or less scientific articulation of such a history – a possibility afforded Hakluyt, as he reminds us repeatedly, by virtue of his immersion and great competence in the literature – one could say, the *culture* – of travel and trade. But what is the model for this history or historiography? On the one hand, the *practical* model is clearly a *textual* one predicated upon the tools and methods of philological and archival scholarship, and it is this methodological innovation that stands as Hakluyt's great achievement, hence Hakluyt's own (literary-)historical significance as archivist, editor, and anthologizer. On the other hand, Hakluyt's *theoretical* historiographical model is essentially the traditional (and conservative) method and epistemology of chronology: events plotted on a totalized and totalizing time-line predicated upon a *telos* of progression and governed by the politics of sequentiality – what one could call the tyranny of chronology.[12]

If there is any sense in Hakluyt of an anxiety occasioned by his theoretical model it quietly emerges near the end of the reader's preface to the first edition, where he addresses what is in fact only the most obvious of its consequences: the evident inability of his writing and the writings which he collects to offer manifest proof of their professed truthfulness. (This is indeed an issue for at least some of the writers of the narratives Hakluyt collects at least some of the time; Ralegh, to name one, addresses this concern – albeit rather obliquely – in his narrative of his voyage to Guiana, even as Columbus a generation before had attempted to finesse the issue of evidence.) Near the end of the preface to the first edition, Hakluyt notes that the narratives he presents make frequent mention of "curiosities" discovered on voyages of exploration and discovery, and that he has himself seen such objects (evidence) first-hand:

And whereas in the course of this history often mention is made of many beastes, birds, fishes, serpents, plants, fruits, hearbes, rootes, apparell, armour, boates, and such other rare and strange curiosities, which wise men take great pleasure to reade of, but much more contentment to see: herein I my selfe to my singuler delight have bene as it were ravished in beholding all the premisses gathered together with no small cost, and preserved with no litle diligence, in the excellent Cabinets of my very worshipfull and learned friends M. Richard Garther, one of the Clearkes of the pettie Bags, and M. William Cope Gentleman Ussier to . . . the Lord Burleigh, high Treasourer of England. (*Principal Navigations* I.xxx)

In this statement, intended to secure the truthfulness of Hakluyt's collected narratives against readerly disbelief or skepticism, we witness a series of exchanges or substitutions that ultimately impacts the anecdote. In the first instance, the objects of discovery ("curiosities") are substituted for the experience of travel itself, as the former have the evident advantage of materiality and portability. Secondly, Hakluyt's own experience of seeing these objects – his sense of "delight" and feeling of being "ravished" – are substituted for the objects which in spite of their having been identified, transported, and collected in one of the cabinets remain inaccessible (or, perhaps, merely *hypothetical*) for the reader. And lastly, Hakluyt's more or less autobiographical writing – his anecdote of having seen these objects – is substituted for the experience of having seen them. These "curiosities" are construed as something like proof, but Hakluyt can only offer the story of his experience of them in the face of their persistent absence (though these evidential curiosities are said to be in England, they are nevertheless not in the hands of the readers). In other words – and as is certainly also the case for the narratives of *Principal Navigations* – the anecdote at hand (Hakluyt having seen Garther's or Cope's curiosities, or Ralegh having seen oysters growing on trees in Guiana) is always held out to the reader as "first-hand," but its actual form is inevitably second- or, even, third-hand. This is the hermeneutic of travel writing more generally: the experience of travel can only be communicated – or, only *approximately* communicated – by virtue of the anecdote offered in the face of an anticipated and perhaps real readerly skepticism and in the disruptive absence of substantive authorial proof. But the textual anecdote is always *written*, substituted for an experience for which it is offered as a near-enough approximation. The anecdote is always, in other words, self-alienated. The anecdote – which is supposed in the logic of travel writing to be self-evident – always inscribes the absence of evidence and the absence (there in the writing) of experience. The anecdote is always figured – can *only* be figured – as *the story of the anecdote*, and in the face of its own belatedness, the anecdote effectively displaces description and offers in its stead (yet another instance of substitution) a narrative. The anecdote works to establish itself so fully within the realm of narrative that it may be seen at times as the very condition of narrativity. And perhaps this is so. Perhaps narrative itself actually is inaugurated in the violent emergence of the anecdote *as a form of historiography*, that moment in which a non-appropriative description is construed as bearing an innate utility. If description is the form of that *uselessness* that exists prior to the very sense of utility, then the narrational – and the anecdote – is the form of supreme use. Description predates the desire to render its object useful; description posits no functional value to its object. The narrational, on the other hand, emplots its object – which can be identical with the object of description, or may even be description itself – within any given plot, each of which is defined by a narrative of utility. This notion of utility is clearly understood in Hakluyt's anecdote in which the entire world – in all its true "distribution," in its resources, products, and markets – is reinvented in the image of universal use: commerce. The theoretical issues pertaining to travel are, then, figured in Hakluyt's prefaces to the first edition of *Principal Navigations* – first in the form of the anecdote at the beginning of the introductory editorial material, and then in the form of the cabinet of curiosities at its conclusion.[13] These serve to bracket, as it were, the actual presentation of the narratives of Hakluyt's text.

One of the most important narratives Hakluyt offers in *Principal Navigations* is Ralegh's *Discovery of Guiana* – a text in which we can trace the deployment of the anecdote under the sign of the narrational. There are two passages in Ralegh's text that stand out in stark contrast to one another, though in both – and between them – one can detect the emergence of the narrational over against the contrary politics of description. The first:

I never saw a more beautiful country, nor more lively prospects, hills so raised here and there over the valleys, the river winding into diverse branches, the plains adjoining without bush or stubble, all fair green grass . . . the deer crossing in every path, the birds towards the evening singing on every tree with a thousand several tunes, cranes and herons of white, crimson, and carnation perching in the river's side, the air fresh with a gentle easterly wind, and every stone that we stooped to take up promised either gold or silver by his complexion.[14]

And the second:

To conclude, Guiana is a country that hath yet her maidenhead, never sacked, turned, not wrought; the face of the earth hath not been torn, nor the virtue and salt of the soil spent by manurance; the graves have not been opened for gold, the mines not broken with sledges, nor their images pulled down out of their temples. It hath never been entered by an army of strength, and never conquered or possessed by any Christian prince. (*Discovery* 507)[15]

While one believes that for Ralegh discovery is emphatically acquisitive[16] (he is out to discover Guiana, he tells us, the "magazine of all rich metals" [455]), he is nevertheless inspired by Guiana's natural beauty. The foregoing description of this natural beauty is perhaps the most lyrical moment in the text. At the same time it is entirely teleological: topographical splendor gives way to biological diversity and beauty, and both yield in turn to the gold or silver the landscape seems to hold out as a promise. It is the teleological nature of this passage that signals what I earlier called the occlusion of description by the narrative of possession. Even within this single passage we can chart its loss. Ralegh's wonder at Guiana's natural beauty is not obviously possessive at the point of its first impression, but this moment (as I suggested earlier) can be a moment of extremely brief duration, and what follows it emerges by the end of the passage as the narrative of possession: the landscape itself holds the much-coveted gold that we know lured Ralegh to Guiana in the first place.

But by the end of the *Discovery*, where the second passage occurs, the relationship between natural beauty and economic utility has become undisguised. Now it is the unspoiled natural beauty of Guiana that not only guarantees wealth but also actually incites one to (a gendered) violence to procure it. The language of description and the *topoi* of the travel book have given way to the language of narrationality and the imperative of the political tract: the text reveals its profound political and appropriative embeddedness, its call for conquest in the face of the other, as a reaction to difference or the incommensurate conceived of as useful.

Response to the incommensurate can be characterized in a number of ways: as surprise, as confusion, as shock. Or as wonder. The latter is the characterization offered by Stephen Greenblatt in his study of European representational practices in the New World, *Marvelous Possessions*. Greenblatt asserts early in his book that wonder is "the central figure in the initial European response to the New World, the decisive emotional and intellectual experience in the presence of radical difference" (p. 14). This arises, in part, from the place wonder held in the period in the fields of philosophy and aesthetics, though geographical discoveries in the early modern period not only are understood through this "central figure" of wonder, but indeed "helped (along with many other factors) to provoke its conceptualization" (*Marvelous Possessions* 19). Greenblatt traces wonder in Descartes and Spinoza, who both – despite other points of non-convergence in their philosophies – consider the salient feature of wonder to be its unique positionality: by virtue of its primacy and the uniqueness of its object, wonder

precedes, even escapes, moral categories. When we wonder, we do not yet know if we love or hate the object at which we are marveling; we do not know if we should embrace it or flee from it. For this reason wonder, Descartes argues, "has no opposite and is the first of all passions." Similarly for Spinoza – in whose account wonder was not, strictly speaking, a passion at all, but rather a mode of conception (*imaginatio*) – wonder depends upon a suspension or failure of categories and is a kind of paralysis, a stilling of the normal associative restlessness of the mind . . . The object that arouses wonder is so new that for a moment at least it is alone, unsystematized, an utterly detached object of rapt attention. (*Marvelous Possessions* 20)

Greenblatt's characterization of wonder corresponds to Derrida's "heterogeneity of a *pre-*" and to my sense of description (as I have used that term here) – each is a primary reaction and neither carries the systems and categories of meaning that I have been calling the narrational. Another way of characterizing the object of description or wonder as "unsystematized" (as Greenblatt does here) is to say that it resides – however briefly – outside or *prior to* meaning. It is once – literally on second thought – we conceive a meaning for this object that it ceases to be "unsystematized." Even if we do not yet know the meaning we suppose adheres in this object, we have nevertheless posited *meaningfulness* for the object and thereby ushered this otherwise incoherent object into the world of the narrational. This is precisely what Greenblatt does next: "The expression of wonder stands for all that cannot be understood, that can scarcely be believed. It calls attention to the problem of credibility and at the same time insists upon the undeniability, the exigency of the experience" (*Marvelous Possessions* 20). To read this passage is to witness the momentous shift from description to narrationality, from anecdote to history: the incommensurate denies understanding not because we do not yet have a system in place capable of discovering its (hidden) meaning, but because it *precedes meaning itself*. Meaning – like ideology – is always a function of the narrational. To say further that the incommensurate calls attention to the problem of credibility is to have already imported it into a particular narrational context within which matters such as credibility and incredulity are themselves possible.

Greenblatt links wonder to the experiences of travel and travel writing, suggesting that the success of the travel text can only be secured if the writer succeeds in communicating wonder credibly: "His work can only be believed if he arouses in his readers something of the wonder that he himself felt, for that wonder will link whatever is out there with inward conviction" (*Marvelous Possessions* 22). Greenblatt continues, "Hence the ease with which the very words *marvel* and *wonder* shift between the designation of a material object and the designation of a response to the object, between intense, almost phantasmagorical inward states and thoroughly externalized objects that can, after the initial moments of astonishment have passed, be touched, cataloged, inventoried, possessed" (*Marvelous Possessions* 22). But as I have argued in terms of Hakluyt, who records his feeling of being "ravished" by New World curiosities, such a system of communication is destined to failure. Or: its success can only be metaphorical. Wonder stands by definition as unavailable to a communication within which it suffers a killing separation from description and new alignment within the narrational.

There is a tension within Ralegh's text that arises out of these competing ideologies of description and narrative, a tension signaled in the very title of the book:

The Discovery of the Large, Rich and Beautiful Empire of Guiana: With a Relation of the great and golden city of Manoa, which the Spaniards call El Dorado . . .

Ralegh's book marks the discovery of Guiana, which is to say the "dis-covering" or "unveiling" of Guiana – in short, its description. In the next phrase, however, we are told that the book is also a "relation" of various locations within Guiana – especially El Dorado (the true object, we know, of Ralegh's interest in the first place) – and a relation of Ralegh's adventures there. While "discovery" suggests description, "relation" suggests the narrational. Ralegh's title and the book that follows operate between both epistemologies: within the epistemology of description as apparently promised in the travel book, and within the epistemology of narrative as deployed in an overtly political text. But if these two epistemologies reside together in some fashion, they do so only provisionally, and not without a certain tension as narrative finally supersedes description as the fundamental discursive (and one could say, philosophical) strategy.

In the opening passage of his *Discovery*, Ralegh literally wastes no time: we are caught up in the moment the passage recounts, drawn into the moment of narrative with no contextual information concerning the journey – its leaders, objectives, ships, provisions, men, authority, etc., all those details that so frequently are taken up in other travel narratives from the period. Ralegh's text simply begins with the movement across the ocean:

On Thursday the 6th of February, in the year 1595, we departed England, and the Sunday following had sight of the North Cape of Spain, the wind for the most part continuing prosperous; we passed in sight of the Burlings, and the Rock, and so onwards for the Canaries, and fell with Fuerteventura on the 17th of the same month, where we spent two or three days, and relieved our companies with some fresh meat. (*Discovery* 454)

Mary B. Campbell comments on Ralegh's opening sentence in her book *The Witness and the Other World: Exotic European Travel Writing, 400–1600*: "His first sentence . . . establishes the intensely and minutely narrative format. Without any preliminary situating of the voyage's events in a larger political–historical context, such as opens the *Journals* of Columbus, he plunges directly into the water . . . Narrativity is the point and exposition secondary."[17] Campbell understands this "narrativity" as something of a genuine response, largely rhetorical in nature, to the discursive demands of the New World, and Ralegh's dilemma as essentially a literary one of attempting "to document another world, without any tradition behind him of simply denotative discourse" (Campbell 222). For Campbell, Ralegh writes his *Discovery* against what she calls "the antinarrative urge toward encyclopedism" that had characterized late medieval travel literature (Campbell 219–20). The New World "necessitated a new rhetoric for reasons having as much to do with perception and inadequate vocabulary as with politics and economics" (Campbell 222).[18] Campbell asks how it was possible "to *express* difference in a genre whose rhetorical mainstay was the analogy and whose Matter had always been the Scripted, the legendary, the elaborately preconceived" (Campbell 225). Given these pressures and demands, Ralegh's text registers the "conceptual birth" of a "new thing in the world" (Campbell 226). In Ralegh, the failure of "useful" description – by way of analogy – leads to an emphasis on narrative: "the only object of which his knowledge can be comprehensive and to which his language can be equal. It is with this experience that he fills the wilderness and his relation" (Campbell 228).[19]

Ralegh's project depends, then, in part upon a repudiation of the purely descriptive (Campbell's "simply denotative discourse"). In spite of the occasional appearance of his fascination with locale and an attendant desire to describe it, Ralegh resolutely insists that his project – both the journey and the text – are not concerned with description. For Ralegh, description is typically impertinent unless it is in the service of his political agenda: his call for the conquest of Guiana. Moreover, Ralegh's sense of pure description places it outside the very formal purview of his text, and he frequently suggests that description can best be communicated by charts and maps – outside, that is, what he tends to think of as narrative:

How all these rivers cross and encounter, how the country lieth and is bordered, the passage of Ximnenes and Berrio, my own discovery, and the way that I entered, with all the rest of the nations and rivers, your lordship shall receive in a large chart or map, which I have not yet finished. (*Discovery* 466)

Every day we passed by goodly branches of rivers, some falling from the west, others from the east, into Amana; but those I leave to the description in the chart of discovery, where every one shall be named with his rising and descent. (*Discovery* 478)

To speak of what passed homeward were tedious, either to describe or name any of the rivers, islands, or villages of the Tivitivas, which dwell on trees. We will leave all these to the general map. (*Discovery* 503)

For Ralegh, description – here construed as the special domain of charts and maps – denotes immediate fact, the unmediated representation of details whose objective status are seemingly beyond dispute. But as I discussed in chapter 3, the very idea of maps as neutral representations of objective fact is entirely illusory; maps, again, are always narrational.

There is of course a world of difference between the *Discovery* as narrative and the description it refuses to own: for Ralegh the latter seems to exist outside interpretation, the former fully embedded within it. To find Ralegh's political interpretation of Guiana, and his own mission there, one needs to attend not only to his narrative but to the narrational structure of the *Discovery*: its anecdotal form. In his dedicatory epistle, Ralegh addresses the rumors spread by his political enemies that suggested – anecdotally – that he never voyaged to Guiana but secreted himself away at home in England and only subsequently fabricated his voyage and his narrative: "I have neither hidden in Cornwall, or elsewhere, as was supposed . . . and the rest were much mistaken who would have persuaded that I was too easeful and sensual to undertake a journey of so great travel."[20] In fact, it is precisely the status as eye-witness account that authorizes the content of the *Discovery*; Ralegh's is no dream of Guiana, but an historical record of his voyage there grounded in his own experience which serves to insure its accuracy and truthfulness. The question of evidence, then, is fundamentally important to his book not merely to refute these accusa-

tions, but (and this is more important) to substantiate his text, to authorize it as *fact*.[21] What is important to note, however, is that evidence for
Ralegh is not the description of Guiana, but rather the *narrative* of his
journey there. In the *Discovery*, narrative is supposed to be evidential, is
understood itself as carrying evidential weight. Of course, this evidential
weight is more than a rhetorical matter, strictly speaking. Indeed, the
narrational is thoroughly ideological in nature. What comes to stand as
proof in Ralegh's text is not the accumulation of details, but rather the
sheer weight and momentum articulated along the axis of their narration,
the *story* of these details.

Ralegh's text is also dependent upon other texts. In offering a genealogical account of the people of Guiana, Ralegh tells us they are descended
from the great princes of the Inca who fled the army of Pizarro. Ralegh
offers as proof the works of Portuguese historians: "I thought good to
make it known that the Emperor now reigning is descended from these
magnificent princes of Peru, of whose large territories, of whose policies,
conquests, edifices and riches, Padro de Cieza, Francisco Lopez and others
have written large discourses" (*Discovery* 460). Ralegh proceeds to tell the
story of Pizarro's conquest of Peru and the escape of thousands of the Inca
to Guiana, and offers to supplement (and authorize) his narrative by
grounding it in "the very words" of these discourses:

And if we compare it [the wealth of El Dorado] to that of Peru, and but read the
report of Francisco Lopez and others, it will seem more than credible; and because
we may judge of the one by the other, I thought good to insert part of the 120th
chapter of Lopez . . . whose very words are these: "*Todo el servicio de su casa, mesa
y cocina era de oro y de plata.*" (*Discovery* 460)

For Ralegh, as this instance makes clear, evidence comes in the form of narrative, as the earlier words of the conquistadors authorize his own. Indeed,
discourse itself is for Ralegh inevitably narrational, and the narrational is
moral and it is moral because it is true.[22] It exists and functions beyond or
in excess of interpretation. It offers direct and unmediated access to the
real. Of course, as Roland Barthes – and a great deal of post-structuralist
theory since – has demonstrated, the "fact" imagined as somehow outside
discourse is wholly illusory:

The fact can only have a linguistic existence, as a term in a discourse, and yet it is
exactly as if this existence were merely the "copy," purely and simply, of another
existence situated in the extra-structural domain of the "real." [History] is doubtless the only type in which the referent is aimed for as something external to the discourse, without it ever being possible to attain it outside this discourse.[23]

Yet it is just these "facts" imagined to exist outside discourse that are
offered to substantiate Ralegh's text, to authorize the text as "factual"

history and to authorize the political imperative of conquest that the text advocates.

As I have suggested above, the anecdote is offered in travel writing as the very mark of the fact. In a manner of speaking, this gesture amounts to a carefully determined choice of genre: what *kind* of literary device or writing will serve best to communicate the facticity of New World experience? While this question is one posed by writers of primary New World discourse, it is at the same time a question asked by "secondary" writers of New World discourse. Todorov begins *The Conquest of America* with a discussion of his choice of genre for his study. Referring to classical oration, Todorov cites the orator's query of his audience's generic preferences: "myth – i.e., narrative – or logical argumentation" (*Conquest* 3). In the age of the book, however, the orator's gesture is of course impossible; one can only hope to appeal to the audience in his or her choice of genre and "to listen to the answer suggested or imposed by the subject itself" (*Conquest* 4). Todorov then declares his choice: "to narrate a history": "Closer to myth than to argument, it is nonetheless to be distinguished from myth on two levels: first because it is a true story (which myth could, but need not, be), and second because my main interest is less a historian's than a moralist's; the present is more important to me than the past." (*Conquest* 4). Todorov believes that by "telling the exemplary story (this will be the genre chosen)" he will best be able to answer the question "How to deal with the other." In his discussion he will "try never to lose sight of . . . its [the story's] tropological or ethical meaning" (*Conquest* 4). Todorov continues, "And in this book, rather as in a novel, summaries or generalized perspectives will alternate with scenes of analysis of detail filled with quotations, and with pauses in which the author comments on what has just occurred, and of course with frequent ellipses or omissions. But is this not the point of departure of all history?" (*Conquest* 4). The connection here between story and moral is both clear and suggestive, and seems to imply that narrative associates in some immediate way with truth, and that, moreover, narrative exists beyond or *outside* argument and interpretation. Todorov suggests, finally, that narrative – what he will later call "exemplary history" (*Conquest* 254) and what I would call the narrational – functions in excess of interpretation and judgment: he need only present this story and its tropological value – its truth, which is unassailable, unproblematical, and moral – will be entirely clear. What we witness here is Todorov's culturally determined privileging of narrative over alternate forms – a maneuver, I want to suggest, that is explicitly disqualified within Todorov's own analysis of conquest.

In the epilog to *The Conquest of America*, Todorov tries to assess the state of our contemporary system of encountering the other and suggests that while colonialism (which includes but is not limited to conquest) is the failure to encounter the other, this crucial epistemological and cultural task is not yet complete, "For the other remains to be discovered" (*Conquest* 247). However, the still recent discovery of the internal other (Rimbaud's "Je est un autre") and our new ways of theorizing alterity (Todorov invokes here both Bakhtin and Levinas) point to *our* desire for equality without identity, difference without superiority/inferiority. Todorov speaks for, in short, a cultural heterology. And here, at the end of his text on conquest and genocide, Todorov asks again about genre:

> The form of disclosure I have resolved upon for this book, that of the exemplary history, also results from the desire to transcend the limits of systematic writing, yet without "returning" to pure myth. By comparing Columbus with Cortés, Cortés with Montezuma, I have become aware that the forms of communication – production as well as reception – even if they are universal and eternal, are not accessible to the writer's free choice, but are correlated to the ideologies in force and can thereby become their sign. But what is the discourse appropriate to our heterological mentality? (*Conquest* 253)

In his study, Todorov has recourse to the *narrative* discourse of the conquistadors, even while acknowledging that in "European civilization *logos* has conquered *mythos*": "I could not separate myself from the vision of the 'conquerors' without at the same time renouncing the discursive form they had appropriated as their own. I feel the need . . . to adhere to that narrative which proposes rather than imposes; to rediscover, with a single text, the complementarity of narrative discourse and systematic discourse" (*Conquest* 253). Todorov then discusses the formal strategies of his book, his interest in reporting facts which only sometimes leads to "general assertions"; submitting some narratives to analysis while others remain "unsubmissive"; and refusing (and repudiating) closure: "And if, at this very moment, I am 'drawing the moral' of my history, it is with no thought of yielding up and 'fixing' its meaning – a narrative is not reducible to a maxim – but because I find it more honest to formulate some of the impressions it makes upon me, since I too am one of its readers" (*Conquest* 254). Todorov argues for a provisional and heterological history of the conquest – and, more generally, the encounter with the other – which speaks *through* his text but is *not* made to speak by him, in a way which does not obtain to power: "For Cortés, the conquest of knowledge leads to the conquest of power. I take the conquest of knowledge from his example, even if I do so in order to resist power" (*Conquest* 254). The subject of Todorov's book remains our present moment: the history of the conquistadors is exemplary not because it "represents a faithful image of *our* relation to the other," but because "it permits us to reflect upon ourselves, to discover resemblances as well as differences: once again self-knowledge develops through knowledge of the other" (*Conquest* 254).

Though entirely different in character, Todorov's heterology as it is here described strikes me as a potentially appropriative one – one in which, while the other does not exist as our image, the other nonetheless exists for our own *use*. This version of the encounter with the other seems at least theoretically able to authorize the (inadvertent) appropriation of the other for our own ideological uses. This can hardly be imagined, properly speaking, as a heterology at all, but rather as another instance of its denial.

In Todorov, "history" appears always to be written elsewhere, never by the active – that is to say, *political* – writer; it can speak *for itself* ("Heterology, which makes the difference of voices heard, is necessary" [*Conquest* 251]). And yet, we know that a truly a-political person is a fantasy, as fantastic, no doubt, as the a-historical person. Todorov's notion of history as a practice appears to be modeled on one of the texts of the conquest that he examines in his book: Bernardino de Sahagún's monumental *Historia general de las cosas de Nueva España*. In this work Sahagún attempts to write a complete description of the religion of the ancient Mexicans to facilitate the conversion of Mexico by European Christians. Yet, according to Todorov there was another (perhaps contrary) motive: "the desire to know and preserve Nahuatl culture" (*Conquest* 223). The *Historia* is gradually expanded to include much of Nahuatl culture, not just its ancient religion, and its information is written in Nahuatl rather than Spanish. Sahagún adds a free Spanish translation of the eye-witness narratives of the first part, in which he aspires to present the narratives themselves, without any intervention or commentary: the path, Todorov says, of "total fidelity, since he reproduces the very speeches that are made to him, and to them *adds* his translation" (*Conquest* 226). Though Sahagún clearly intends absolutely no interpenetration of the two voices that "speak" in his *Historia*, Todorov proceeds brilliantly to demonstrate the numerous ways in which interpenetration of the voices occurs. I will focus on only one of these here: the intervention of Sahagún's voice in the narrative of human sacrifice, which had been offered by Sahagún, Todorov asserts, as intending "no value judgment, but no interpretation either; we are reading pure description" (*Conquest* 230):

Their masters pulled them up and dragged them by the hair to the sacrificial stone where they were to die. Having brought them to the sacrificial stone, which was a stone of three hands in height, or a little more, and two in width, or almost, they threw them upon it, on their backs, and five [priests] seized them – two by the legs, two by the arms, and one by the head; and then came the priest who was to kill him. And he struck him with a flint [knife], held in both hands and made in the manner of a large lance-head, between the breasts. And into the gash which he made, he thrust his hand, and tore from [the victim] his heart, and then he offered it to the sun and cast it into a gourd vessel. After having torn their hearts from them and poured the blood into a gourd vessel, this the master of the slain man himself received, they started the body rolling down the pyramid steps.

(*Historia* III.2, qtd. in Todorov, *Conquest* 230)

But in spite of the desire for non-intervention, Todorov argues, this narrative is not "uncontaminated" by Sahagún: "The Indians had no need to express themselves in this way among themselves; such discourse is powerfully determined by the identity of their interlocutor . . . Then is this . . . version of the rite the zero degree of intervention? We may doubt this . . . because the very notion of zero degree is perhaps illusory" (*Conquest* 230–31).

Sahagún's liability, then, is Todorov's as well. The attempt at descriptive history is perhaps inevitably contaminated by the very fact of its teller, as description gives way to narrative: Sahagún tells his own story – he is a European, and an invasive reporter of "strange" New World practices – even as he seeks to separate and silence himself. Self-consciousness appears not to be a guarantee against intervention and re-invention.

The implicit cultural bias in Todorov's book is further revealed in his discussion of an alleged Spanish "technological superiority," which Todorov identifies as the decisive factor in the conquest – both in terms of Spanish improvisational ability and, more importantly, their possession of written language. Even though Todorov readily acknowledges elsewhere in his book the fact that "the prejudice of superiority is an obstacle in the road to knowledge" (*Conquest* 165), he nevertheless insists upon this Spanish "technological" superiority: "There is a 'technology' of symbolism, which is as capable of evolution as the technology of tools, and, in this perspective, the Spaniards are more 'advanced' than the Aztecs (or to generalize: societies possessing writing are more advanced than societies without writing), even if we are here concerned only with a difference of degree" (*Conquest* 160). Todorov's suggestion here that Amerindian cultures were inferior (technologically) because, unlike Europeans, they lacked written language is entirely erroneous. Again, Todorov's interpretive maneuvers themselves betray a certain cultural bias. In terms of written language, the difference between Amerindians and Europeans is not that the latter had it while the former did not, but that the latter did not recognize Amerindian written language because it was non-alphabetic. Todorov, it seems, makes a similar mistake.[24]

Todorov pursues what he believes to be the repercussions of his techno-supremacy, and while his analysis is lengthy and complex, it is sufficient here to mark what cannot fail to be – in spite of his disclaimers to the contrary – a certain cultural (ideological) bias. Todorov fails to submit to his own critical acumen the assumptions implicit in this pronouncement concerning discourse (here the discourse of evolution as a progressive model of human affairs) and its interlocutor: Todorov occupies a position from which technology – and indeed evolutionary models altogether – are understood as necessarily advantageous and desirable. With this *linear* conception of time Todorov identifies himself once again with the discourse of the conquistadors whose faith in (Christian–temporal) linearity was virtually unimaginable to the ancient Mexican's conception of time.

The point upon which Todorov's argument turns is narrative and narrational. While Todorov discusses at some length Aztec concern with speech, he identifies their primary concern as the desire to interpret, and offers as emblematic of this the trials by which chiefs were chosen: they are presented with figurative expressions which they had to interpret. Failure to do so correctly resulted in severe corporal punishment. Todorov offers the following comment: "Like the victims of the sphinx, the future chiefs are confronted with this dilemma: to interpret or die (though differing from certain characters of the *Arabian Nights* whose law is, instead, 'Narrate or Die!' But no doubt there exist narrative civilizations and interpretive civilizations)" (*Conquest* 78). This is clear enough: Aztec culture is interpretive (it is later characterized in essentially negative terms: it is ritualistic, for example, and slavishly tied to the past), while other – Spanish – culture is narrative. It is this narrative nature of Spanish culture that allows for the improvisational skill of the Spaniards (and Cortés in particular) that Todorov offers – along with written language and symbological superiority – as chief and decisive reasons for the conquest.[25]

The narrational nature of Todorov's argument culminates (to invoke the formal language of narrative) in his thoroughly teleological sense of history in which one's current condition is understood as the (logical) end-product of a certain narrative which becomes clear and obvious in its trajectory but which is, finally, wholly constructed. We can say of Todorov as he says of Sahagún that his zero degree of intervention is perhaps illusory as "discourse is powerfully determined by the identity of [its] interlocutor." In Todorov's text, the attempt "to let history happen" without authorial intervention is largely contaminated by a cultural privileging of the narrational; the theory of the supremely communicative, transparent, and objectively true and moral seems suspect. The voices his text seeks to present do not simply speak outside or beyond his interpretation – representation – of them. The voices of his heterological study are still finally his own.

Any historicism – such as Todorov's – founded upon a faith in the objective truth value of historical artifacts – or, even, historical "events" – is destined to a problematical tautological status: the "fact" that is understood as true is the fact to which historical meaning has already been ascribed. This is true of any historicism that understands history as a narrative.[26] We might well echo Nietzsche's description of the non-existence of "facts" when we say that there is no such thing as history as such; it is always necessary to begin with a meaning in order that there can be history. Or, there is no such thing as the historical "event"; it is always necessary to begin with a narrative in order that there can be an event.

In the remaining pages of this chapter I would like to turn to a consideration of the sort of historicism practiced by new historicists – particularly in relation to the anecdote. In new historicism, "fact" and history tend to be located in the anecdote, even though its entire enterprise is in part an attempt to demonstrate the constructedness of both "fact" and "history" – what Louis Montrose calls "the historicity of texts and the textuality of history."[27] While the ambition of such a project is to make evident the historical embeddedness of both the historical subject and object, new historicism nevertheless lays surprisingly confident epistemological claim to a history imagined to exist *out there*. New historicism seeks the opportunity in which to make history happen, and yet this history is understood as inhabiting a space that is somehow beyond discourse, as evidenced in the postulation of the anecdote as a "found object," or in the notion that new historicism can clear a space in which to hear the voice of the other.[28] The project, then, of new historicism is evidently a heterological one. History, as Todorov suggests and Michel de Certeau argues, is perhaps the most profound attempt to understand the other, and new historicism aspires to a similar objective. And yet, the access new historicism has to these voices is mediated by – or is in fact *predetermined* by – the narrative it would tell; the voice of the other is inexorably one's own. By this measure new historicism fails to escape the liabilities of what we could call the philosophy of history. The very possibility of a philosophy of history is entirely dependent upon a narrational understanding of history and the world. Without an implicit over-riding faith in narrativity, there cannot be a philosophy of history, in the traditional sense of the term. The great philosophical models of history are available because of the master-narratives each chooses to employ: from Providentialism, to Hegelian dialectical history, to Marxist dialectical materialism, "history" is understood as the progressive exfoliation of one master-narrative or another. While one can offer critiques of any of these master-narratives, and while one can in fact critique the idea of the master-narrative itself (such as Lyotard does when he describes post-modernism as an "incredulity toward metanarratives"),[29] I want to argue that these models of causality have in common a narrational vision of history – in large part because they have a narrational vision of time itself. Bound to a philosophy of dialectics, to the notion of an extra-discursive space, to the desire for causal explanation, to a dependence upon and faith in evidence and to the mandates – or tyranny – of chronology, history becomes the narrative it will tell. In the end, *narrative* is the master-narrative. And we are never content to believe that history is not *for us*.

The idea that history is ours and that it is for our use is what empowers historicisms of various sorts. As such, historicism is constantly seeking more sophisticated and powerful ways to put history to our use, to put history to work. History, then, seems poised, available, and awaiting our appearance. In this way it is like early European visions of America as voluptuously available for a conquest made possible by an epistemology founded on the value of use. Ralegh's transitive discoveries, Cortés's interpretive conquest, critical and theoretical heterologies in which the other is fashioned into an object for our own use, these are the spoils and the costs of the conquest of history. For it is in fact to the narrational that these are sacrificed. And the alternative? A history that exists only *for itself*. While I do not want to dispute the "facts" of history, I do mean to say that its events (its record of that birth or death, its record of the rise in price of this or that commodity) exist only for themselves and not for us – that our belated access to history is always barred. History, strictly speaking, remains *unthinkable*.

In his essay "The History of the Anecdote: Fiction and Fiction," Joel Fineman identifies the anecdote as that which formally "determines the practice of historiography."[30] We see this in the uses to which the anecdote is put in new historicism. It is often introduced in order then to introduce a set of issues or texts that are at stake in the given essay – more at stake, as it were, than the anecdote itself. In this use the anecdote is strategically deployed principally to deny strategy, though it is, finally, the very mark of strategy. The anecdote is offered as a found object that exists in the real, and in some hypothetical extra-discursive field. The anecdote needs to seem unmotivated. Fineman refers to this appearance of the anecdote as "its characteristic air of reporting, haplessly, the discoveries it happened serendipitously to stumble upon in the course of undirected, idle rambles through the historical archives" (Fineman 52).

Critics do indeed "stumble upon" and "find" objects in the archives that might contribute to their work, but the idea of the status of this object as *found* is completely specious. Indeed, the archive itself – its establishment as an institution, its sources of funding, its relation to the state – as well as the objects in it, are anything but unpremeditated. The archive is clearly an organized production – however haphazard and chaotic it may be – of what we agree to call the past. Yet the idea that the anecdote is actually a found object is no doubt operative within not only new historicist use of the anecdote, but also in the narrational structure of the anecdote itself and the anecdote in historiography. The anecdote is offered as ideologically and politically neutral. It is, so it says, merely a matter of historical fact. But the anecdote and, for that matter, narrational history altogether are never ideologically or politically neutral. Thus Fineman writes on new historicism:

the term "New Historicism" initially carried with it a somewhat polemical air, for the literary criticisms and literary histories that pronounced themselves New Historicist, and that thereby understood their own critical practices to amount to actions performed, quietly enough, in the name of history, presented themselves as overdue corrections of, or as morally and politically motivated reactions against, the formalism – more precisely and more pejoratively, the "mere formalism" [of new criticism, structuralism, and post-structuralism]. (Fineman 51)

From here Fineman turns to a discussion of Thucydides and his invention of "a scientific view of history" that makes possible both the "regularizing, normativizing, essentializing laws of historical causation by reference to which it becomes possible to fit particular events into the intelligible whole of a sequential, framing narrative," and a defense of "the eternal *usefulness* of his history" (Fineman 52, my emphasis). It is the anecdote, Fineman argues, that makes this possible. Fineman seems, then, to agree with only the second of my two observations of the nature of the anecdote and its uses – i.e., that the uses of the anecdote can indeed be ideologically and politically charged – and not with the first: that the anecdote *itself* is never value-free, never represents a zero-degree intervention. This view is essential to Fineman's argument, and I will quote him here at some length:

the anecdote, a specific literary form, is important, and this because, I want to argue, the anecdote determines the destiny of a specifically historio-graphic integration of event and context. The anecdote, let us provisionally remark, as the narration of a singular event, is the literary form or genre that uniquely refers to the real. This is not as trivial an observation as might at first appear. It reminds us, on the one hand, that the anecdote has something literary about it, for there are, of course, other and non-literary ways to make reference to the real . . . that are not anecdotal. On the other hand, it reminds us also that there is something about the anecdote that exceeds its literary status, and this excess is precisely that which gives the anecdote its pointed, referential access to the real . . . . These two features, therefore, taken together – i.e., first, that the anecdote has something literary about it, but, second, that the anecdote, however literary, is nevertheless directly pointed towards or rooted in the real – allow us to think of the anecdote, given its formal if not its actual brevity, as a *historeme*, i.e., as the smallest unit of the historiographical fact.

(Fineman 56–57)

Fineman continues his discussion of the anecdote and historiography and makes the point, in fact, that it is precisely the anecdote that constitutes the *site* of the very possibility of historiography:

the anecdote is the literary form that uniquely *lets history happen* by virtue of the way it introduces an opening into the teleological, and therefore timeless, narration of beginning, middle, and end. The anecdote produces the effect of the real, the occurrence of contingency, by establishing an event as an event within and yet without the framing context of historical successivity, i.e., it does so only in so far as its narration both comprises and refracts the narration in reports. (Fineman 61)

It is this "opening" (Fineman will call it variously a "dilation" and, invoking the language of psychoanalytic theory, the "orifice") that established the possibility of history: "This double intersection, the formal play of anecdotal hole and whole, an ongoing anecdotal dilation and contraction of the entrance into history through the opening of history that lets history happen . . ." (Fineman 61).

While Fineman understands the political and moral uses to which the anecdote and historiography can be put, he seems not willing to accept the notion that the anecdote *as such* carries with it an equally significant ideological valence. He agrees that the use of the anecdote is made to seem unmotivated – the serendipitous by-product of "idle rambles through the historical archives" – the anecdote, I would say, as found object. And yet, he does not question the status of the anecdote in its relation to history. Indeed, he argues that the anecdote makes history happen, that the object (the anecdote) exists literally beyond interpretation in what I maintain can only be posited as an extra-discursive field. Objects or anecdotes, I would argue, simply cannot exist outside discourse, cannot simply exist as found objects, fragments (as it were) of the real. They are themselves always and in every instance the by-products of interpretation. The "actual" historical object – if it existed at all – can no longer be said to exist *for itself*: the narrative, say, of a dream recorded by a sixteenth century person, has the distinct difference in *our* (historiographical) discourse (*as* an anecdote) of being offered as evidence – as, in effect, a quotation. There are, of course, countless ideological constructs and motivations that enable us to understand that account of the dream as itself notable. But again, as Barthes reminds us, that which is notable can only be identified as such tautologically: what is noted derives from the notable, but the notable is only that which is worthy of being noted.

The "citation" of the anecdote has a status analogous to that of historical documents. In *The Writing of History*, Michel de Certeau discusses the status – or, more appropriately, the *creation* – of historical documents. De Certeau suggests that objects of the archive are appropriated *as documents* and are not, strictly speaking, found, but instead created. While de Certeau refers here to the "technological" production of documents, his idea of the production of documents out of objects can be equally true of the production of anecdotes:

In history, everything begins with the gesture of *setting aside*, of putting together, of transforming certain classified objects in "documents." This new cultural distribution is the first task. In reality it consists in *producing* such documents by dint of copying, transcribing, or photographing these objects, simultaneously changing their locus and their status. This gesture consists in "isolating" a body – as in physics – and "denaturing" things in order to turn them into parts which will fill the lacunae inside an a priori totality. (de Certeau 72–73)

Citing the work of Jean Baudrillard on the "collection" as the practice of creating a "marginal system" in which we place these "documents," de Certeau identifies this process of production as an instance of the creation of a category of things upon which we "confer . . . the status of 'abstract' objects of knowledge" (de Certeau 73). This process, then, effectively removes ("exiles") these things from the real world (de Certeau's word is "practice," though I would also say "history"). These, then, *become* the basis of historiography; understood as the very stuff of history, these *become* historical "facts." And yet, their status as "facts" or found objects or "events" (de Certeau's critique of documents is in fact quite similar to his critique of the historical "event"), is wholly illusory:

Far from accepting "data," this gesture forms them. The material is created through concerted actions which delimit it by carving it out from the sphere of use, actions which seek also to know it beyond limits of use, and which aim at giving it a coherent new use. It becomes the vestige of actions which modify a received order and a social vision. The establishment of signs offered for specific treatments, this rupture is therefore neither uniquely nor from the first the effect of a "gaze." A technical operation is necessary. (de Certeau 73)

It is this "technical operation" that characterizes what I have been calling the production of the anecdote – both in its own (narrational) manifestation, and in the larger narrational and ideological uses it is made to serve. The anecdote is never simply found, but always created.

This chapter has thus far been devoted to discussing this process of the creation of the anecdote – especially within New World discourse. I will continue by turning now to the work of Stephen Greenblatt – which has already played an important role in my discussion – work that (perhaps more than that of any other writer identified with the new historicist project) has been devoted to the anecdote. It is in *Marvelous Possessions: The Wonder of the New World* that Greenblatt's enduring interests in the anecdote and the New World converge.

Greenblatt begins *Marvelous Possessions* with a personal anecdote. He tells of being in Marrakesh and listening "uncomprehendingly" to a storyteller's tale. "In the peculiar reverie that comes with listening to a language one does not understand," Greenblatt writes,

I allowed my mind to wander and discovered that I was telling myself one of the stories from the Arabian Nights, the tale of Sinbad and the roc. If it is true, as Walter Benjamin writes, that every real story "contains, openly or covertly, something useful," then that tale, of diamonds, deep caverns, snakes, raw meat, and birds with huge talons, must have impressed itself upon my prepubescent imagination as containing something extremely useful, something I should never forget.

(*Marvelous Possessions* 1)

While this "utility . . . has remained hidden," Greenblatt is nevertheless "reasonably confident that it will someday be revealed." He remains, he tells us, "possessed by stories and obsessed with their complex uses" (*Marvelous Possessions* 1). The book that these words introduce manifests this possession/obsession – even on a structural level: the book's chapters are built upon anecdotes, which Greenblatt identifies as "*petites histoires*, as distinct from the *grand récit* of totalizing, integrated, progressive history, a history that knows where it is going" (*Marvelous Possessions* 2). Greenblatt's text, then, claims here explicitly that it does not know where it is going and in this regard comes to resemble medieval and Renaissance travel narratives written by voyagers "who thought that they knew where they were going and ended up in a place whose existence they had never imagined": both are "rarely if ever interesting at the level of sustained narrative and teleological design, but gripping at the level of the anecdote" (*Marvelous Possessions* 2). While such texts may well have some "sense of overarching scheme," their strength lies in "the shock of the unfamiliar, the provocation of an intense curiosity, the local excitement of discontinuous wonders." Anecdotes are, finally, "the principal register[s] of the unexpected and hence of the encounter with difference," which are then offered as "*representative* anecdotes . . . significant in terms of a larger progress or pattern that is the proper subject of history perennially deferred in the traveler's relation of further anecdotes" (*Marvelous Possessions* 2–3). For Greenblatt, anecdotes stand

among the principal products of a culture's representational technology, mediators between the undifferentiated succession of local moments and a larger strategy toward which they can only gesture. They are seized in passing from the swirl of experiences and given some shape, a shape whose provisionality still marks them as contingent – otherwise, we would give them the larger, grander name of history – but also makes them available for telling and retelling. (Marvelous Possessions 3)

In terms of what he calls "my own traveler's anecdotes," Greenblatt declares them "bound up with those that I study, shaped by a singular longing for the effect of the locally real and by a larger historicizing intention that is at once evoked and deflected" (*Marvelous Possessions* 3).

In this more or less theoretical situating of the place of the anecdote, Greenblatt stages the production of the anecdote and the production of the cabinet of curiosities discussed earlier in terms of Hakluyt's dedicatory epistle to his *Principal Navigations*: the anecdote is valorized precisely because it is construed as a piece of history and, moreover, because it answers the same demand as the cabinet of curiosities for the "shock of the unfamiliar, the provocation of an intense curiosity, the local excitement of discontinuous wonders." What I have been arguing are the covert ways in which the anecdote betrays a utilitarian – and narrational – valence become here virtually transparent: the anecdote (like stories and like the narrational more generally) becomes significant precisely because it can lend itself to such uses. And yet, Greenblatt's invocation of Benjamin's essay "The Storyteller" and the message it evidently sends him promising an essential usefulness (or "utility") borne by stories perhaps introduces into Greenblatt's discussion (if not his "theory") more than he intends. Benjamin indeed celebrates the story, but for him this celebration is largely melancholic as he is convinced that "the art of storytelling is coming to an end" (Benjamin 83). The end of storytelling results from a global failing and loss of "our ability to exchange experiences" – as if, Benjamin suggests, we have lost "the securest among our possessions" (Benjamin 83). One of the reasons for this – and, therefore, one of the things that the end of storytelling itself tells – is that "experience has fallen in value" (Benjamin 83–84).[31] With the falling off of the "communicability of experience" comes the related phenomenon of the insufficiency or the belatedness (Benjamin calls it an "old-fashioned ring") of offering "counsel" – the "usefulness" referred to here theorized as the "nature of every real story . . . [that it] contains, openly or covertly, something useful . . . a moral . . . some practical advice . . . a proverb or maxim" (Benjamin 86).[32]

For Benjamin, the earliest "symptom of a process whose end is the decline of storytelling" is the emergence and "rise of the novel at the beginning of modern times," whose fundamental distinction from the story – and it is this that contributes, ultimately, to the decline of storytelling – is "its essential dependence on the book." This is an issue of critical importance: the storyteller's art is oral, while that of the novelist "neither comes from oral tradition nor goes into it," with the result being the novel's profound inability to communicate experience – a phenomenon that arises from the novelist's absolute isolation: "The birthplace of the novel is the solitary individual, who is no longer able to express himself by giving examples of his most important concerns, is himself uncounseled, and cannot counsel others. To write a novel means to carry the incommensurable to extremes in the representation of human life" (Benjamin 87). But the inexorable rise of the novel, which for Benjamin takes place only very gradually over many centuries, is not the only – nor perhaps the most disheartening – transformation in the form of communication that has contributed to the loss of storytelling.[33] This new transformation – linked with the history of the rise to power of the middle class "in fully developed capitalism" – only now begins to exert its influence and "confronts storytelling as no less a stranger than did the novel, but in a more menacing way . . . This new form of communication is information" (Benjamin 88). Information has become an overwhelming form of communication, a form that both claims a real-world truthfulness and a self-evidential status: "Information . . . lays claim to prompt verifiability. The prime requirement is that it appear 'understandable in itself.'" This understandability is, Benjamin says, the mode and the goal of information, with the result that "no event any longer comes to us without already being shot through with explanation" (Benjamin 89).

Benjamin's discussion of the loss of storytelling, the rise of both the novel and, more damningly, information, strikes me as an uncannily apt characterization of what I have been describing as the "story of the anecdote." If the anecdote is made to function in new historicism – or in Greenblatt's text in particular – as a form of the story or of storytelling, then by virtue of its very nature as a *textual* effect it violates Benjamin's definition of storytelling which is used (at least in this instance) as its theoretical defense. Just as the novel violates the oral nature of the story, so the written anecdote violates the essentially oral nature of the story it is meant to figure. To reproduce a bit of what one implicitly or explicitly claims is history as a figure for that history – or as Greenblatt has it, for the "larger historicizing intention that is at once evoked and deflected" – is to violate the very nature of the story, is to produce as text that which by definition is non-textual. At the same time, this gesture (for perhaps that is what the use of the anecdote in new historicism is) runs the further risk of so completely transforming the "story-ness" of the anecdote as to reinvent it in the guise of what for Benjamin is its nemesis: information. Like information for Benjamin, the anecdote in new historicism both claims verifiability (it is always at hand, always *locatable* within the archive) and is offered as "understandable in itself." The consequence of this new informationalism – like the consequence for storytelling – is that nothing we encounter (in the new historicist world) is saved from "already being shot through with explanation." We saw another manifestation of this will to absolute explanation in our collective unwillingness or inability to accept something like a textual error in traditional textual scholarship, as discussed in chapter 2. In the face of our critical writing, nothing stands as inexplicable. But the value of the anecdote – like the value of information – is fleeting, for it "does not survive the moment in which it was new. It lives only at that moment; it has to surrender to it completely and explain itself to it without losing any time. A story is different. It does not expend itself. It preserves and concentrates its strength and is capable of releasing it even after a long time" (Benjamin 90).

As deployed in new historicism, the anecdote is made to renounce its relation to the story and to project in its place a new embodiment of the narrational: information novelized. In this regard, then, one could say that Greenblatt's use of the anecdote – and, for that matter, Todorov's as well (though his term is "exemplary history") – work quite contrary to the ways in which they are intended. For in neither case can the anecdote be said to

offer history itself, nor a space within which history can be made to happen
or the other made to speak – unless at the considerable theoretical risk of
deflating (and not "deflecting") the anecdote into the merely informational.
Grounded in the conviction that the anecdote is no less implicated in the
liabilities of the *grand récit* against which Greenblatt hopes to define it, and
the further conviction that the anecdote – by virtue of its narrational nature
– carries with it its own implicit and teleological philosophy of history that
serves to link rather than to distinguish it from the progressive and essentially Hegelian historicisms it seeks to revise, the newness of new historicism or the success of either of these heterological criticisms appears to me
very much in doubt. Perhaps another way of saying this is to suggest that
neither Todorov nor Greenblatt is, strictly speaking, writing *criticism* any
longer, but instead is engaged in the production of novels. If they were not
these novelist–historians, as opposed to storyteller–chroniclers (keeping in
mind Benjamin's distinction between the chronicler who is relieved from the
obligation of explanation and therein free to offer only interpretation, and
the historian who is compelled at every turn to produce explanation) then
both would be "content . . . with displaying [the "happenings" of history]
as models of the course of the world" (Benjamin 96).

The final point I would like to make concerning Greenblatt's discussion
and use of the anecdote in his study of early modern Europeans and the
New World has to do with his suggestion, quoted above, that serves to link
his study with early travel writings in the model of homology: both are
structured anecdotally, which is supposed to mean, among other things,
that neither has a true sense of where it is *really* going. This suggestion is
a romantic one – and, perhaps, like so much in Greenblatt's work, an
appealing and seductive one – but its effect serves to occlude rather than
to illuminate the theoretical work to which it is dedicated. While the idea
perhaps rings true that Columbus, for example, did not really have an idea
where he was truly going (though of course he very famously had quite a
specific idea of where it turns out he never went), this was certainly not the
case for the *texts* Columbus produced. To claim that Columbus's texts
essentially wander (like Columbus is imagined to have wandered into the
New World) or that travel writings wander, is to mistake a textual embodiment of experience – or what Benjamin would call the *story* – for the experience itself. This is to confound travel and writing; like maps and the
worlds they figure, travel and writing indeed exist in a relation of extreme
proximity, but they are not the same thing. Unlike travel (or even wandering) the text is constructed *after the fact* – not from the point of view of
a given present tense from which a turn, say, to the north or to the south
may seem equally valid or likely, but rather from the point of view of

remembrance which serves to construct the notion of the "rightness" or "wrongness" of any northward or southward turn one may have taken. Benjamin makes a similar point in terms of the time-structure of the novel, and the reader's interests in it:

"A man who dies at the age of thirty-five," said Moritz Heimann once, "is at every point of his life a man who dies at the age of thirty-five." Nothing is more dubious than this sentence – but for the sole reason the tense is wrong. A man . . . who died at thirty-five will appear to *remembrance* at every point in his life as a man who dies at the age of thirty-five. In other words, the statement that makes no sense for real life becomes indisputable for remembered life. The nature of the character in a novel cannot be presented any better than is done in this statement, which says that the "meaning" of his life is revealed only in his death. But the reader of a novel actually does look for human beings from whom he derives the "meaning of life." Therefore he must, no matter what, know in advance that he will share their experience of death . . . How do the characters make him understand that death is already waiting for them – a very definite death and at a very definite place? That is the question which feeds the reader's consuming interest in the events of the novel . . . What draws the reader to the novel is the hope of warming his shivering life with a death he reads about. (Benjamin 100–1)

In order for Greenblatt's suggestion that his text does not know – there in the Introduction – where it is going, to be true, his book literally would have to be something like a perambulation, wandering, something like a story: a striking out from shore, as it were, with nothing but the storyteller's art to propel it forward more or less blindly into the night.[34] But we know that his text – even there in the Introduction when it claims explicitly that it does not know – indeed knows precisely where it is going. Or, more correctly, *where it has been.* For the text – unlike the wandering travel or voyage it strives so much to be like but can never finally actually become – has been completed already. The suggestion offered as if beforehand but literally as an afterthought (for Introductions to texts, like anecdotes and like narrative, are always belated) that the book does not know where it is going stands as a sort of nostalgic fantasy for what may well be in the end the already lost world of stories and storytelling:

When I was a child, my favorite books were *The Arabian Nights* and Richard Halliburton's *Book of Marvels*. The appeal of the former . . . lay in the primal power of storytelling . . . The appeal of Halliburton's *Book of Marvels* is less easy to explain . . . I suppose that my suburban soul, constricted by the conventionality of the Eisenhower 1950s, eagerly embraced the relief that Halliburton offered, the sense that the real world was full of wonder . . . At a certain point I passed from the naïve to what Schiller calls the sentimental – that is, I stopped reading books of marvels and began reading ethnographies and novels. (*Marvelous Possessions* 1–2)

In the face of this loss of storytelling Greenblatt strives for its resurrection, but such struggling only serves to mark the passing of the story as it lies discarded for the more analytical and explanational politics of the critic's info-novel.

If Todorov and Greenblatt write info-novels in response to New World discourses, it is because they stand committed – both in political and ethical terms – to exposing the costs of such discourses: in Todorov the death of the Mayan woman thrown to the dogs, in Greenblatt the invasive effects of European representational strategies on New World inhabitants and culture, and for both the breakdown of the encounter with the other into apocalyptic conquest and genocide. Calling their work "info-novels" is not to be construed as a condemnation, nor (strictly as a matter of information) a criticism. It is, rather, a call to a more explicit theorization of what we mean when we talk about history, and what we mean when we talk about the other in history. At the same time, my comments should perhaps stand as an appeal for less explanation. If info-novels are characterized (and to an extent disabled) by the novelist's desire to explain "the meaning of life" – as opposed to the storyteller's satisfaction with the articulation of "the moral of the story" – then let these remarks register a certain resistance to the notion of this "meaning" supposedly embedded in life. To be a novelist (and, therefore, to be a certain kind of critic) is to have granted a primary faith in the presupposition of meaning. But as I have tried to suggest throughout this chapter (and indeed throughout this book), such a notion is itself the very hallmark of a narrational projection. I will revise Nietzsche one last time: it is always necessary that there be a narrative in order that there should be meaning. In other words, the faith in the presupposition of meaning is under-written – indeed, it is *produced* – by the *a priori* projection of a narrative that is by definition totalizing and teleological. This is the domain of the novelist, and not the storyteller. When we consider this in the context of the New World, or in the context of heterological discourse, what emerges is a practice of writing that remains insufficiently responsible to the other, a practice of writing that has not learned its own valuable lessons against the politics of appropriation and the requirement of a responsibility to the "heterogeneity of a *pre-*." To take up an anecdote or a fragment of exemplary history from the New World and place it informationally within one's own discourse dedicated to novelistic exhaustive explanation – even if to condemn such colonialist work on the part of a Columbus, a Cortés, or a Frobisher – is still to claim otherness as one's own, is still to claim *possession*, and as such stands as another manifestation of the will to sameness.

5   Browne's skull

My gorge rises at it.   (*Hamlet*)

For Sir Thomas Browne, America (and the entire New World, more generally) stands as the very mark of otherness – distant, ancient, immensely
wealthy (America figures in the opening of *Hydriotaphia*, for example, as a
great treasure and great "*Antiquity*" that "lay buried for a thousand
years)."[1] In one of his most curious and charming pieces, "A Prophecy
Concerning the Future State of Several Nations," Browne predicts a
wealthy and illustrious future for America:

The prophecy

When New England shall trouble New Spain.
When Jamaica shall be Lady of the Isles and the Main.
When Spain shall be in America hid,
And Mexico shall prove a Madrid.
. . .
When America shall cease to send out its Treasure,
But employ it at home in American Pleasure.
When the new World shall the old invade,
Nor count them their Lords but their fellows in Trade.
. . .
Then think strange things are come to light,
Whereof but few [eyes] have had a foresight.   (*Works* vol. III. 103–4)

In his explanatory commentary on his own verses, "The Exposition of
the Prophecy," Browne speaks of that moment when America will retain its
own treasure and "rather employ it to their own advantages, in great
Exploits and Undertakings, magnificent Structures, Wars or Expeditions of
their own," and predicts that even Europe itself may one day be the target
of American strength, pride and aggression:

That is, When America shall be so well peopled, civilized and divided into
Kingdoms, they are like to have so little regard of their Originals, as to acknowledge
no subjection unto them: they may also have a distinct commerce between themselves, or but independently with those of Europe, and may hostilely and pyratically
assault them. (*Works* vol. III. 107)

Browne's vision of the future of America as the equal and rival of the "Old World" can be considered, perhaps, prophetic. But at the same time it bespeaks the very will to sameness discussed in the preceding chapter; it constitutes, anachronistically, something approximating the Old World's last and final possession of the New World. The New World reappears, though this time not as the fantastic other but rather as another version (the ghost?) of the Old. Browne's "prophecy" works – surprisingly – toward the production of the New World as an *artifact* of his Europe. This process of what I will call *artifaction* is central to Browne's literary and scientific career and forms the central focus of this chapter in which I trace the narrational discourse of artifaction both in Browne's own writings and in two later versions (one from the nineteenth century, another from the early years of the twentieth) of the pseudo-science of phrenology. Across these various practices one can detect a movement along a narrational trajectory from a theory of the relation between the body – even, and *especially*, the dead body – and identity, to the emergence of such scientisms as "race" and "racial craniology."

I

In 1982, Polish-born and naturalized British subject Andre Tchiakowsky, classical musician (1955 winner of the prestigious Chopin Prize, Warsaw), and Shakespearean theater *aficionado*, died of intestinal cancer. Among its bequests, Tchiakowsky's will stated that his skull was to be removed, cleaned, and donated to the Royal Shakespeare Company with the express intention of serving (acting?) as Yorick's skull in an RSC production of *Hamlet*. The terms of this bequest were honored, as attested both by Tchiakowsky's undertakers and by the RSC. The story of Tchiakowsky's bequest was published by the United Press International, along with a brief discussion of his life-long secret desire to be an actor, making Tchiakowsky's first "professional" histrionic gesture a true (if minor) international media event.[2]

I would like to focus on a number of issues that inform this "Shakespearean" narrative of national identity, theatricality, and death. In particular, I am interested in the status of the dead body and identity as they are figured in skulls – Tchiakowsky's "real" skull and Yorick's "fictional" one – and the extent to which the skull, by virtue of surviving death, continues to embody (or figure) the identity of its "owner." Tchiakowsky's desire to play Yorick, in other words, may have been an expression of another desire: life after death. In playing Yorick, Tchiakowsky's skull will achieve such an immortality – but only to the degree to which the skull continues to embody Tchiakowsky. In this scenario (fantasy), the skull always figures its "owner" by virtue of staging his or her presence. In so doing the skull seems to negate the passage of time; the skull and the identity believed immanent in it inhabit something like a perpetual present tense. As such, the skull simultaneously comes to occupy an ironic position as it attempts to invest a corporeal object with a version of permanence that is by conventional definition unavailable to corporeal objects: the skull figures life. We are more accustomed to seeing the skull invoked as a sign of death, as *memento mori*. Tchiakowsky's dream is a fantastic one, then, founded upon a faith in some version of bodily immortality that aspires to nothing less than a recuperation of vitality, presence, and permanence from within a semiotics of death and absence.

Tchiakowsky's skull – to whatever extent that it *is* his once it has been cleaned and prepared, and while it is "sitting in a cardboard box in Stratford . . . treated with preservatives" (UPI story) – figures both his identity, and the desire to exchange the status of his own skull as real for that of Yorick's as unreal. But what *is* the status of a human skull that functions as a theatrical representation of a real skull? Does it lose some of its own reality? When, tomorrow or next season, an RSC actor holds Yorick's skull, will it in any way signify – even vestigially, as a trace – Andre Tchiakowsky? If it does figure Tchiakowsky (*if* it does) that trace will not only be a material remainder of what *was* Andre Tchiakowsky, but also the narrative reminder of his strange (his Hamlet-like) bequest, preserved in a newspaper account, and now in this discussion.

Tchiakowsky chooses a theater as the site for the posthumous staging of his body and his identity within the persistently real, and yet the theatrical nature of this staging serves to render problematical the very status of the skull-as-real. These concerns, however, are not limited to the skull in the theater, but obtain as well when we consider the skull – Tchiakowsky's, let us say – outside the theater of representation. If we can inquire into the status of the real skull fictionalized in the very moment of its representation, then we can just as easily ask about the status of the un-representing skull, the skull-in-itself. But the skull-in-itself is, finally, no less fictive than the skull-in-representation (Tchiakowsky playing Yorick). The narrative of Tchiakowsky's skull embodies an articulation not of the body itself, but rather of its discursive nature. Indeed, it serves to demonstrate that the body as object never exists immediately, but rather is intelligible only through mediation – through writing, or through certain cultural practices. In a word, through discourse. The body is at one moment pure materiality (as incoherent, perhaps, as Hamlet's "quintessence of dust"), and in the next moment it becomes meaningful only by virtue of its insertion in narratives that are intended to generate its meaning and significance.

In this way, the body (in culture, as in language) is necessarily always bracketed by an implicit pair of quotation marks, even as recent discussions and retheorizations of "race" insist upon explicit quotation marks. Both the "body" and "race" can be said only to exist within discourse, and never objectively in "nature."[3] In the course of this chapter I will consider this bracketing of the body – or, more specifically, the skull – and the ways in which various attempts to understand the skull are enabled only once an over-riding narrative of the production of meaning is deployed. The principal narrative that emerges in the literature I discuss in this chapter is the complex series of acts that, taken together, are dedicated to the production of artifactuality. This process of artifaction, as I will call it, shares a common heritage with the emergence of the scientific method in the early modern period. As we shall see, the human skull becomes the object *par excellence* of the scientific discourse of artifaction called phrenology and its later (and more insidious) manifestation, "racial craniology." In the latter of these, the matter of "race" becomes the explicit focus of phrenology, a cultural practice modeled on science that arose within the same historic moment as the rapid expansion of the British Empire, and in the service of which the study of the human skull becomes the very ground for the justification of a racist colonial agenda. All this is enabled, as I suggested, by the preliminary process of artifaction – the execution of a set of interpretive and theoretical procedures dedicated to the production of narratives of meaning. It is this practice of generating signifying narratives that then constructs a meaning or a set of meanings that is staged in the grave-digger's scene in *Hamlet*:

> GRAVE.: Here's a skull now hath lien you i'th'earth three and twenty years.
> HAMLET: Whose was it?
> GRAVE.: A whoreson mad fellow's it was. Whose do you think it was?
> HAMLET: Nay, I know not.
> GRAVE.: A pestilence on him for a mad rogue! A poured a flagon of Rhenish on my head once. This same skull, sir, was Yorick's skull, the King's jester.
> HAMLET: This?   [Takes the skull.]
> GRAVE.: E'en that.[4]

"Whose was it?" Hamlet asks the grave-digger of the skull cast up in the excavation of what will be Ophelia's grave. The use of his past tense in this question is curious: the skull *is*, but the matter of ownership/possession (and even of Yorick "himself") *was*. In this scene the skull oscillates between the past and the present: it used to be Yorick's, and yet it persists beyond or without Yorick, and as such becomes an apt object for the grave-digger's and Hamlet's very different questions and musings. Yet, in the earth "three and twenty years," the skull has been no one's: it has not been

Yorick's (indeed, it has not even been recognized as a skull). Neither has the skull yet been (re)possessed either by the grave-digger – for whom the skull is less *memento mori* than an occasion for sardonic recollections, and Yorick less a lost loved one and more a "whoreson mad fellow" – or by Hamlet, for whom the skull occasions first a philosophical discussion of the materiality of the body, and then an equally material revulsion: "He hath bore me on his back a thousand times, and now – how abhorred in my imagination it is. My gorge rises at it. Here hung those lips that I have kissed I know not how oft" (5.1.179–83).[5] For the skull does change "ownership": it was first Yorick's, and then became no one's, but then the grave-digger's, and then Hamlet's. (In the more than three hundred years of production, this scene – of Hamlet with "his" skull – has come to stand both as a kind of monument to and as a representation of *Hamlet* itself.) At the same time, the scene of Yorick's skull dramatizes the invention of the scientific method and enacts the production of the artifactual. Before the scene, as the skull lay buried in the earth, it literally had no significance. Strictly speaking, it had no significance even once it was dug out of the earth. The skull only accrues significance (and then not a solitary but rather multiple meanings) once it is created as an artifact, and subsequently interpreted artifactually – such as when the grave-digger identifies the skull as Yorick's, a "whoreson mad fellow" who had once doused him with Rhenish. Hamlet picks up the production of artifactuality when he picks up the skull and narrates a different set of associations and meanings: a former intimate and playmate, complete with lips and a strong back, with his "flashes of merriment," but all serving only to highlight for Hamlet the inanimateness of the skull in hand. But even though the skull remains silent it is nevertheless considered meaningful, even if the content of that meaning is the subject of speculation or debate.

This desire to fend off incoherence through the narrative production of meaning characterizes our traditional – narrational – epistemological claims on material objects. In fact these epistemological claims can themselves become the groundwork for wide-ranging claims to knowledge and certainty in the non-material world, as well. The notion of the author – which has undergone such radical critique (one could say annihilation) in the wake of post-structuralism – was a construct founded upon a particular narrationality having to do with humanism, essentialist individualism, the emergence of capitalism, and the "discovery" sometime in the early modern period of the self imagined as a sovereign and autonomous subject. The celebrated "death of the author" (a phrase cast in the semantics of narrative) really amounts to a rejection of the narrative(s) that served to conceptualize and codify that most modern of figures, the author. The *meaning* of "author" – in other words – is produced narrationally out of the material objects ascribed to a particular individual: plays by Shakespeare, for instance. In a very compelling sense, if Shakespeare is (or was) an author, it is because of a particular, generally stable and fixed collection of material objects, the plays, which as material objects produce the narrative – or competing narratives – of authorship: Shakespeare the hack, Shakespeare the deer-poacher, Shakespeare the venture capitalist, Shakespeare the national genius, and so on. Yet the processes and politics of artifaction are not limited to material objects. Surely the idea "Shakespeare" (even as early as the seventeenth century) is just that, an *idea* – a fragment of the non-material world posited with great certainty by our narrative to exist somewhere. Or, at least, the idea begins this way, but only until it gets caught up in narrative production – that willful creation of Shakespeare as narrative, Shakespeare as "Shakespeare" – not merely a construct, but indeed an *artifact* of a certain set of narratives.

Whatever Shakespeare thought himself to be, he certainly never thought of himself as an "author." He quite famously left nothing "authorial" behind, such as manuscripts, and he had no clear interest in the publication of his work – the very facts for which he is sometimes condemned by certain writers who would prefer Shakespeare to have been involved not only in the production of theater, but in the quite different practice of the production of texts and the production of authorship.

If material objects submitted to narrational production can effectively produce the artifaction of fragments of the non-material world (if thirty-odd plays can engender "Shakespeare") then this newly forged artifact can, in turn, produce a kind of non-material aura for material objects – plays, certainly, but also monuments, tombs, and bones. Hence the famous prohibition inscribed upon Shakespeare's monument in Stratford's Holy Trinity Church designed to preserve an aura of hallowedness:

> GOOD FREND FOR JESUS SAKE FORBEARE
> TO DIGG THE DUST ENCLOASED HEARE:
> BLESTE BE THE MAN THAT SPARES THESE STONES,
> AND CURST BE HE THAT MOVES MY BONES

What this effectively does is produce Shakespeare's bones – actual material objects – as *artifacts* of the non-material "Shakespeare," just as Tchiakowsky had imagined his skull-as-Yorick would produce something like immortality for him.

But narratives of meaning, perhaps like historical periods or epistemes, are never enduring but rather are constantly in the process of establishing themselves only to be challenged, revised, even changed altogether. The narrative of "Shakespeare" sketched here endures largely unchallenged until mid-way through the nineteenth century when we begin to see a new attention focused on Shakespeare, on "Shakespeare," and, even, on Shakespeare's bones. Complete with a flood of rival-author theories and stories of conspiracies, ciphers, secret societies and corporate authorship, the latter half of the nineteenth century witnessed a virtual campaign of proposals for the disinterment of Shakespeare's remains. The earliest principal advocate was ironically not a devoted Shakespearean, but rather Delia Bacon (founder of the so-called Baconists), who argued that a corporation of Elizabethan courtiers headed by Sir Francis Bacon was the true author of the works attributed to Shakespeare. Delia Bacon is also famous for her vigil in the shadows of the Holy Trinity Church in Stratford, awaiting the proper moment to break open Shakespeare's grave, a story she writes of in a letter to Nathaniel Hawthorne.[6]

Throughout her work on Shakespeare, Bacon insists that her methodology is entirely scientific, and that the results she presents should not be understood as hypotheses, but rather as matters of scientific fact. This arises in part from Bacon's belief that she was living in a scientific age, an age in which traditional beliefs and conventional methods would necessarily give way to scientific inquiry and the absolute clarity afforded by its methods. In "William Shakespeare and his Plays: An Inquiry Concerning Them," published in *Putnam's Monthly Magazine* in 1856, Bacon argues that hers is the age that will welcome the obvious objection to the very idea of Shakespeare as the actual author of the plays: "the age which has found, and labeled, and sent to the museum, the skull in which the pyramid of Cheops was designed . . . the age in which we have abjured our faith in Romulus and Remus, – is surely one in which we may be permitted to ask this question."[7]

Bacon attributes the longevity of the Shakespearean mistake to the non-scientific character of his age: "at the time when these works were issued, all those characteristic organizations of the modern ages, for the diffusion of intellectual and moral influences, which now everywhere cross and recross with electric fibre the hitherto impassable social barriers, were as yet unimagined" (Bacon 130). But this is a new age, the age of science and technology in which we are able to see with greater accuracy and power: "To-day, there is no scholastic seclusion so profound that the allied voice and action of this mighty living age may not perpetually penetrate it. To-day, the work-shop has become *clairvoyant*" (Bacon 130).[8]

Such "science," however, is not limited to Bacon's own moment or her own theory, but originally arose within the plays themselves, and from the hand of the unnamed philosopher whom she calls the "*one*" (Bacon 155) who first brought the scientific imagination to bear on the works of nature and the works of culture, "laying bare, in its cold, clear, pure depths, in all their unpolite, undraped scientific reality, the actualities which society, as it is, can only veil, and the evils which society, as it is, can only hide and palliate" (Bacon 142). Bacon's call, then, is a call to continue the scientific work begun in the plays, the first step of which is the proper reading (or decoding) of the plays themselves.

Bacon's scientific philosophy seems to have generated a defensive response on the part of Shakespeareans, and we see (particularly in the 1870s through the 1890s) a reactive rallying cry from them for the disinterment of Shakespeare's remains precisely because they believe him to be none other than the great English writer whose name and place in history Delia Bacon and other anti-Stratfordians of various convictions had sought so desperately to erase. In the 1883 book, *Shakespeare's Bones: The Proposal to Disinter Them*, C.M. Ingleby offers an argument fully illustrative of the Stratfordian argument to disinter. Unlike the removal to Pennsylvania of the remains of William Penn, which "had already a more suitable resting-place in his native land," there are certain cases in which it is "justifiable to exhume a body recently buried . . . in order to find such evidences as time may not have wholly destroyed, of his personal appearance, including the size and shape of his head, and the special characteristics of his living face."[9] Ingleby dismisses any possible familial objections to such acts, and as for the rights of the subject "if he can be said to have any," they pose not a bar, but rather serve as a prompting: "we may surely reckon among them [the deceased's rights] the right of not being supposed to possess such objectionable personal defects as may have been imputed to him by the malice of critics or by the incapacity of sculptor or painter, and which his remains may be sufficiently unchanged to rebut" (Ingleby 3). Ingleby's ostensible subject is those "objectionable personal defects" he believes he sees in artistic representations of Shakespeare, particularly the Gheerart Janssen bust that forms part of Shakespeare's tomb: "I think it self-evident that there is some little derangement of natural proportions in those features" (Ingleby 34). In this regard, Ingleby's condemnation of the bust is akin to such assaults by anti-Stratfordians, who found the man figured in the bust a comically improbable candidate for the authorship of the plays. But the similarity here is deceptive, for Ingleby objects to the *accuracy* of the sculpture, while Bacon and the anti-Stratfordians object to its *argument*. For Ingleby the bust is of the correct man, it is just not a very fair likeness, while for Bacon and her fellow skeptics, it is the man represented more or less accurately in the bust that is not a fair representation of the national genius figured in the plays.

The true object, however, of Ingleby's discomfort over the "personal defects" potentially encoded in representations of Shakespeare is not, finally, an aesthetic one, but rather one prompted by the sort of faith in the myth of national genius that underwrites the place of Shakespeare in the

popular imagination, and to which Ingleby and to a large degree all pro-
ponents of disinterment subscribe. What is at stake in Shakespeare's
remains – particularly his skull – is not the test of accuracy they would presumably afford viewers of sculpture and portraits of Shakespeare, but
rather the claim to the particular character of national genius Shakespeare
was said to embody. Ingleby's interest in Shakespeare's remains marks his
implicit faith in the notion that bodies are (in some sense) texts in which we
may read character. In this regard Ingleby does indeed come to resemble
the phrenologists whose philosophy his rhetoric so clearly echoes. But
Ingleby is not, strictly speaking, a phrenologist – at least not in the original
sense of the term. He is, rather, a believer in another form of quasi-science
that believes the body signifies not only inwardly – that the skull, for
example, can tell us about the individual – but also outwardly – that the
skull can tell us about "race." It is this latter form that most interests both
Ingleby and Bacon. For Bacon, the works attributed to Shakespeare constitute "products of the national life," works that themselves "have given
our English life and language their imperishable claim in the earth, that
have made the name in which they come to us a word by itself in human
speech" (Bacon 101).

Like Tchiakowsky, Bacon's sense of national identity and feeling is,
strictly speaking, adoptive. Bacon was American and her fondness for
England and the affinity she feels with English culture is more a function
of sentiment than of fact. She writes in her October 1856 letter to
Hawthorne (the same one in which she tells of her vigil at Shakespeare's
tomb in search of the documents, which she calls "memorials," she imagines it to hold) of her relation to England: "I am a great deal more at home
here than I am in America – I tell all the people here, that I see, that they
need not call me 'a foreigner.' My fathers helped conquer this country, and
I have as good a right here as they have."

Bacon argues that this name – Shakespeare – is simply inaccurate, that it
serves to cover the true identity – "this master spirit of our race" (Bacon
111) – of the author (or, sometimes, authors) of the plays. Part of Bacon's
strategy is to discredit the historic Shakespeare for his allegedly obvious
inadequacy as a candidate for the authorship of the plays, "the very wine
of all our life . . . and gold of all the ages" (Bacon 112). Shakespeare (the
"Stratford poacher" [Bacon 102], "this Jack Cade" [Bacon 114], "Traitor
and miscreant!" [Bacon 117]) lacked not only the necessary training and
education to write the plays, he was also *by nature* incapable of such splendor. Neither properly educated not literally a scholar, Shakespeare was
merely one of "that dirty, doggish group of players" represented in *Hamlet*
(Bacon 137). Hamlet himself is construed as wholly disdainful of them,
with the "very tone of his courtesy to them, with its princely condescension,

with its arduous familiarity, only serving to make the great, impassable social gulf between them the more evident" (Bacon 137). Bacon's objective here may seem entirely class-motivated, and to an extent it is, but the over-riding prejudice against this Shakespeare is one, finally, of heritage, genealogy – in a word, of breeding:

With such an origin as this, how was it possible to note, not in this play only, but in all the Shakespeare drama, what otherwise we could not have failed to observe, the tone of the highest Elizabethan breeding, the very loftiest tone of that peculiar courtly culture, which was then, and but *just* then, attaining its height . . . a culture which required not the best acquisitions of the university merely, but acquaintance with life, practical knowledge of affairs, foreign travel and accomplishments, and, above all, the last refinements of the highest Parisian breeding. (Bacon 138)

Bacon's Norman prejudices are revealed here and Shakespeare's inadequacy is enlarged from class and breeding to, finally, something like "race."[10] Bacon's quest is accordingly revealed as both an argument concerning the authorship of a particular set of plays and as the desire for racial refinement and exultation: "and to this hour his bones are canonized, to this hour his tomb is a shrine, where the genius of the cool, sagacious, clear-thoughted Northern Isle is worshipped, under the form of a mad, unconscious, intellectual possession – a dotard inspiration, incapable of its own designs, wanting in the essential attribute of all mental power – self-cognition" (Bacon 119–20). This Shakespeare emerges as painfully inadequate to his reputation – in spite of the name, in spite of the tomb and its monument, in spite of "the laboring conceptions of the artists whose business it is to present his apotheosis to us," an effort, Bacon declares, that is inevitably and *by nature* doomed to ludicrous failure:

Enlarge the vacant platitudes of that forehead as you will; pile up the artificial brains in the frontispiece to any height which the credulity of an awe-struck public will hesitate to pronounce idiotic . . . how could the old player and showman be made to sit the bird of Jove, so comfortably as he does, on his way to the waiting Olympus?
(Bacon 124)

It is no wonder that Bacon would like to open Shakespeare's grave – in part (as she argues) to discover manuscripts she believes to be hidden there, but also because her quasi-phrenological predisposition inclines her to believe that the remains themselves *are* texts that would speak the "scientific" truth of her theory of authorship and her theory of "race."

Like Ingleby's "Shakespeareanism," Bacon's science is founded in part upon her faith in the body as a legible signifier of some larger meaning that is allegedly manifest in the world (the plays attributed to Shakespeare are transcendent masterpieces, their author's genius stands for English national genius clearly visible in England's global colonial supremacy) but which is perhaps only verifiably and scientifically accessible through the body (hence Bacon's intense and conflicted desire to open Shakespeare's tomb). But the relation posited here between signifier and signified – between body and national genius and "race" – is not of course a natural and inevitable one. Indeed, it is not quite a viable one. Such theories as Ingleby's and Bacon's say that they observe natural fact – the skull, say – and this natural object speaks a certain truth – national genius, for example. And yet, what in fact occurs is quite the reverse: though they claim to find truth in the natural object – the bodily remains – that "truth" is already posited within that object *through the process of artifaction*. The materials for such a science have always to be created through artifaction that occurs within a historical narrative. Put another way, the skull does not give us immediate access to the person or to "race" precisely because the skull itself makes sense only within a narrative of the past that already defines person and "race."

The terms deployed and the issues at stake in my characterization of Ingleby and Bacon do not pass with the end of the nineteenth century but persist (some would perhaps say interminably) into the twentieth century. There are two notable instances of the extension of Ingleby's or Bacon's concerns into the realm of racial eugenics that begin with the scientific–phrenological analysis of the skull of a seventeenth-century English writer presumed to represent an example of the national genius conventionally defined by Shakespeare: Sir Thomas Browne. Miriam Tildesley and Sir Arthur Keith each attempt to produce narratives of meaning for the skull of Sir Thomas Browne. For Tildesley, this project serves, in the final analysis, as the occasion for a discussion of "racial craniology," and her study as an attempt to secure a place for Browne's skull-form within the two categories (which she takes to be related) of "normal" and "English." Keith's project, on the other hand, is a self-conscious attempt to redeem phrenology as a science, and as such his discourse on Browne's skull serves as a test case of the limits of phrenological knowledge and emergent hormone theory. Both writers, I will argue, are deliberate in their practices of artifaction. Indeed, their work is wholly enabled by artifaction which in turn clears the way for the narrative production of meaning.

In their particular ways both Tildesley and Keith represent contributions to what was by the 1920s in which they wrote the more or less dead field of *classical* phrenology. But both bring to this field a new urgency. In part, this urgency arises from a renewed interest in the accurate description of skull types made possible by the emergent field of statistical medical analysis. At the same time, this interest is fueled by other contributing factors, including the rise of psychoanalytic theory which in its own classical formulation argued for a semiotic relation between body and mind (psyche) and which eagerly anticipated that future, though inevitable, moment when science would finally reduce all psychological characteristics to chemical and physiological truths about the brain.[11] The reinvention of phrenology as a discourse on "race" that the works of Tildesley and Keith represent and to which they contribute can also be seen as a reaction to the early twentieth-century rise of European fascism – an arch form of nationalism explicitly (and fanatically) linked to presuppositions concerning "race" and ethnicity. To these contributing factors I would also add a third: the emergence of mature capitalism as a world power – together with its notions of the rights of ownership, subjectivity, and "race." Together these factors serve to contribute to a new and powerful combination of science and imperialism that is deployed globally from particular centers of social (and military) power. In the discussions of Tildesley and Keith that follow (as in earlier discussions of Benjamin's reaction to the emergence of mass and impersonal destruction in World War I, or in Dover Wilson's reaction to the Bolshevik revolution) in which I will pay very close and careful attention to the philosophical, intellectual, and textual strategies they employ, only our immediate focus is on phrenological science, but by this science I do mean to implicate a much wider range of social and critical practices. In the works of Tildesley and Keith – and Sir Thomas Browne, in a discussion of what he calls "intuitive Physiognomical knowledge" to be taken up in the chapter's final section – we can glimpse the dynamics of the varied and often competing processes of artifaction in the service of the narrative production of meaning.

II

Physiognomy outlives our selves, and ends not in our graves.

(Thomas Browne, *Hydriotaphia*)

In August 1840 in St. Peter Mancroft, Norwich, the vault containing the remains of Sir Thomas Browne was broken open while workers (grave-diggers) were preparing an adjacent burial vault for the interment of the body of Mrs. Bowman, deceased wife of the then incumbent, Reverend John Bowman. The events immediately following this incident are somewhat shrouded in uncertainty, though this much is clear: some time during the four days in which the coffin was exposed and the remains accessible, Browne's skull was stolen from the tomb, along with a few evidential locks of hair and the identifying coffin plate bearing a Latin inscription. The skull's whereabouts remained a mystery for the next five years until it reappeared in 1845 and was presented to the Norwich Hospital Museum. Browne's skull remained in the possession of the museum until 1922, when, after years of complaints from St. Peter Mancroft officials and the popular press, as well as a good deal of quoting from Browne's own eloquent protestations – chiefly from *Hydriotaphia* – against the abhorrent abuses that might befall one's bones, the skull was reinterred in a public ceremony in the chancel at St. Peter Mancroft.

During the years of its second appearance (1840–1922) Browne's skull was subjected at least twice to more or less careful, and more or less "scientific" study: a plaster cast of the skull was made in 1840; and in 1922 a series of castings of the skull was made, as well as several brain-casts. There were also multiple photographs of the skull. In 1923, a year after the skull had been reinterred, both the 1840 and the 1922 casts were themselves subjected to an extensive "craniological" study by Miriam Tildesley, first published in *Biometrika: A Journal for the Statistical Study of Biological Problems*, then reprinted as a monograph in 1923.[12]

Tildesley's study is prefaced with an "Introductory Note" by Sir Arthur Keith, Conservator of the Museum, Royal College of Surgeons, who would later go on to write his own scientific (i.e., phrenological) study of Browne's skull. Keith records having been asked by the Norfolk and Norwich Hospital to make "an exact and permanent record of [the skull's] form and features" (Tildesley 1). Both the request made of Keith and his own methodological approach to it attest to the apparent scientific nature of his inquiry. Keith's first task was to "reproduce" the skull. And yet, no sooner is the skull "reproduced" (that is, casts are made of its interior and exterior as a way of affording Keith a set of working models) than the scientific epistemological model itself breaks down – or rather, gives way to another sort of inquiry: "After successful plaster casts had been made of the outward form of the skull and of its brain cavity . . . I set out to make an anatomical examination and soon realized that this was the least part of my task. Every detail in the history of the skull had to be reinvestigated to make certain of its authenticity" (Tildesley 1). Keith's scientific inquiry gives way immediately to an *historiographical* one. Or, more precisely, the scientific inquiry must await the results of historical inquiry, and, in fact, can be said to depend utterly upon the historical inquiry. In the face of the historical challenge, Keith's task seems daunting, indeed. How does one establish the "authenticity" of a skull? And what does such a task represent? The skull in question was undoubtedly real and actual human remains, though this was not the case for Tildesley, whose object of inquiry was not a skull, but various plastic and photographic representations of presumably the same skull. But whose? The question, then, of authenticity is actually a question of ownership – or rather, possession: who used to own or possess this skull? But does one really ever *own* a part of one's body on the model of a property claim?

The very idea of a property claim to one's body is, in fact, an historically specific response to the virtually ubiquitous question of the nature of the mind–body relation: "Our bodies are with us," notes Peter Brooks, "though we have always had trouble saying exactly how."[13] Conventionally for Christian thinkers, one is thought *to inhabit* the fallen and corrupt body, thereby reifying the notion of a fundamental division between body and mind (or soul). But this theory begins to give way in the early modern period with the emergence of what will come to be called capitalism. Within the capitalist ideology we begin to see a newly configured relation between the mind and the body predicated upon proprietary rights in a world in which one does not simply reside in a body but altogether *owns* it. We see this in the writings of Descartes as he constructs this new relation of mind/soul to body: "It was also not without reason that I believed that this body, which by a certain particular privilege I called mine, belonged to me more properly and strictly than any other."[14]

If this question of the ownership of the body raises complications, what of the personal ownership of what *used to be* a part of one's body? The dead Thomas Browne can make no claim on what used to be his skull. In fact, the skull exists in relation to Browne only attributively, in language and in history. Or, to put it another way, the belief that the skull is/was Browne's is purely historical. As this dilemma makes clear, the status of the skull is always historiographical and only secondarily – belatedly – scientific. And if this status is ever scientific, it is so only after a certain historiographical discourse has deemed the skull sufficiently available to scientific inquiry. Only the historical renders the scientific possible.

Faced with the obvious difficulties of this task, Keith resolves this crisis of authentication by virtue of a systematic and scientific appeal to documentary and – more importantly – pictorial representations of Thomas Browne: "It became necessary to collect and collate all facts relating to portraits and representations of the great Norwich Physician. Registers, libraries and private collections had to be searched for data bearing on his personality and on his lineage" (Tildesley 1).

Keith's task of "authenticating" the skull thus depends upon the gathering of biographical data that would be used to screen the pictorial images for the "correct" one, which would then be used, in turn, to read the skull itself. While this would seem to place the *scientific* nature of Keith's (and Tildesley's) project in some jeopardy, Keith insists on its scientific integrity and its explicitly scientific methodology: the empiricist and statistical study of the skull in order to determine its relation to the brain, the mind, and, finally, the character of Sir Thomas Browne. Tildesley's project (which she, as "research worker," took over from Keith once he had fallen ill – a series of events that Keith believes readers of Tildesley will come to consider "a blessing in disguise" [Tildesley 2]) itself stands as a monument to the scientific method, and represents, Keith claims, "the best kind of scholarship – one which illustrates the right application of laboratory methods to historical enquiry and to anatomical pursuits" (Tildesley 2).

Keith concludes his brief preface by assuring the reader that although Browne's skull is no longer available (since reinterment in 1922), we will always have Tildesley's book, a "faithful record of what the outward appearances of the Norwich physician really were" (Tildesley 2). Browne's skull stands as a material representation of the man – in fact, as the most complete and true representation – and as such becomes in Tildesley's book the truth against which all other representations are judged. With the skull we are at another representational remove. But this twice-removed representation is, paradoxically, monumentalized in Keith's formulation in which Tildesley's text stands as Browne's monument and, moreover, stands in immediately for Browne's skull and, mediately, for Browne "himself."

Tildesley begins her book by identifying the two principal issues that serve to define and organize her inquiry: (1) the study of Browne's skull will further knowledge in the field of racial craniology (the attempts "to measure the degree to which various racial characters in the mental and physical domains tend to be associated together"); and (2) her book will help demonstrate the degree to which cranial study can offer particularized knowledge about a given individual – "To what extent do various mental and physical characters tend to be associated together *in the individual*? Can the body really tell us anything about the mind of a man, and if so, how much?" (Tildesley 3). Tildesley recognizes that while the latter was the very question that "the palmist, the physiognomist, and the phrenologist" vainly (and perhaps foolishly) sought to answer, there is no substantial reason why we ought to abandon our efforts to explore scientifically the mind/body relation, informed, as they are, by *new* technological and scientific advances. Tildesley says of the phrenologist, with whom, despite her ultimate dismissal of his efforts, she has the most in common, "His methods were empirical, and have proved misleading. But was his basic idea that it was possible to establish some logical connection between the inward and the outward entirely at fault?" (Tildesley 4). In order to answer this question, Tildesley declares it necessary to determine the degree of association between:

(1) the mental faculties and the proportions of the various parts of the brain; and then on the degree of association, doubtless getting weaker at each remove, between
(2) the mental faculties, and the modelling of the brain surface,
(3)   "   "   and the contours of the cranial cavity,
(4)   "   "   and the outer surface of the skull, and lastly,
(5) the mental faculties, and the living head.

(Tildesley 4)

Here Tildesley marks out the *scientific* nature of her inquiry, which she is again at pains to distinguish from more traditional phrenological study, and suggests that the ultimate goal is the correlation of the mental faculties with "the living head." And yet, though perhaps least promising of results, it is this notion of "the living head" as the true grounding of Tildesley's craniology that serves as her epistemological objective. Tildesley suggests that her craniological study of Browne will be all the easier, and therefore something of a test case, because both Browne's skull and Browne's "self" are readily available to Tildesley's science:

The pairs of characteristics which it is most desirable to study together are precisely those concerning which the data are fewest. To this branch of science, therefore, our records of Sir Thomas Browne make an especially valuable and welcome contribution, since here we know the cranial cavity from our casts, and the mind of the man from his books. (Tildesley 4)

Tildesley's entire project as defined here depends upon the now much-discredited notion that texts figure or embody their authors. As discussed in chapter 2, the lessons of post-structural theory and Foucauldian criticism (among other contributing factors) have taught us to be wary of the idealist and essentialist nature of this simplistic (and romantic) equation of text and author. Indeed, in the aftermath of the "death of the author," texts (to revise Tildesley's conventional notion) can be said only to embody that death.

Tildesley believes that one of the immediate benefits of her study of Browne's skull will be that its results could be used to test popularly held beliefs concerning the actual or supposed relationships between the skull and the man. Chief among these beliefs is the traditional idea that "a low and receding brow involves a low mentality" (Tildesley 5). Although Tildesley reserves discussion of this issue until later in her study, this question of the "low-brow" was one that deeply concerned those who viewed Browne's skull (plate 11), and thought they saw in its receding forehead some profound paradox: how could such a skull belong to such a mind?[15]

Tildesley recounts the inadvertent opening of the tomb by workers preparing the adjacent vault, as well as the series of letters and articles in the local Norwich press describing – often with conflicting details – the vault and Browne's remains. A piece in the 29 August 1840 *Norwich Mercury* tells of the accidental opening and viewing of the remains:

While the persons employed in opening the ground for the interment of the late Mrs Bowman were at their work, they accidentally struck a coffin and exposed the corpse, which proved to be that of the great Sir Thomas Browne. The features it is told us were perfect, and especially the beard. Sir Thomas was accounted one of the handsomest men of his time. The circumstances becoming known the men deemed it best to cover the remains immediately. (qtd. in Tildesley 33–34)

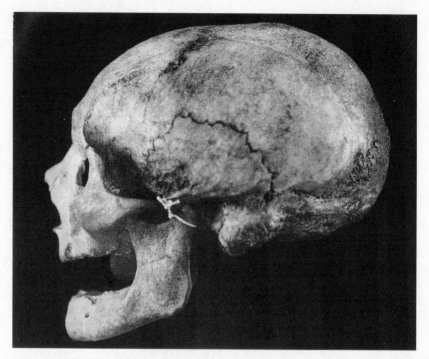

Plate 11 Sir Thomas Browne's skull, left profile, from Miriam L. Tildesley, "Sir Thomas Browne: His Skull, Portraits and Ancestry," in *Biometrika: A Journal for the Statistical Study of Biological Problems* 15 (1923), pp. 1–76.

John Wortley, one of the Norwich citizens who saw the remains, offers a corrective letter to the editor which appeared in the next number of the *Norwich Mercury*, September 5:

Observing in your paper last week a paragraph stating that the remains of Sir Thomas Browne were found in a state of great preservation, I beg leave to correct the report given by your correspondent, that the head and the features were perfect, – such was not the case, nothing more was found than in ordinary instances, the bones being perfectly bare; the skull was of the finest conformation, the forehead being beautifully developed. (qtd. in Tildesley 34)

This letter itself prompted yet another correction: Robert Fitch's letter was printed in the September 12 number of the *Mercury*: "Sir, Allow me to correct the errors of your last week's correspondent with respect to Sir Thomas Browne's relics. It is true that no trace of the 'features' remained, but the 'beard' was in good preservation, and of a fine auburn colour; the forehead was remarkably small and depressed; the head unusually long" (qtd. in Tildesley 34).

Another account appears in *Norfolk Chronicle*, also on September 12, which offers more detail, as well as more discussion:

The bones of the skeleton were found to be in good preservation, particularly those of the skull. The brain was considerable in quantity but changed to a state of *adipocere* – resembling ointment of a dark brown hue . . . With respect to the conformation of the head, we are informed that the forehead was remarkably low, but the back of the cranium exhibited an unusual degree of capaciousness.

(qtd. in Tildesley 34–35)

The viewing of Browne's remains, as these conflicting accounts suggest, was a complicated matter. The first narrative depicts a perfectly preserved body; the second, a typically decomposed body, but one whose signs (e.g., the "finest conformation" of the skull and the "beautifully developed" forehead) seem to guarantee something like a formerly perfect body; and the third and fourth describe the decomposed body and, with special attention and focus, the unusually shaped head. It is the question of the shape of Browne's forehead and what that shape signifies that organizes subsequent discussions of Browne's skull. We see in this a profound shift from an understanding of the body (or its remains) as essentially anonymous and essentially meaningless materiality to a theory and a practice that seek to infuse meaning (and sometimes even identity) into otherwise incoherent bodily remains. At a certain point the living body ceases to house or constitute identity and meaning; perhaps that point is death. Or, perhaps that point is the moment beyond which we are no longer able or no longer interested in assigning (however we choose to do so) any *immateriality* to the body which "exists" in excess of it. The scientific endeavor described here – which at the same time is an historiographical endeavor – is to recover some approximation of this immateriality in the absence of which the body *is* simply meaningless. Robert Fitch is puzzled because Browne's skull ("low" and "depressed") tells him certain facts about Browne that he may not be able to assimilate to his (pre)conception of Browne. Hamlet finds the skull notable only after it has been ascribed to the long-absent and much-missed Yorick. In some ways, the matter of the skull – or, more largely, the matter of the body – is precisely concerned with absence. It is the apparent absence which "infuses" the immaterial that triggers the scientific/historiographic endeavor to ascribe meaning, to "restore" the immaterial in the very face of the material presence.[16]

Tildesley argues that the *Chronicle* narrative was also written by Robert Fitch, an argument that depends upon the significant similarities between the *Chronicle* piece and a letter written by Fitch to Thomas Amyot, Treasurer of the Society of Antiquaries, of which Fitch was a member. Tildesley is inclined to believe the details of the last three narratives, particularly when it comes to the form and shape of Browne's skull. And yet, despite her own investment in offering positive proof in her own study of the skull, Tildesley is concerned that the Fitch documents can offer only "negative proof" of their truth: only that they are consistent, and that they were never contradicted in the local media (Tildesley 36). In the face of the evident inadequacy of this "negative proof," Tildesley turns to an investigation of "the character and reputation of the witness who furnishes us with two [of the narratives], and probably also with the third": Robert Fitch (Tildesley 36). Fitch, we are told, was a prominent citizen of Norwich; a partner in a chemist/druggist firm; Sheriff of Norwich; member of several societies, including the Norfolk and Norwich Archaeological Society, the Society of Antiquaries, as well as a fellow of the Geological Society; something of a famous collector; and churchwarden at St. Peter Mancroft: "If one reflects on the characteristics that are implied by this record, one concludes that ability, observation, capacity for detail, a mind alive to many interests and energy in the pursuit of these were prominent among them" (Tildesley 36). Fitch would seem to be Tildesley's ideal eye-witness. And yet, Tildesley discovers "an incident that . . . throws another side-light upon his character" (Tildesley 37). Tildesley reminds us that in his letter to Amyot, Fitch tells of having himself taken impressions of Browne's coffin-plate "without implying," Tildesley notes, "that he had removed the plate in order to do so" (Tildesley 37). Fitch reportedly claimed to have returned the plate to the church sexton, though the plate was only recovered after Fitch's death in 1895, discovered in a "secret well" in his desk (Tildesley 37). Tildesley concludes:

We gather, therefore, that Mr. Fitch's antiquarian zeal sometimes led him to take steps which he was not afterwards prepared to admit, and even went so far as to deny. This incident may lead us to question the entire suitability of Mr. Fitch for the office of churchwarden, but does nothing to call the value of his evidence as antiquarian in question. That he was a keen antiquarian his works do testify, and where the two interests clashed, we see it was not the latter that gave way. (Tildesley 37)

Grounded, then, in large part upon Fitch's reputation as a reliable antiquarian, Tildesley is willing to accept his descriptions of Browne's skull as accurate. She offers as further corroboration the plaster cast of the skull made in 1840–41, presented to the Norwich Castle Museum in October 1841 by Charles Muskett. Muskett, like Fitch, had antiquarian ambitions of his own, publishing in 1850 an illustrated folio, *Notices and Illustrations of the Costumes, Processions, Pageantry, etc. formerly displayed by the Corporation of Norwich*. From evidence available, Tildesley concludes that the original of both Fitch's descriptions and the plaster cast was indeed Browne's skull, taken (for whatever reason) from his opened crypt sometime between August 10 and August 14, 1840: "The skull which has been preserved as that of Sir Thomas Browne for more than seventy years in the

Norfolk and Norwich Hospital Museum answers to every point of the description left on record by Mr. Fitch and we identify it as the original of the cast given by Mr. Muskett" (Tildesley 39).

Tildesley discusses various objections to the identification of the skull as Browne's. Chief among these objections, both for the frequency of its telling, and for the curious way in which Tildesley summarily dismisses it but nevertheless continues to be informed by its *telos*, is the suggestion that the skull in question could not have been Browne's by virtue of its small and receding forehead. Tildesley retells an anecdote of an American surgeon who, upon being shown the skull, "laughed heartily and replied that for his part he should class it as that of a Peruvian!" (Tildesley 41). However ridiculous this "trans-Atlantic joke" might be (though Tildesley never explicitly objects to its manifest racism), it stated suspicions nevertheless shared by many. For those who have difficulty "associating the low forehead of Sir Thomas Browne with the high intellectual capacity he evidences," Tildesley baldly claims: "I suggest that it is their previously-conceived ideas on this subject which need revision: a high brow does not invariably denote intelligence nor is it a necessary condition of the same" (Tildesley 41–42).

Tildesley recognizes the limitations of classical phrenological theory, suggesting that although its results would afford us invaluable insight to the correlation of physical and mental characteristics, they can only carry us so far in our desire to know the individual from the body. In this inquiry, Tildesley asserts, we often depend on physical characteristics that the skull alone does not reveal completely:

More unconsciously however, doubtless more truly and to a far greater extent we base our mutual judgments upon the expression of the living face, upon features which are not determined by the shape of the bony framework alone.

We do not feel we know a man unless we know what he looks like, and our curiosity is very strong in the case of men dead and gone whom we have learnt to know in part through their actions or their works. (Tildesley 5)

Tildesley considers the system of pictorial representation by which historically we have gratified this desire to know the face. This knowledge necessarily comes to us filtered through the "medium of the artist – perhaps of several artists, of various schools, of varying skill and truthfulness, their work coloured by differing individual mannerisms" (Tildesley 5). While Tildesley here laments the obvious difficulties imposed by "second-hand" knowledge, she never questions the system of representation itself; for Tildesley the portraits vary from one another only in relation to the presumed face, which stands as the thing itself, unmediated, and coexistent with mind and identity. The only matter of the portraits, then, is the matter of their relative *truthfulness* to this face/mind: "If we place them side by side, we realise how imperfectly some of the portraits at any rate must have transmitted the exact appearance of the original: if one speak truth on this point the others cannot, but which is the truest?" (Tildesley 5). This dilemma, which according to Tildesley's argument is typical of our relationships to "men dead and gone," can be remedied "to some extent in the case of Sir Thomas Browne" precisely because we "possess" the skull: while the "skull alone cannot tell us all we wish to know about the living head . . . the skull and the portraits together can do much" (Tildesley 5).

The discussion of the portraits is a long and elaborate examination of the various pictorial representations of Sir Thomas Browne, or those alleged to be representations of him. Tildesley's first task is to distinguish between portraits made from life and all others which are descended from them. Tildesley examines three types of portraits: painted portraits (the Norwich portrait, the Royal College of Physicians portrait, and the Bodleian portrait); engraved portraits (the Van Hove engraving for the 1672 *Pseudodoxia Epidemica*; the Vandrebanc – or, Van der Banck – image for the 1683 edition of *Certain Miscellany Tracts*; and the Robert White engraving for the 1686 *Collected Works*); the painted miniature (the Buccleuch miniature), and a pencil ("plumbago") drawing in the National Portrait Gallery. From her essentially genealogical investigation, Tildesley decides (though not without some qualification) that all three engravings are almost certainly descended from a single source, which is probably the Buccleuch miniature. Of the painted portraits the Bodleian is dismissed as a posthumous rendering (c. 1730) from the miniature; and the RCP portrait – perhaps like the miniature itself – is declared a descendant from the Norwich portrait, which stands, evidently, as the ultimate source of all subsequent authentic images of Browne – "the grandfather," Tildesley declares, "to these lesser fry" (Tildesley 16).

One of the principal issues in this discussion of the portraits and the claims each makes for from-life authenticity is the matter of Browne's forehead. The Van Hove engraving (plate 12) is the only portrait of Browne known to have been executed in his lifetime (though Tildesley makes the reasonable yet not absolutely proven argument for from-life authenticity for the Norwich portrait and the Buccleuch miniature), and from it Tildesley focuses on the sloping forehead, which is either reproduced in descendants of this portrait, or rather radically revised. The Van Hove and the miniature are similar images, though Tildesley regards the engraved portrait as less aesthetically pleasing than the miniature, and, given what Tildesley says we know of Browne from his literary works, probably less accurate:

The Van Hove engraving is harsher, harder, and more angular than the miniature . . . The curve of the upper lip is exaggerated into a sharp angle; the eyebrows are heavier . . . The eyes are larger and more sombre; the whole expression is forbid-

Plate 12 *Sir Thomas Browne*. Line drawing by F. van Hove, 1672.

ding, whereas that of the miniature is sweeter, and accords better with what we know of the character of the philosopher. (Tildesley 10)

The Van der Banck engraving (plate 13) is also "less admirable," and among its other characteristics, "the backward slope of the forehead is considerably modified." On this score, the Robert White engraving is "kinder to the slope of the receding forehead, than are Van Hove and the miniature-painter" (Tildesley 11).

Plate 13 *Sir Thomas Browne*. Line drawing by P. Vanderbank, 1683.

Tildesley considers the Royal College of Physicians portrait, and sees a family resemblance between it and the portraits so far discussed (plate 14). But this image is decidedly *not* the source, but a rather liberally reconceived descendant:

I ask the reader to look at this towering forehead, this conventional and rather wooden countenance, long and narrow; high foreheads were no doubt as popular

Plate 14 *Portrait of Sir Thomas Browne*. Unknown artist. Royal College
of Physicians, London.

then as today, and what artist, copying from this, would give his own production the
low and sloping brow found in the miniature and Van Hove, or even reduce the
height of it to the dimensions found in Van der Banck and White?. . . The more one
studies these portraits, the more obvious it becomes that the painting at the Royal
College of Physicians is the expression of the artist's own idea of what it would have
been more becoming in Sir Thomas Browne to have looked like. Whether he was
right or no, it is certain that he has nearly improved him out of all resemblance to
himself if the miniature be near the truth. And on this point it will no doubt be safe

Plate 15 *Portrait of Sir Thomas Browne* (?). Unknown artist. Wellcome Institute Library, London.

to fall back upon the same canon as obtains in literary criticism: where two versions differ, the more awkward and difficult is the correct one. I am afraid we must accept Sir Thomas Browne's disturbing forehead! (Tildesley 13–14)

Tildesley discusses another portrait said to be of Browne in the Wellcome Historical Medical Museum (plate 15). On the back of this portrait are affixed two pieces of paper with writing on them, one in script and one printed. The script reads, "Sir Thos. Browne, Kt. M.D., Author of Religio Medici and other learned works. Practised in Norwich." The printed lines, evidently a fragment of a description, read,

st   from   which a mezzotint   was   aped by Simon,
ssion   of   Wm.   Douglas,   Esq.   of   Teddington, near
  h it to its present possessor, Sir John Lister Raze,
    efield, Yorkshire, for the sum of £400.

Tildesley notes that while this description fails to name the portrait's subject, her investigation has nevertheless yielded a startling conclusion: the Wellcome portrait corresponds "with a mezzotint by Simon, not of Sir Thomas Browne, but asserted to be of Shakespeare!" (plate 16). Borrowing from Abraham Wivell's 1827 study, *Inquiry into . . . Shakespeare's Portraits*, Tildesley quotes Edmund Malone's 1790 *Shakespeare's Works*:

About the year 1725, a mezzotinto of Shakespeare was scraped by Simon, said to be done from an original picture painted by Zoust, or Soest, then in the possession of T. Wright, painter, in Covent Garden . . . I have lately seen a picture in the possession of – Douglas, Esq. at Teddington, near Twickenham, which is, I believe, the very picture from which Simon's mezzotinto was made. (Tildesley 22)

An earlier discussion offered by James Boaden in his *Inquiry into the . . . Portraits of Shakespeare* (1824) both denies Malone's identification of Douglas's painting as the Soest original, and offers a conflicting set of dimensions (20 inches by 16). Wivell responds by offering a brief history of the Douglas painting, including a memorandum from Douglas himself which asserts that the painting was sold to its "present possessor, Sir John Lister Raye, Bart. of the Grange, near Wakefield, Yorkshire, purchased [from] me for four hundred pounds" (qtd. in Tildesley 22). Tildesley turns to the Wellcome portrait and identifies it as "another version of the [Soest] picture, and we also see correspondence with the details of the mezzotint" (Tildesley 23). Tildesley is now ready to offer a reconstruction of the partially obscured printed paper affixed to the back of the Wellcome portrait. Noting that the name "Kaye" is misspelled in the Douglas memorandum (as "Raye"), and maintaining that "our completed lines must begin exactly underneath one another" (Tildesley 24), Tildesley offers to "reconstruct the original somewhat as follows":

W^m. Shakespeare
From a portrait by G. Zoust from which a mezzotint was *scraped by Simon, at one time in the posse*ssion of Wm. Douglas, Esq. of Teddington, near *Twickenham, who parted with* it to its present possessor, Sir John Lister Raze, *Bart., of The Grange, near Wake*field, Yorkshire, for the sum of £400.

While Tildesley cannot be completely certain about her reconstruction ("Possibly the opening words as we have restored them are not correct . . .

Plate 16 After Gerard Soest, *William Shakespeare*. Engraving by J. Simon (*c.* 1731).

As to the remainder of the restored portion, we have little doubt that it follows closely the missing original"), she is certain that the Wellcome portrait was not the Douglas portrait, though she is equally certain that the two pictures are related: "Thus the Wellcome portrait . . . is identified as one of the various 'Zoust Shakespeares'" (Tildesley 24). This portrait, thought to be of Thomas Browne, may well be one of a group of images said to be of Shakespeare. But Tildesley does not think she has "discovered" another portrait of Shakespeare in an alleged picture of Browne: "Is it possible that we have by chance exposed an error two hundred years old? Are the Zoust Shakespeares perhaps all portraits of Sir Thomas Browne?" (Tildesley 24). Tildesley reminds us that the Soest original "has long been discredited as a reliable presentment of Shakespeare" and that the only evidence we have that Soest even attempted to paint Shakespeare is Simon's word on the mezzotint itself, produced more than forty years after Soest's death (Tildesley 24).[17] But this, of course, does not prove that the image is of Thomas Browne ("as the writer of the manuscript label on the picture has left no written justification of it as far as we know, he too may have been one of the class we have just had reason to condemn" [Tildesley 25]), and for any more compelling evidence to help in deciding this matter, Tildesley can only turn to internal evidence in the painting itself. But the internal evidence is ambiguous at best, and certainly not conclusive: the painting seems to resemble both the Norwich painting of Browne and the Chandos painting of Shakespeare, though more heavily the former (with the exception of the "high and rather perpendicular forehead"); the picture depicts a subject with hair, though all of Shakespeare's portraits represent him as (partially) bald, though the Wellcome hair fails to suggest a relationship with any of the Browne portraits. Tildesley's only recourse in the face of such ambiguous information, is to turn to a more promising – a more *scientific* – means of analysis:

we should hesitate very greatly to affirm, on the evidence, that the MS. label [identifying the Wellcome portrait as an image of Thomas Browne] speaks the truth. But since we cannot absolutely prove that it does not, from the data so far considered, we must submit it, together with all others that are not clearly proved to be either copies of known portraits of Sir Thomas, or else portraits of some-one else, to the test of the skull. (Tildesley 25)

Tildesley's reinvention of the Wellcome portrait as a relative of the images of Shakespeare reveals that what had earlier emerged as an aside concerning Shakespeare's bones was not an isolated event, nor was it merely tangential to Tildesley's project. After having described her methodology, Tildesley offers the following comment: "If we could also have the skull of Shakespeare before us for a short time, what vexed problems that too would resolve!" (Tildesley 5). Tildesley evidently offers this thought as an aside, an interesting but finally not entirely pertinent fantasy. And yet, the dream expressed in this single sentence carries a great deal of historical and cultural significance. Indeed, the references to Shakespeare – first the dream of his bones, and then the lengthy discussion of his relation to the Wellcome portrait – indicated a particularly strong investment in the discourse of national character – something that will be later in Tildesley's racial-craniological study crucially relevant and important.

Tildesley wants to compare the 1840–41 skull cast (which had various imperfections of workmanship and execution) with the 1922 records in order to establish further the identity – or the *original* – of both. Tildesley can compare the earlier cast only with *records* from 1922, and not, of course, with the skull itself, which had been reinterred in 1922. In theory, Tildesley's records – consisting of photographs and another plaster cast – are insinuated in her scientific discourse only as *figures* of what she takes to be Browne's skull, while within the practice of her comparativist study of the early cast and the subsequent records, they (in fact *both* the 1840–41 cast and the 1922 records) are made to function *literally*. This is admitted quite freely in the text: like the 1922 photographic images of the skull, the 1840–41 cast has

been photographed from vertical, lateral and occipital aspects. These terms each carry with them an exact definition of the position required of the skull: it must be adjusted to the "horizontal," the "sagittal," and the "vertical" planes respectively, and these planes are determined by certain important points on the skull – the nasion, bregma, lambda, auricular points and orbital point. (Tildesley 47)

These are the standard procedures for determining the contours of the skull. And yet, Tildesley points out that the 1840–41 cast, created with purely phrenological objectives in mind, simply does not afford some of these rudimentary skull reference points:

Since the 1840–1 cast lacks malar bones and therefore the orbital point, gives no indication of the whereabouts of the bregma, and does not allow us to locate the lambda or nasion with any exactness, we are reduced to appreciative methods in orienting it for the camera. Thus we cannot guarantee that skull and cast will be photographed from exactly similar, but from only approximately similar, points of view, and we must bear in mind, when comparing the results, that a slight shifting of the view-point means a slight – possibly more than a slight – alteration in the outline presented. (Tildesley 47)

In the ensuing comparison between the 1840–41 cast and the 1922 photo-graphic and plastic records, the best Tildesley can hope for is an *approxima-tion* of scientific accuracy – only a *figural* scientific certainty. The 1840–41 cast and the 1922 photographs can only attain a relationship to each other figuratively: one can only ever be a trope of the other, either in the model of metaphor or in the model of simile. An undeniable tropicality underlies Tildesley's science, which, ironically, is at least in part dedicated to the elimination of tropism within the world of scientific/mathematical dis-course:

It is interesting to note here the general principle which holds in such cases: that photograph-outlines (and outlines are the chief part of what this cast will give us) can give convincing evidence of identity of shape, but, given a certain resemblance between the objects represented, cannot give convincing evidence against it! If the outlines differ, it may be due either to difference of shape in the objects, or difference of position; if they are alike, the chances are overwhelming that this is due to identity of shape. (Tildesley 47)

The comparison between the cast and the skull yields a correspondence that Tildesley asserts could only result if the cast and the skull were identical. Tildesley wants to rewrite the nature of the cast–skull relationship: due to statistical analysis, the relationship is no longer figural, but literal: the cast and the skull become (in Tildesley's discourse) identical. This is the central "fact" of Tildesley's study – the fact that allows for such ideas (and phrases) as submitting the portraits to "the test of the skull," or the title to the study's fifth section, "The Portraits and the Skull Compared." Tildesley acts, then, as if we could compare the portraits *directly* to the skull, when the skull is in fact literally inaccessible, or accessible only figuratively. It is this act of radical substitution (skull=cast=skull=Browne) that allows Tildesley's entire project. Moreover, it is this explicit acceptance of this substitution (made in spite of – or rather, in opposition to – tropicality) that empowers Tildesley's science altogether.

Once Tildesley has secured the identity of all the plastic and photographic records with Browne's skull, she can then proceed to interrogate the portraits for representational "accuracy," using the "skull" (i.e., the results of her statistical analysis of the casts and photographs) as the measure. For the purposes of the comparison, "the cast of the skull has been photographed at 'three-quarter face'" (plate 17), a position "the same as in the Norwich and miniature portraits as nearly as this could be estimated" (Tildesley 52), though she admits the possibility exists in this approximated orientation for "enough difference to be misleading" (Tildesley 52).

The principal characteristic of Browne's skull, Tildesley maintains – much like those first "eye-witness" accounts of the remains found in the crypt in 1840 – is the low forehead, which cannot be disputed, though a second characteristic that emerges from her statistical analysis of the skull – its narrowness – is more open to interpretation. The forehead as represented in the portraits need not be narrow, as the narrowness of Browne's forehead ("Browne's minimum forehead breadth measured between the temporal ridges, was considerably less than the normal") was really a matter of the forehead above the eyebrows: "Thus the width of the frontal at the level of the upper margins of the orbits is more normal than it is higher up. We shall therefore not expect the face to look unusually narrow at the level of the eyebrows" (Tildesley 52–53). The living head, as Tildesley refers to it, would appear to have a low forehead, though not necessarily an excessively narrow one, and the cheekbones "would project somewhat,"

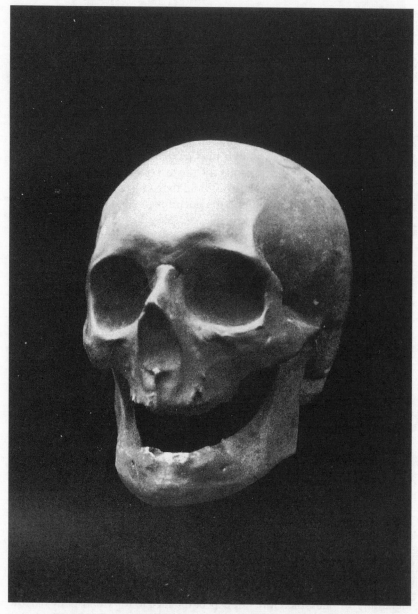

Plate 17 Cast of Sir Thomas Browne's skull (1922), from Miriam L. Tildesley, "Sir Thomas Browne: His Skull, Portraits and Ancestry," in *Biometrika: A Journal for the Statistical Study of Biological Problems* 15 (1923), pp. 1–76.

and the nose would be "either prominent or aquiline . . . depending upon the shape of the cartilage" (Tildesley 53). With this description afforded by the "skull," Tildesley immediately dismisses the Wellcome portrait:

It is quite certain that Sir Thomas Browne's forehead *cannot* have looked like the one shown in this portrait. If we had other evidence to prove that this was intended for his portrait, the picture itself would not be disproof, for many misrepresentations, intended and otherwise, can find their way into a portrait. But if this picture looks to the evidences of its own features to support a very doubtful claim, it looks in vain. (Tildesley 53)

The remaining portraits – the Buccleuch miniature, the Norwich painting, and the plumbago drawing – are all more frank in their presentation of the low forehead, though, Tildesley maintains, "None of the artists has been *quite* candid about the depressed forehead of the subject; but the miniature seems to have disguised the depression least" (Tildesley 53). But the final decision of authenticity – which was, after all, one of the organizing questions of the study to begin with – is not simply a matter of faithfulness to one (albeit a prominent and defining) characteristic; the plumbago drawing, for example, is relatively honest in its representation of the depressed forehead, but less so in terms of its fullness (breadth); and the miniature, for all its fidelity to the uniqueness of the forehead in its angle of declension and its characteristic narrowness, is less true in its representation of the nose as in the miniature it is "neither aquiline nor prominent, and we are sure it must have been one of these, in life" (Tildesley 54). While strident, Tildesley's conclusion is nevertheless equivocal:

Summing up then, we surmise that the Norwich portrait is most like its subject in the shape of the nose; that it shares with the miniature the recommendation of being truthful in the temporal region of the brow, which the pencil portrait does not; that it and the plumbago drawing seem rather more faithful – though not conspicuously so – in the region of the cheek-bones; but that the miniature is the one which gives us the truest indication of the slope of the forehead. (Tildesley 54)

This suggests the final inauthenticity of *all* the portraits, with the only "true" one being a hybrid version of all of them.

It is worthwhile noting here that Tildesley appends to her study a discussion of the then recently discovered L'Estrange portrait of Thomas and Dorothy Browne (plate 18), which Tildesley sees – belatedly – as the very image her analysis of Browne's "skull" had predicted:

we find at last, in this picture, a head which answers in every detail to what the skull would indicate as the appearance of the living head. The nose long and slightly aquiline, the cheek-bone projecting, the forehead normally broad at the level of the eyebrows, but retreating and narrowing abruptly; and, above all, exhibiting a lowness that no other portrait examined thus far has matched. Here we have the forehead that we knew a faithful portrait must shew, and the back of the head has a capacious appearance which is also confirmed by the skull. (Tildesley 76–77).

Plate 18 Joan Carlile, *Portrait of Lady Dorothy Browne and Sir Thomas Browne*, 1650. L'Estrange portrait. National Portrait Gallery, London.

After her comparisons with the portraits, Tildesley's text makes its perhaps inevitable strategic move of shifting her immediate emphasis from an analysis of the "skull" to an analysis of Browne's ancestry, concluding it to have been "7 parts Cheshire (with infusion from Lancashire and Flintshire), 1½ parts Herefordshire, 1½ parts Essex, 1 part Middlesex, and 5 parts unknown but probably of the home counties" (Tildesley 56). Only after we progress through this section of the study and reach the next section – "Study of the Skull" – does the agenda behind the concern for ancestry become clear. Tildesley's interest is in establishing a truly comparativist portrait of Browne's skull, and to that end employs two sets of craniological measurements from seventeenth-century London skulls (known as the Whitechapel and Moorfields groups). In her choice of these two series, Tildesley considered and finally rejected two other series – the Hythe (Kent) and Rothwell (Northants) series – not only because they are significantly smaller samples, but because they represent a particular "racial" stock less likely to be as "cosmopolitan" as Browne's, or as a London sample.

The value of Browne's "skull," then, is no longer that it can be read as a text signifying (in some fashion) the mind and character of Browne the writer/philosopher; rather, the skull is important because it offers a supposedly well-documented instance of a racially determined cranial type. In this regard, Tildesley's self-imposed distance from phrenology comes more clearly into focus: Tildesley is finally not concerned with the relationship between the skull and the brain – or even more remotely still, the skull and the mind. Instead of a discussion (of whatever sophistication) concerned with the regions of the brain and their relationship to mind, Tildesley's racial craniology is finally concerned with "pure" measurements, statistical analysis articulated against standard deviations, shape rather than significance of shape: average cranial height, average cranial capacity, average cranial circumference.

Within this selected population – only *metaphorically* the proper population for this sort of study of Browne's "skull" – the character of Browne's skull appears unremarkable: "in the great majority of characters he is entirely normal and usual" (Tildesley 60). As for Browne's apparently low forehead, Tildesley's analysis provides a significant revision of the conventional explanation that first reinvents "lowness" as a matter of bone rotation, and then places Browne's cranial type within a certain predictive calculus of frequency of occurrence:

Sir Thomas Browne's low forehead is therefore not due to a flattened frontal bone, but to one which is rotated further backwards. The degree of rotation may be measured by the bregmatic angle . . . For Sir Thomas Browne, this is 38.2°; for the type, 47.1°. Measured by the appropriate s.d., 3.36°, this or a greater degree of rotation of the frontal is seen to be likely to occur in only 1 in 248 of the population.

(Tildesley 65)

Tildesley concludes her racial craniological comparison by summarizing those peculiar characteristics of Browne's "skull":

It was quite normal as regards length and maximum breadth, but was deficient in height, this deficiency occurring in the height of the vault above the horizon of the nasion. Its circumference . . . is quite normal. Of the major proportions of the skull, those in which height is a factor . . . are unusual. The breadth of his forehead is significantly smaller than the average breadth, but the skull widens rapidly at the temples, and . . . attain[s] normal maximum breadth in the region where the maximum usually occurs . . . The breadth at the back of the head is thus significantly greater than usual, and, the length of the head behind the vertical through the auricular passages having also an excess over the normal which borders on significance, the small capacity of the skull in the frontal region is compensated for by increased capaciousness at the back, with the result that the total capacity of the skull comes within the normal range. (Tildesley 66–67)

Tildesley's study succeeds here in placing Browne's skull within the range of "normal" for English males. Near the conclusion of her study she

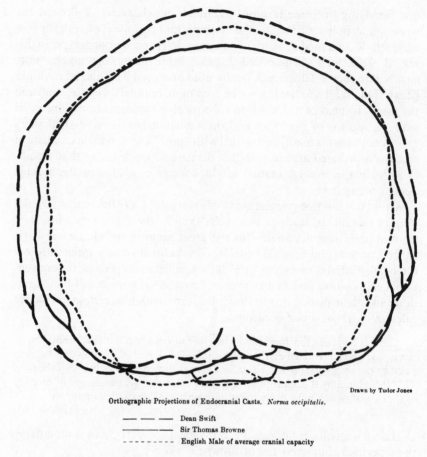

Drawn by Tudor Jones

Orthographic Projections of Endocranial Casts. *Norma occipitalis.*

— — — — Dean Swift
—————— Sir Thomas Browne
- - - - - - - - English Male of average cranial capacity

Plate 19 Orthographic projections of endocranial casts of Sir Thomas
Browne and Jonathan Swift (*Norma occipitalis*), from Miriam L.
Tildesley, "Sir Thomas Browne: His Skull, Portraits and Ancestry," in
Biometrika: A Journal for the Statistical Study of Biological Problems 15
(1923), pp. 1–76.

introduces a "report" on the endocranial cast of Sir Thomas Browne, executed by G. Elliott Smith, which likewise concludes that Browne's cranial
capacity was within this "normal" range. To demonstrate this Smith introduces orthographic projections of the three brain casts from Browne, Dean
Swift (whose was "of large size"), and "a modern English skull picked at
random from . . . the Anatomical Department of University College"
(Tildesley 67) (plates 19 and 20). Smith compares the capacities of the three
casts, and determines Browne to fall between Swift, on the one hand, and

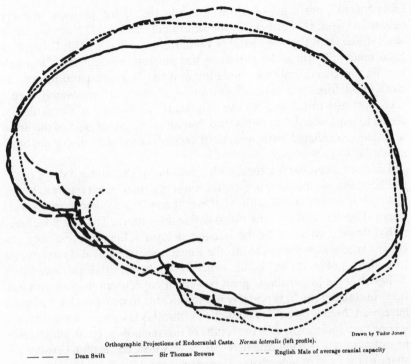

Orthographic Projections of Endocranial Casts. *Norma lateralis* (left profile).

Drawn by Tudor Jones

— — — — Dean Swift   ———— Sir Thomas Browne   - - - - - English Male of average cranial capacity

Plate 20 Orthographic projections of endocranial casts of Sir Thomas Browne and Jonathan Swift (*Norma lateralis*), from Miriam L. Tildesley, "Sir Thomas Browne: His Skull, Portraits and Ancestry," in *Biometrika: A Journal for the Statistical Study of Biological Problems* 15 (1923), pp. 1–76.

the "random English skull," on the other, declaring, "There is nothing in the peculiar features of the cast indicative of exceptional or particular development of brain" (Tildesley 67). The effect of this comparison, however, is not simply to place Browne within the "normal" range, but also to place him within a particular hierarchy: Browne's brain was of peculiar but nevertheless average or even above average capacity when compared to the "random" English man whose brain was of "normal" shape but somewhat small in capacity. On the other hand, Browne's slightly above average cranial capacity is more or less dwarfed by Swift's enormous capacity. Thus we have the hierarchy of British types: beginning with the "random" entirely average man we *progress* to Browne's peculiar but still exceptional skull, then on to Swift's manifestly expansive brain.

Tildesley summarizes her four principal findings: (1) only the Buccleuch miniature and the Norwich portrait are authentic (though perhaps not independent) portraits of Browne, with the latter perhaps actually descended from the former; (2) the skull reinterred in 1922 was the same skull stolen from Browne's vault in 1840, from which the 1840–41 cast had been made; (3) where the various other portraits misrepresent Browne's receding forehead, only the miniature and the Norwich painting are "as close to the form that in life draped the skull as we can reasonably expect such portraits to be; and (4) the significant "peculiarity of the skull . . . seems to suggest a defect of marked development in that part of the brain intimately correlated with powers of concentration and discrimination" (Tildesley 68).

Tildesley is confronted, then, with a paradox: if the outward shape of the skull can tell us something about "the mind of a man" what it tells us in this instance is incompatible with what we "know" from that man's textual traces. Tildesley can see only two possible resolutions. The first possibility is that Browne, who was "in the first place a lover of literature and not a scientist," who was never elected to the Royal Society, who "did not hesitate to make a public avowal of his belief in witchcraft" did not necessarily demonstrate in his writings "great powers of concentration or discrimination" and therefore "it is possibly not reasonable to demand that [he] must have been 'high browed'" (Tildesley 68). But this is dismissed in favor of a second conclusion: "to take the results of this memoir as confirming earlier investigations which indicate that there is very little correlation between the shape of the head or indeed of the brain cavity and the mentality of the individual" (Tildesley 68).

Tildesley, citing an earlier *Biometrika* article on the skull of Jeremy Bentham that determined "it [Bentham's skull] was essentially mediocre with no outstanding characters which might be associated with marked intellectuality," decides that her study "seems to indicate that the skull of another man of genius can depart from general mediocrity in a few isolated characters, and in some of these reach a form which current opinion describes as a 'low type' of skull": "Thus the second solution, and to us the more reasonable one, may be summed up in the words that Sir Thomas Browne's skull supports the conclusion that the correlation of superficial head and brain characters with mentality is so low as to provide no basis for any prognosis of value" (Tildesley 68).

When considered in light of its opening statement on the nature of its project and its ambitions, Tildesley's conclusion comes as something of a shock. Tildesley's study reveals the epistemological limits of phrenological or craniological study in determining the relationship between mental abilities and the shape and conformation of the skull. But Tildesley's text, as I have tried to suggest above, is throughout aware on some level of its own inevitable failure; it is this sense of the limitations of the study that accounts for its various discursive strategies and maneuvers: the deflection into the matter of portraits, the turn to an elaborate and detailed discussion of ancestry. Tildesley's text always surprises us, though it never surprises us with a viable phrenological/craniological discussion, and ends *sotto voce* with the dismal prognosis for scientific and predictive phrenology.

Tildesley's conclusion could not have been welcomed by Sir Arthur Keith, the physician, writer, and Conservator of the Museum, Royal College of Surgeons. While Keith did offer a laudatory preface to Tildesley's study, his ambition for the phrenological endeavor – as evidenced both in that preface and in his subsequent writings – seems not to have been wholly satisfied. His praise of Tildesley, in fact, is qualified and guarded: her work demonstrates the "right application of laboratory methods to historical enquiry and to anatomical pursuits (Tildesley 2), and her study has the effect of preserving the physical image of Browne.

In some ways, Tildesley's text succeeds only in being a descriptive one; in this regard it succeeds in what Keith in the preface had identified as his original charge "to make an exact and permanent record of its form and features" (Tildesley 1). And yet, for both Tildesley and Keith, this project stands merely as the necessary first step in a larger project: for Tildesley it is the larger project of racial craniology; for Keith it is the larger project of what he will come to call "scientific phrenology."

In 1924 Keith delivered and then published his University of Edinburgh Henderson Trust Lecture, entitled *Phrenological Studies of the Skull and Brain Cast of Sir Thomas Browne of Norwich*. In this work, published two years after and as a response to Tildesley's study, Keith wastes no time in identifying his method as phrenological: "Of all the men who have made for themselves a sure place in the history of English Literature, there is none who lends himself to the phrenologist with such promise as Sir Thomas Browne, the Norwich physician," whom Keith identifies in his opening paragraph as a man "of pure English ancestry" (Keith 1).[18]

Keith's work begins, in effect, where Tildesley's leaves off. While Tildesley's project, Keith suggests, was entirely devoted to establishing the "authenticity" of the skull, Keith's will be a "search for a solid basis of fact on which a scientific phrenology might be built" (Keith 2). The Henderson lecture allowed Keith the opportunity to complete his study which had been deferred – into Tildesley's hands, and into Tildesley's conclusion. Keith is unequivocal in declaring his scientific – and *textual* – project: "It was my ambition to make the skull of Sir Thomas Browne a text from which I might preach a sermon concerning the forces which mould the skull and brain into their several forms, and to illustrate the methods I had devised to measure and elucidate the nature of the forces which are involved" (Keith 2).

Keith begins with a personal recollection that establishes the nature of Keith's life-long – and complicated – engagement with phrenology:

In my youth I was seized by the doctrine promulgated by the pioneer phrenologists of Edinburgh – George Combe and his younger brother, Andrew. As was the case with Dr. Andrew Combe, I thought Nature had dealt rather meanly by myself as regards size and form of head, and I could not help envying her liberality in this respect towards some of my class-fellows and rivals. One particular form of head which was not uncommon at Aberdeen University in those days, and still is, held a high place in my esteem; it was particularly common amongst students from the Highlands. This head was long, with flat sides; it was evenly balanced on the neck, the occiput projecting well backwards, while the forehead was square and upright.

(Keith 2–3)

And yet, even given this profound esteem for particularly shaped heads, Keith confesses that his school experience "sadly disturbed [his] phrenological beliefs" since "some of my finest heads . . . turned out to be 'duds'; one of my ablest teachers had a decidedly receding forehead; I saw men with mean heads become prominent prizemen" (Keith 3). In the face of such irrefutable (though wholly anecdotal) evidence, Keith does not decide that phrenology itself was invalid, but that it merely stood in need of serious improvement and updating; Keith remains, he declares, "sustained . . . by a positive assurance that some day Gall's dream of a science of phrenology must come true" (Keith 3).

Keith cites his two fundamental reasons for believing not only in the viability, but in the inevitability of a phrenological science: the evolutionary trajectory of the human brain toward both increased size and greater faculties, and the localization of specific functions to specific areas of the brain. "The human brain," Keith declares, "has certainly been evolved along physiological lines" (Keith 4). It is Keith's faith in these two fundamental (though by no means *natural*) beliefs that under-writes his vision of a new phrenology: "If these things are true, then, when our knowledge of the human nervous system is perfected, it will be possible by a mere inspection of a brain to assess the mental potentialities of its owner. This is the ultimate goal of the scientific phrenologist" (Keith 4).

This passage is notable both for its clear and hopeful statement in the inexorable teleology of Keith's sense of evolution and his profound confidence in the inevitability of an eventual fullness of phrenological knowledge, and for its privileging of the brain in Keith's phrenological science. The quick and sure glance at a *brain* – and not a skull – will simultaneously determine mental faculties and guarantee the phrenological epistemology. This belief marks either a profound shift in the methods and theory of phrenology from the desire (as we saw in Tildesley) to discover the nature of the unseen by virtue of a semiotics of the seen (the apprehension of the nature of the brain and its abilities by virtue of the careful study of the skull), or it marks a profound slippage in Keith's discourse, causing him to say "brain" when he intended "skull." But there is more to this latter possibility, of course, than "merely" a linguistic error (whatever that could be): to privilege the brain over the skull, as Keith seems to do here, is to invert the *telos* of phrenology – to relegate the skull (traditionally the object of phrenology) to the position of secondary importance. There is the further problem for Keith's study that while he here privileges the brain over the skull, he will later reverse this, and privilege the skull over the brain. In fact, Keith's text wavers precisely between these two different – and perhaps antithetical – determinations. And herein lies what will in fact turn out to be the primary (but by no means the conscious) structuring principle of Keith's text which constitutes itself – particularly in moments of theoretical and epistemological crisis – in the oscillation between two different models of the production of the mind. Keith will even locate the phrenologist's crux at the intersection of this complex and ambiguous skull–brain: "Phrenology cannot be called a science until we have exposed the machinery which regulates and co-ordinates the architecture of brain and skull" (Keith 5).

After these preliminary and more or less theoretical declarations on the nature of scientific phrenology, Keith begins his discussion of Browne by foregrounding a consideration of Browne's temperamental and intellectual characteristics ("We cannot discuss the cranial characters of Sir Thomas Browne unless we bring to our task a knowledge of the workings of his mind" [Keith 5]). As Tildesley had done in her study, Keith too posits a wholly unproblematical relationship between "men" and texts. For his part, Keith emphasizes Browne's "meditative and contemplative" nature, labeling him "a spectator of life rather than a man of action" (Keith 5). Browne is identified as "a product of high civilisation" who nevertheless "retained all the credulity which characterises the brain of primitive races of men" (Keith 6–7). Keith aims to make sense of this rich and sometimes surprising temperamental disposition by way of his new phrenology.[19]

Keith had earlier mentioned the peculiarity in shape of Browne's skull, retelling the anecdote of a "visitor, on examining the specimen, [who] exclaimed that he would rather ascribe the skull to a flat-headed Indian than to a genius like Sir Thomas Browne" (Keith 2). Keith clearly wants us to repudiate this comment; how could a "flat-headed Indian" and the genius of Sir Thomas Browne be compared at all? It is the self-evidently preposterous nature of this comparison that seems to offend Keith, not that Browne may have been "flat-headed" (indeed, Keith accepts this as the very impetus for his own study), nor the racist slur against "Indians" for whom "flat-headedness" is evidently more a description than an insult. Moreover, it would seem to go without saying that any "flat-headed" individual could in no way make any claim to as illustrious a life or as splendid a literary career as Browne. "Flat-headedness" would by nature (so the argument goes) render any such success physically impossible. And yet (as I will argue below), it is this image of the "flat-headed Indian" that returns near the end of Keith's study to frustrate the very claims for scientific phrenology that Keith hopes to make.

Once his project ("to place the study of the human skull on a more rational basis") and its object (the "head-form of Sir Thomas Browne" [Keith 7]) have been thus displayed, Keith turns to a discussion and then a demonstration of his new methods by way of which he will construct his scientific phrenology. Keith's principal methodological innovation is his decision to study – and represent – the skull oriented along a newly defined axis, what Keith calls the "sub-cerebral plane," which he thought to be an improvement over the traditional craniological "Frankfort plane" orientation illustrated, for example, in Tildesley's graphic representations (plate 21). Keith argues that the Frankfort plane – which represents a line "drawn through two points: one is the lowest point on the sill of the orbit or eye-socket, the other is on the upper margin of the ear-passage" [Keith 9]) – is essentially useless for true phrenological study since it is not derived from structurally meaningful cranial characteristics and can therefore only function as "purely an axis of the face" (Keith 9). For Keith, the subcerebral plane is the appropriate axis of orientation because it represents structurally pertinent information: "This line corresponds approximately to the floor of the cavity which contains the cerebral hemispheres, the parts of the brain serving as the seat of all man's higher mental faculties" (Keith 7).

But, as Keith himself states, this structural value of the subcerebral plane is only approximate, and, moreover, the characteristic of the subcerebral plane that makes it both most valuable and most viable is the fact that one can discern it from the outward characteristics of the skull: "It is quite true that certain parts of the cerebral hemispheres descend below this line . . . but it is the nearest approach to the actual cerebral floor *which is attainable from indications on the surface of the skull*" (Keith 7, my emphasis). In other words, Keith can offer us no assurance of the validity of the subcerebral plane either to represent the actual cerebral floor, or to have a true value beyond its ease of association with outward "indications" on the skull. On this score it seems that the old Frankfort plane succeeds at least as well as Keith's subcerebral (it can be discerned from outward characteristics of the skull), and probably better in terms of its ability to represent something like the actual cerebral floor. The distinction – prejudiced in nature – that powers Keith's use of the subcerebral plane as a near-enough approximation of the true cerebral floor is his privileging of the upper areas of the brain as "the

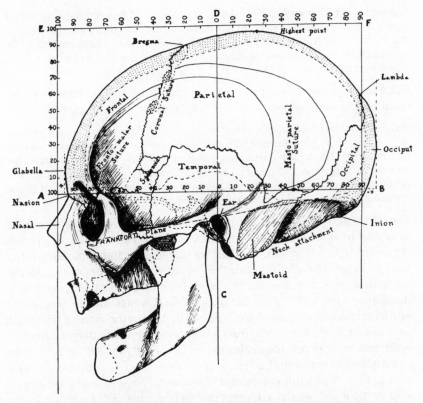

Plate 21 Drawing of the skull of Sir Thomas Browne, in profile, from Sir
Arthur Keith, *Phrenological Studies of the Skull and Brain Cast of Sir
Thomas Browne of Norwich*, Edinburgh, 1924.

parts of the brain serving as the seat of all man's higher mental faculties"
(Keith 7). To determine orientation of analyses and representations of the
skull thus is to orient the skull in terms of what we *conjecture* or *believe* to
be "man's higher mental faculties." Indeed, it is only a certain kind of linear,
hierarchical, and, finally, teleological thinking that identifies human identity
with these amorphous and ambiguous "higher mental faculties."[20]

Another of the effects of orientation along the subcerebral plane, especially in the instance of Browne's skull, is to alter what we think of as the
shape of the skull, and its relative relationship to more "normal" skull
dimensions and measurements. With the subcerebral orientation, Browne's
skull appears (visually and numerically) both less flat on the crown, and less
deep in the occipital area. After detailing the measurements of Browne's
skull, Keith offers the following description:

that part of Sir Thomas Browne's skull which contained his cerebrum was placed unusually far back in the head, and had a low and flat roof. If one were to conceive that his head had been plastic in youth, and that pressure had been applied to the forehead in a backward and downward direction, such a conformation of head would have been produced. (Keith 10)

But Keith's greater concerns are theoretical in nature, and he is quick to point out the fictional nature of this "explanation" of skull shape:

But we know that a head shaped as his was, is not produced by pressures acting from the outside, but by living forces which exert their pressure from within. We shall see that the shape taken by the developing skull depends on two sets of forces: the growth of the brain as a whole and of its several parts on the one side; the growth of the bones, which enclose the brain, and the manner in which they react to the expansion of the parts within the skull on the other. (Keith 10)

The effects of this brain–skull growth dynamic caused in Browne "the brain to expand to an unusual extent in a backward direction and to give a receding aspect to this forehead. We shall see that it also caused the sides of the skull to bulge" (Keith 10). Keith then declares, quite in opposition to the theoretical account he has just offered on the internal forces that determine the shape of the skull, "Thus the brain of Sir Thomas Browne was forced into a curious and unusual shape" (Keith 10). Within the space of this single page of text, Keith has moved from a numerical representation of Browne's skull, to a more purely linguistic description of it ("low and flat roof"), to a mythological account of external forces that could be conceived to have changed but finally did not change the shape of Browne's skull, to a revision of the myth of external forces into his doctrine of the internal forces and pressures that shape the skull, to the image of Browne's brain "forced into a curious and unusual mould."

Keith confuses these two models of explanation for the shape of Browne's skull and he does so precisely because neither version is fully compatible with what his science says he will find. On the one hand, the brain is said to determine the final shape of the skull. This is problematical for Keith's study because it would be the equivalent of identifying a problem with Browne's brain – erratic or abnormal growth – which would then account for the shape of the skull. On the other hand, the skull shape is predetermined, and its shape determines in turn the shape of the brain. This option is also problematical because to accept it would be tantamount to abdicating hope for *any* effective relation between skull shape and the character of the brain. For Keith, both positions or theories are unacceptable, and rather than accept either he opts for an unclear (con)fusion of both.

Positing the constriction and shaping of the brain by the forces of the skull is incompatible with that part of Keith's new phrenology that states it

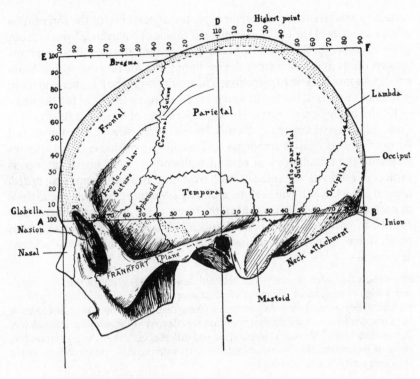

Plate 22 Drawing of the cast of Jonathan Swift's skull, in profile, from Sir Arthur Keith, *Phrenological Studies of the Skull and Brain Cast of Sir Thomas Browne of Norwich*, Edinburgh, 1924.

is the brain that shapes the skull. This is not an unimportant theorem for Keith's scientific phrenology; indeed, it is this belief in the (trans)formative power of the growing brain that enables Keith's new phrenology altogether. To help illustrate this notion, Keith invokes a comparison of Browne's skull to that of Dean Swift, whose skull bears the marks of a particular brain expansion: where Browne's brain grew "in a backward direction" producing a pronounced "back-headedness or opisthocephaly" (Keith 10), Swift's brain grew in a more clearly upward direction (plate 22). Keith discusses the results of the "upward expansion" of Swift's skull, including a similar lift upward of the neck area and a decreased forward projection of the face. "By pursuing physiological clues," Keith determines, "we do find rational explanations of craniological features" (Keith 12).

Another effect, Keith argues, of brain growth along a particular line of development is the appearance of the forehead, which was, of course, of special interest to traditional phrenologists. But rather than indicating a certain characteristic or character type, the appearance of the forehead is wholly a matter of the forces exerted on its angle of emergence from the root of the nose. So, for Swift, whose brain grew upward, the frontal bone merely rotated on its axis to a greater degree than it did for Browne, whose brain grew in a more backward direction. The results would be a higher and more prominent forehead for Swift, and a lower, receding forehead for Browne.

Keith's tactic here is telling. He has in the skulls of Swift and Browne two quite unusual specimens – Swift's for its sheer size and volume, and Browne's for its relative smallness and peculiarity of shape. In his attempt to secure the foundations of scientific phrenology, and his simultaneous project of retaining the value of both Swift and Browne as eminent *British* men of letters, Keith will seek to mollify the extraordinary characteristics of both skulls, pushing each toward the mean which lies between them. This entails, in part, reinventing the figure of "Dean Swift" as a man whose "high dome" is not an absolute indicator of high humanistic values and sensibilities:

It is not, as the older phrenologists believed, that the lofty dome of the Dean signified a high development of organs of veneration, benevolence, and hope – at least we know they were never exercised to a striking degree. Nor does the low crown of Sir Thomas Browne indicate that his brain was devoid of these higher attributes of the human brain. All that is implied by the differences is that the corresponding parts of their respective brains unfolded or expanded in different directions within their respective heads. (Keith 14)

If it is true that this is all that Keith can imply in his study, then his hopes for a scientific phrenology would seem all but dashed as such a science could only ever aspire to be a descriptive and not a predictive discourse at all. Yet Keith finds his salvation in the pathology of "that strange disorder of growth known as Acromegaly" and in an emergent hormone theory. In people who suffer from acromegaly, new bone is laid down along existing bone, resulting in a pronounced thickening of bone wall of the skull while the underlying brain structures remain unaffected. Acromegaly, then, would seem to present a serious challenge to traditional phrenology in that "Under the influence of this strange disorder the markings which the older phrenologists employed as guides to the development of certain mental faculties, have been transformed, and yet the convolutionary pattern of the patient's brain remained unchanged" (Keith 15).

Acromegaly is important for Keith and his scientific phrenology not because it serves to illustrate non-internal and non-external forces brought to bear on the skull – indeed, this is something Keith needs to overcome – but because it offers evidence for a systemic model of skull–brain growth and formation dependent upon and to a great extent determined by hormones. Acromegaly can be attributed to certain undetermined dysfunctions in the pituitary gland, and it is the pituitary that "throw[s] into the circulating blood certain substances – hormones – which have the power to stimulate and also to regulate the growth of all structures of the body – including bones. The pituitary gland has a power to mould – or to assist in moulding – the phrenological markings of the skull" (Keith 15). Keith seeks to revise the theory of the "old phrenologists" who argued that temperament had to be considered in "the interpretation of a man's mental faculties" by offering a chemical explanation of temperamental characteristics: "we now seek to explain temperament, and all that is implied by temperament, on the basis of hormone-theory" (Keith 16).[21] With this shift from structure to substance, from brain–skull formation to hormone-theory, Keith saves scientific phrenology, though he saves it not as a practice but as a theory, and as a theory, moreover, predicated upon deferral. Unlike traditional phrenologists, we cannot accept external skull markings as absolutely indicative of the brain (or the mind) in large part because for us the skull is no longer itself the object of scientific inquiry but instead simply a sign that represents the informing truth of chemically induced temperamental characteristics.

To demonstrate this new theory (which could not now properly be called "phrenological"), Keith turns to two skulls of famous men: Robert the Bruce and Robert Burns, both of whom (like Keith) were Scots. As for the former, Keith declares "[t]here is no doubt as to Bruce's racial type" (Keith 16). Keith offers precise measurements of this skull, including its cranial capacity of 1540 c.c., "60 c.c. above the average man's." Keith declares, "The Bruce, it will be seen, was big-headed":

Thus the skull of Bruce was of a size and strength which is but seldom seen amongst men; he was big-brained. It would be the strength and configuration of the face rather than the size of the brain that would weigh with most students if they sought to hazard a guess as to the nature of the man of which such a skull had formed part. We should suppose him to have been a forceful leader of men . . . Those features, which come out under the taint of Acromegaly, appeared in him as normal healthy products. The strong and heavy chin, the massive angles of the lower jaw – the prominent jowls, the pronounced nose, the strength of the eyebrow-ridges, the robustness of the whole visage, indicate a man of strength, power, and resolute action. (Keith 17–18)

Quite in contrast to Keith's study thus far, what emerges in this fierce portrait as truly significant is the face, and only secondarily the skull. The effective consequence of the Bruce's big-headedness is his even more imposing face. In Keith's science, the skull relinquishes it primacy to those characteristics that to conventional phrenology had always been secondary.

As for his second specimen, Keith declares, "Robert Burns had a massive brain, it measured at least 1680 c.c. – 200 c.c. more than the average

Scotsman, 140 c.c. more than the great King of Scotland, 150 c.c. more than in the most witty of Deans, and 160 c.c. more than in the meditative Sir Thomas Browne" (Keith 19). While standard phrenological theory would suggest that the size of Burns's brain indicates he would have had more than his own share of "benevolence, veneration, and hope," Keith considers it "impossible to find facts in the life of the poet to suggest his richness in these qualities" (Keith 19). This leads to a crucial question: "What value are we to attach to volume of brain?" Keith's answer to this question is perhaps inevitable:

If the brain were merely an intellectual organ, it would be difficult to explain why the brain of Robert Burns was bigger than that of Dean Swift. One might infer that the brain is an emotional as well as intellectual organ, and that such mass as is seen in the case of Robert Burns is connected with the intensity with which all emotions – all those primitive functions which have come down to us from animal ancestry – are felt, realized, and enjoyed. A big brain may not signify the possession of high intellectual faculties or of genius, but only a capacity for appreciating and realising the sources of emotional enjoyment. (Keith 19–20)

In order to move toward his conclusion Keith turns to a discussion of his methodology "rather than to lay stress on the conclusion I have reached by the way" (Keith 20). This tactic seems largely diversionary, serving to shift attention away from what is clearly emerging as phrenology's deconstruction and to refocus it on a discussion of the minutiae of methods for ascertaining cranial measurements. But the damage already has been done, and in spite of several additional pages of numbers and drawings, phrenology awaits only the reappearance of Keith's "flat-headed Indian" to lapse into general incoherence.

After detailing what he calls "brain spread" (Keith 21) and difference in brain shape that result from normal "remodelling" of the brain through late adolescence, Keith reminds us that we have "no reason to suppose that such alterations in the shape of the several parts of the brain change in any way their capacity for work" (Keith 25). To illustrate, Keith returns to what had been since the disinterment of Browne's skull nothing but a racist joke:

Indians of America compressed their children's heads so that in some cases the brain expanded sideways over the ears; in others, so that it grew upwards and backwards into the form of a sugarloaf; but the radical transformation in shape of brain thus brought about had no apparent effect on the manner in which the organ carried out its actions. (Keith 25–26)

The "flat-headed Indian" who before served to make the racial, intellectual, and aesthetic superiority of Sir Thomas Browne here stands as manifest proof against such notions and against the discourse of scientific phrenology that sought to substantiate it. There is no correlation between skull shape and brain function. In the aftermath of this revelation which Keith does not explicitly acknowledge but toward which his text inexorably moves, Keith succeeds not in the invention of his new science but rather in entirely displacing both its object and its methodology.

The true object, then, of Keith's phrenology is, strictly speaking, hormone-theory, and the external characteristics of the skull only serve to mark coincidentally the action of hormones as they go on to produce temperament or character. This deferral in the object of phrenology – which is imagined as receding further into physiology and science – necessitates for Keith a similar deferral in the moment at which phrenology becomes truly scientific: it is not until we are able to explain hormone-theory that we will be able to conceive of phrenology as the predictive discourse Keith imagines it to be. While scientific phrenology, then, is deferred and not guaranteed in Keith's study, its goal remains intact: "to examine the head of a living child, by sight, touch, and X-ray transillumination, and to thus form an accurate estimate of the development of its brain as a whole and of its various parts, and from this knowledge of the brain infer the abilities of the child"(Keith 30).

Despite such optimism for his project, Keith's new-model phrenology has indeed determined the limits of phrenological theory, beyond which lies a chemically based physiological system within which skull or facial characteristics bear only an incidental relation to temperament. Or, more damning still, as the true object of Keith's science is transformed into hormones and hormone theory, correspondences between outward features and inward forces can be correlated only in the model of a pathology, as Keith's discussion of acromegaly suggests. The "dream" of phrenology is in the end only a dream, though Keith evidently refuses to recognize this. At the conclusion of his study, Keith defends his decision not to pursue a wide range of traditional phrenological subjects, including the relative and absolute size of the various lobes, the designating of specific areas of the brain in terms of their dominant functions (sight, hearing, motion, etc.). Keith suggests that such a discussion finally would not have been altogether productive, nor necessarily to the point:

Even if I had dealt fully with all of these matters, we should not, in our present knowledge of the brain, have been any nearer to an explanation of the peculiar abilities of the author of *Religio Medici*. To the reader, this may appear to be an admission that phrenology is merely a doctrine, not a science. This is not the view I take. Our knowledge of the use of the various parts of the brain is only dawning; we know, only in the most imperfect way as yet, the exact functional significance which is to be attached to the numerous areas which anatomists, physiologists, physicians, and surgeons have mapped out on the surface of the brain. Until this knowledge ripens, we can only grapple with the grosser feature of the brain and of the structure in which it is lodged, the skull. (Keith 30)

The image Keith offers here of the fruits of scientific phrenology gradually ripening in our determined progression toward absolute scientific physiological knowledge is illustrative of his seemingly indomitable faith in the narrationality of the inevitable (and natural) progress toward scientific truth. With the passage of time, Keith promises, we will enjoy a corresponding fullness of knowledge.

Keith's faith in science and the scientific method bears the marks of a particular kind of modernity – one that seeks (phenomenologically) to access the "real" by way of the "natural." Of course, Keith's "natural" is in fact a highly artificial construct, and the "real" he seeks to access holds close truck with certain forms of racism and nascent fascism (as was the case, too, with Tildesley). The genealogies of such expressions of "science" trace back through the particulars of any given science to the underlying practices of artifaction that I have described here – even back to the moments of the emergence of modernity and modern science in the seventeenth century. All science – perhaps all forms of knowledge – arise only after the processes of artifaction; the skull is only a skull once it has been produced as an artifact. Only once this process has occurred (a process which is always provisional and subject to revision or rejection) is any object (or any conceit) secured narratively *as an object of science*. This is not to say, however, that any science *necessarily* produces a narrative that is negative in its implications, such as phrenology is in Tildesley and Keith, whose works would lead to the scientific institutionalization of racism and an accompanying discourse of racial supremacy. Science does not necessarily produce fascism, but fascism is one of the narratives for which science (a narrative-producing machine) can be put to work and to which science may bear some important structural resemblances. But fascism is only one of the narrational embodiments artifaction takes, and among its countless possible trajectories we could include any number of other manifestations – including ones dedicated, for example, to the discrediting of phrenology, or the repudiation of racism. These narratives are, it is important to note, no less constructed and artificial than the phrenological one is, but they are distinct from the various narrationalities I have discussed in this book, and unlike them, they are entirely more self-conscious of their deployment of narrative, and do not make the mistake of construing the effect of narrative for its primary object.

In the final section of this chapter I will turn to the deployment of artifaction and the narrational in the works of Sir Thomas Browne, who himself was interested in the meaning of the body and its remains in death as figured in one of his most famous and important works, *Hydriotaphia; or Urn-Burial*. In some ways Browne – especially in *Hydriotaphia* – stands at the opening of the era of modern science and to that extent his works mark an

approximate beginning of the processes of artifaction and science I have
argued are so important in Tildesley and Keith. In Browne, artifaction and
science are deployed in an attempt to transcend time and as such his work
offers an example of what happens generally when writers want to talk about
history – to stand somehow outside time, whether in a moment of religious
ecstacy, or within an historicist comprehension of the movement of history,
or within a phrenological analysis of "race" through time. One telling difference that distinguishes Browne from the phrenologists is that while their
science effectively removes the fact of death from their inquiry (just as for the
anatomist death itself is removed from the field of anatomy), for Browne,
death becomes the central figure of artifaction, science, and transcendence.[22]

III

To be knav'd out of our graves, to have our sculs made drinking-bowls, and our
bones turned into Pipes, to delight and sport our Enemies, are Tragicall abomina-
tions, escaped in burning Burials. (*Hydriotaphia*)

Keith's text on Browne's skull offers a scientific discourse predicated
upon a system of reading by which the body is turned into a textual artifact; when deciphered properly, this artifactual body–text will reveal from
the "outside" the character that it in some manner houses on the "inside."
Another way to say this is that Keith offers a system of narration by which
an inner meaning can be deduced from certain external clues – or, one's
story can be ascertained by virtue of the narrative clues it displays in the
manner of signs. Both Keith's science and his narratology are semiotic in
nature and serve to reveal an over-riding investment in the narrational, even
as his new-model phrenology is in fact the old phrenology conceived explicitly as an historiographical discourse.

In *Christian Morals*, Browne describes the historical benefits to be had
from an ideal life and suggests that a life of sufficient length – 100 years, the
equivalent of one-sixtieth of the projected duration of the created world –
devoted to careful observation and inquiry would yield a result similar to
the one Keith envisions:

In such a thred of Time, and long observation of Men, he may acquire a
Physiognomical intuitive Knowledge, Judge the interiors by the outside, and raise
conjectures at first sight; and knowing what Men have been, what they are, what
Children probably will be, may in the present Age behold a good part, and the
temper of the next; and since so many live by the Rules of Constitution, and so few
overcome their temperamental Inclinations, make no improbable predictions.

(*CM* 465)

Browne imagines here – like Keith (and like Tildesley before him) – a
knowledge that can have historical as well as predictive value. This theory

has at its foundation two guiding assumptions: that knowledge is essentially *semiotic* in nature, and that such knowledge is created *in a dialectic with time*. These informing conceptions serve as organizing principles for Browne's great project of the articulation of a system or theory of what I will call knowledge-in-time. Browne's theory – like Hamlet's – comes to depend entirely upon the discursive production of artifactuality. Like Tildesley and Keith, Browne's theory is enabled by the careful and systematic articulation of an interpretive or analytical strategy that only becomes available once it has founded the artifact, once it has, in other words, extracted from the world a particular feature that it will then submit to the logic – or the tyranny – of narrative. While the central interpretive act for Tildesley and Keith is the placing of the "found" artifact – the skull – in history, for Browne, the artifact becomes history itself which is then inserted into a *"Physiognomical* intuitive knowledge" that finally makes sense of the world. Browne creates a scientific discourse predicated upon certain notions of time and knowledge and dedicated to the articulation of a narrative – and a narratively meaningful – world, one able to coexist with and within God's created universe.

In *Christian Morals*, Browne argues that we are, in some sense, charged with the task of historical study:

Think not thy time short in this World since the World it self is not long. The created World is but a small *Parenthesis* in Eternity, and a short interposition for a time between such a state of duration, as was before it and may be after it . . . However to palliate the shortness of our Lives, and somewhat to compensate our brief term in this World, it's good to know as much as we can of it, and also so far as possibly in us lieth to hold such a *Theory* of times past, as though we had seen the same.

(*CM* 471)

Browne goes on to discuss the benefits to be had from such a theory, describing in particular the way in which such knowledge would serve to extract us – or, to free us – from time: "He who hath thus considered the World," Browne writes, "may conceive himself in some manner to have lived from the beginning, and to be as old as the World; and if he should still live on 'twould be but the same thing" (*CM* 471).[23]

Human existence, then, is not merely a matter of inhabiting the brief *"Parenthesis* in Eternity," then passing through death into Eternity; it is also a matter of knowledge. But we know that in our fallen state, true knowledge is extraordinarily difficult to attain. The one certain path to true knowledge is, of course, death, and the access it allows the saved to a kind of fullness of knowledge from the vantage point of God's Eternity:

There is yet another conceit that hath sometimes made me shut my bookes; which tels mee it is a vanity to waste our dayes in the blind pursuit of knowledge, it is but attending a little longer, and wee shall enjoy that by instinct and infusion which we endeavour at here by labour and inquisition: it is better to sit downe in a modest ignorance, & rest contented with the naturall blessing of our owne reasons, then buy the uncertaine knowledge of this life, with sweat and vexation, which death gives every foole gratis, and is an accessary of our glorification. (*RM* 148)

Browne's sentiments in this passage seem, on the one hand, quite genuine: his Christian faith had taught him, in an aphorism to which he frequently alludes, that "all is vanity." And yet, on the other hand, Browne seems to intend these words in the "soft and flexible sense" he identifies in his preface "To The Reader," as one instance of the "many things delivered *Rhetorically*, many expressions . . . meerely *Tropicall*" (*RM* 60). Indeed, Browne's efforts throughout his literary career stand as a coherent project dedicated quite explicitly to the pursuit of knowledge in particular forms and of the construction of a *theory* of human knowledge, especially understood in its dialectical relation to time. What this suggests, of course, is that death – while yet the great liberating event of our lives – is only *one* point of access to knowledge. Or, death and subsequent knowledge in eternity do not constitute the *only* imaginable narrative of human existence. Browne articulates a complementary (and parallel) narrative in which human existence-in-time may itself afford a point of access to knowledge. In many ways, Browne's ambitious *Pseudodoxia Epidemica* stands as an apt representation of his epistemological project: it is a monument both to history's so-called "Vulgar Errours," and to Browne's faith in the idea of human knowledge.

Browne is quite explicit in his understanding that any study of the world is necessarily an *historical* study in that the world itself is a manifestation of God's providence and can therefore be understood as an expression (effect) of God's will (the prime cause). To the extent that historiography of any description is essentially a study of the relation of cause and effect, Browne's literary project was at least in part historiographical. The version of causality that Browne constructs is a more or less orthodox Christian one that places God in the customary position of the prime cause, and from whom all other – or secondary – causes issue. Browne's Christian historiography constructs a wholly *caused* universe – a universe in which such potent demons as chance, accident, and fortune simply do not exist: "there is no liberty for causes to operate in a loose and stragling way, nor any effect whatsoever, but hath its warrant from some universall or superior cause" (*RM* 83). A necessary conclusion, then, of this theological historiography is that not only are all events and effects entirely caused, but also that every particular essence is itself caused by and in the mind of God, "by which each singular essence not onely subsists, but performes its operation" (*RM* 84).[24]

For Browne, all knowledge is therefore causal knowledge, and any understanding – of religion, or of the world – is therefore an *historical* understanding. However, Browne makes clear that there are two important provisos to this basic tenet of his theory of knowledge and causality. First, while natural reason is innate in all of us and therefore available to us, true knowledge is in no such sense a function of nature and therefore necessarily available by means as natural, say, as recollection. To the contrary, true knowledge begins with what seems like a decidedly "unnatural" event, with the willful act of forgetting:

> Would Truth dispense, we could be content, with Plato, that knowledge were but Remembrance; that Intellectuall acquisition were but Reminiscentiall evocation, and new impressions but the colourishing of old stamps which stood pale in the soul before. For, what is worse, knowledge is made by oblivion; and to purchase a clear and warrantable body of Truth, we must forget and part with much wee know.
>
> (*PE*, "To the Reader" 1)

Browne continues in this opening paragraph to describe the epistemological project of the *Pseudodoxia*, couching his conceit in imagery (taken from astronomy and cosmology) of the universe as a complex and precise machine:

> Our tender Enquiries taking up Learning at large, and together with true and assured notions, receiving many, wherein our reviewing judgements doe finde no satisfaction; and therefore in this Encyclopaedie and round of knowledge, like the great and exemplary wheeles of heaven, wee must observe two Circles: that while we are daily carried about, and whirled on by the swindge and rapt of the one, wee may maintaine a naturall and proper course, in the slow and sober wheele of the other. And this wee shall more readily performe, if we timely survey our knowledge; impartially singling out those encroachments, which junior compliance and popular credulity hath admitted. Whereof at present wee have endeavoured a long and serious *Adviso*; proposing not onely a large and copious List, but from experience and reason, attempting their decisions. (*PE*, "To the Reader" 1)

It will emerge later in this chapter that this image of the universe as a perfect machine is crucial to Browne's entire theory of knowledge-in-time. To anticipate here what later will be discussed more fully, let me say that the success of Browne's knowledge-in-time depends upon his ability to create the possibility of a parallel system by which human existence-in-time can coexist with God's eternity, but temporally and on its own terms. If Browne's image of God's eternity is the universe as machine, what will stand as Browne's image for his own "created world" is the perpetual motion machine theorized and described in *Pseudodoxia Epidemica*.

The second (and more problematical) proviso to Browne's theory of knowledge is the understanding that knowledge and causality are not only unnatural, in a strict sense (and therefore "artificial," as Browne uses that term), but both are vulnerable to Satan's evil manipulations and corruptions. In the fourth chapter of Book I of the *Pseudodoxia*, Browne details "the nearer and more Immediate Causes of popular errours," including "Misapprehension, Fallacy, or false diduction, Credulity, Supinity, adherence unto Antiquitie, Tradition, and Authoritie" (*PE* 22). Browne discusses the four principal fallacies (derived from Aristotle and the logicians): "*Petitio principii. A dicto secundum quid ad dictum simpliciter. A non causa pro causa.* And *fallacia consequentis*" (*PE* 24). The second of these – "when from that which is but true in a qualified sense an inconditionall and absolute verity is inferred" (*PE* 25) – is of special significance to us here.[25] For Browne, all error in the world emanates from Satan and his originary act of error and transgression.[26] Browne construes Satan's fundamental evil as created out of his deliberate corruption of the relationship between signs and things signified. In his temptation of Christ, for example, Satan (self-consciously employing the second fallacy cited above) uses scripture against Christ, offering him the opportunity to call the angels to his assistance. Browne argues that this evil derives from a transgression that is, in a manner of speaking, *textual* in nature:

Thus the divell argued with our Saviour, and by this he would perswade him he might be secure if hee cast himselfe from the pinacle: for said he, it is written, he shall give his Angels charge concerning thee, and in their hands they shall beare thee up, lest at any time thou dash thy foot against a stone. But this illation was fallacious, leaving out part of the text, He shall keep thee in all thy wayes; that is, in the wayes of righteousnesse, and not of rash attempts: so he urged a part for the whole, and inferred more in the conclusion, then was contained in the premises.

(*PE* 25–26)[27]

Browne sees this line of argumentation as a prime instance of Satan's confounding of sign and signified, and it is our own subsequent confusion of this relation that constitutes the essential form of error and the principal bar to true knowledge: "By the same fallacie we proceed, when we conclude from the signe unto the thing signified" (*PE* 26).[28] By this analysis Browne is able to explain similarly produced (historical) errors: the adoration of icons, the Catholic faith's erroneous belief in the transubstantiation of the host, and the Jewish insistence upon proper observance of the Sabbath even at the cost of condemning Christ for healing the sick on the Sabbath, or of their refusal to defend themselves in response to Pompey the Great's assault upon them on the Sabbath (*PE* 26).

If Satan's primary capacity for evil and for seducing us into sinfulness resides in his generally successful historical project of corrupting the relationship between sign and signified, then by definition all acts of human interpretation – all attempts to understand causality – and thus all forms of human knowledge are put promiscuously at risk. If within human understanding signs and signifieds adhere only in a satanic fashion, then all knowledge is thereby given the lie.[29] How, then, does it come to pass that

Browne should dedicate his life to the articulation of a theory of knowledge? How does it come to pass that Browne should voluntarily – and not without significant and manifest optimism – "wander in the America and untravelled parts of truth" (*PE* 3)?

Browne effects a recuperation of knowledge through the production of the theory of knowledge-in-time articulated within a practice of artifactuality. Browne theorizes knowledge-in-time as that possibility that will allow simultaneously the gathering of human knowledge in our fallen state and the renegotiation of existence-in-time in a new fashion. Traditional Christian theology suggested that there were only two possible conditions of existence: human time (which I will call, following Browne's usage, "duration") and God's eternity (which one could call "true duration"). Browne poses the possibility of a third alternative: knowledge-in-time, that knowledge which successfully negotiates the crisis of the incompatibility of human time and God's eternity. In Browne's theory, knowledge becomes possible because it is saved from mere duration. As a consequence, all knowledge is historical – or artifactual – by virtue of Browne's vantage point "alongside" time. What enables Browne's theory of knowledge-in-time is the idea that true knowledge begins as a purified historical knowledge and that this purified historical knowledge then enables a predictive knowledge that is God-like to the extent that it constructs narratives from a point of virtual timelessness analogous to God's eternity. All such human knowledge therefore is artifactual and archaeological, and to the extent that both these consist entirely of the deliberate process of artifaction and the subsequent articulation of signifying narratives (history, for example), all knowledge is narrational. In this way, Browne's theoretical position comes to resemble (parallel) God's own, but where human knowledge is narrational, God's knowledge exists outside of time and therefore outside of narrative.

As we saw in the opening paragraph of *Pseudodoxia Epidemica*, Browne rejects the Platonic notion that knowledge is a function of memory. In fact, time is clearly characterized as knowledge's nemesis; time corrupts knowledge, and duration corrupts them both: "And wise men cannot but know, that Arts and Learning want this expurgation [of error]: and if the course of truth bee permitted unto its selfe, like that of Time and uncorrected computations, it cannot escape many errours, which duration still enlargeth" (*PE* 4). Unlike error, time is not satanic – either in conception or in origin: for Browne time is a fact of God's creation, a fact of God's providence. Of course, Browne's faith in the doctrine of the "Eternal present" insists that God himself is distinctly outside time.[30]

The effects of time, however, are construed as evil *as if* by time's very nature. Browne is careful here to avoid heretical theorizing – he never doubts, for example, that Adam and Eve were both created in(to) time and also created (to borrow Milton's phrase) "sufficient to stand." Supposing that Adam and Eve could have remained unfallen is still to place them fully in time, though had they not transgressed they would never come to suffer the evils of time, particularly its tendency to corrupt. In other words, while time is divine in its origin (only God could create time), it is nevertheless a fact of *created* existence, and as such is distinct from God: humans exist in time while God exists outside time. Human existence, therefore, is narrative in nature while God's is not. But if human existence is narrative then its "truth," as it were, is always at risk due to Satan's interventions on behalf of disorder and incoherence which confound the basic structure of narrative meaning – the relation of sign to signified. In order for Browne to secure meaning in the world he must reconceive the nature of time itself.

Browne's preliminary step in this process is to re-create time as an artifact of human existence. Browne's understanding of time ultimately calls for a more sophisticated definition than had historically been available. Time is not simply the passage of present moments into the past, nor is it simply an entity whose "presence" is by definition inexorably illusory as "it" always exists either conjecturally in the future, or historically in the past, and the present so fleeting as to be non-existent: "What hath escaped our Knowledge falls not under our Consideration, and what is and will be latent is little better than non existent" (*CM* 449).

The project of re-creating time as an artifact of human existence does not represent an entirely unprecedented strategy for Browne's (scientific) works were routinely involved in what can be called generally the discourse of artifactuality. For Browne, the urns discovered at Old Walsingham in Norfolk, for instance, have significance because his discourse on them – like Hamlet's on Yorick's skull, or like Tildesley's and Keith's on Browne's skull – *produces* them as artifacts. *Hydriotaphia* more generally can be understood as the articulation of a practice, if not a theory, of artifactuality. *Hydriotaphia* creates the urns and their human contents as artifacts of a past human existence, but this past human existence can only be made to signify for Browne once it itself has been re-produced in the image of the urns – in the image, that is, of the artifact. In order for Browne to do this, he must theorize the very notion of time if he is to come to terms with the idea of the historical past, the notion of futurity, and the human remains of the urns which seem now to stand as that which links the past and the future through the present moment. *Hydriotaphia* functions, then, as much as a discussion of time as of death, and as such continues the work of the theorization of time that had begun in *Religio Medici*: "nor can I thinke I have the true Theory of death, when I contemplate a skull, or behold a Skeleton with those vulgar imaginations it casts upon us; I have therefore enlarged that common *Memento mori*, into a more Christian memorandum, *Memento quatuor novissima*, those foure inevitable points of us all, Death, Judgement, Heaven, and Hell" (*RM* 116).

Within Browne's Christian metaphysics and theory of time, death is understood as the portal through which we pass into everlasting life and stands, therefore, as the most significant and meaningful act of life. The Pembroke manuscript of *Religio Medici* offers a careful and important modification of this conventional position, making clear the distinction Browne needs to draw – and one that is essential to his theory of knowledge-in-time – between physical death (one can consider this Browne's version of *pagan* death)[31] and Christian death:

I have therefore forsaken those strict definitions of Death, by privation of life, extinction of naturall heate, separation &c. of soule and body, and have fram'd one in hermeticall way unto my owne fancie; *est mutatio ultima, qua perficitur nobile illud extractum Microcosmi* [death is the final change, by which that noble portion of the microcosm is perfected], for to mee that consider things in a naturall and experimentall way, man seemes to bee but a digestion or a preparative way into that last and glorious Elixar which lies imprison'd in the chaines of flesh. (*RM* 110)

But the fact of death leads Browne to his consideration of temporality – especially as he ponders the bones and other relics he finds in the urns: "Time which antiquates Antiquities, and hath an art to make dust of all things, hath yet spared these *minor* Monuments. In vain we hope to be known by open and visible conservatories, when to be unknown was the means of their continuation and obscurity their protection" (*Hydriotaphia* 306). Not only is the method traditionally employed to resolve at least some of the questions the presence of the bones raises, that is, antiquarianism,[32] found to be wholly inadequate to the task ("But who were the proprietaries of these bones, or what bodies these ashes made up, were a question above Antiquarism" [*Hydriotaphia* 307–08]), the very persistence of the bones *and nothing more* renders the hoped-for monumentality (of burial, of "diuturnity") hopeless: "But to subsist in bones, and be but Pyramidally extant, is a fallacy of duration" (*Hydriotaphia* 308). Browne continues, "Circles and right lines limit and close all bodies, and the morall right-lined circle, must conclude and shut up all" (*Hydriotaphia* 309).[33]

In pagan time – in mere duration – death is monumentalized because death leads nowhere, unlike in Christian time in which monumentalizing death becomes a meaningless gesture precisely because death leads to a profound apotheosis – what in *Hydriotaphia* Browne calls "Christian annihilation, extasis, exolution, liquefaction, transformation, the kisse of the Spouse, gustation of God, and ingression into the divine shadow" (*Hydriotaphia* 314). In Christian time, the body in death has a promissory value to be redeemed by God on the last day when souls and bodies are reunited, either for reward or for punishment. The discussion of the follies of human ambition for "diuturnity" culminates in Browne's famous crescendo:

And since death must be the *Lucina* of life, and even Pagans could doubt whether thus to live, were to dye. Since our longest Sunne sets at right descensions, and makes but winter arches, and therefore it cannot be long before we lie down in darknesse, and have our light in ashes. Since the brother of death daily haunts us with dying *memento*'s, and time that grows old it self, bids us hope no long duration: Diuturnity is a dream and folly of expectation. (*Hydriotaphia* 311)

The antidote to death – which is itself the antidote to life – is God's eternity, with which, Browne says in *Religio Medici*, "I confound my understanding: for who can speake of eternitie without a soloecisme, or thinke thereof without an extasie?" (*RM* 72). Time, Browne argues, is something that we can understand ("'tis but five dayes elder then our selves"), but not God's eternity: "*I am that I am*, was his owne definition unto *Moses*; and 'twas a short one, to confound mortalitie, that durst question God, or aske him what hee was; indeed he only is, all other have and shall be, but in eternity there is no distinction of Tenses" (*RM* 72). It has been our inability to comprehend eternity and the suspension or eradication of "Tenses" that has so confused our understanding of "that terrible terme *Predestination*," which does not mean simply God's foreknowledge "of our estates to come," but rather is "a definitive blast of his will already fulfilled . . . [for] what to us is to come, to his Eternitie is present, his whole duration being but one permanent point without succession, parts, flux, or division" (*RM* 72–73).[34]

Browne's celebration of the "Eternal Present"[35] culminates in the following passage, in which the narrator comes to occupy now his eternal position in heaven which has been guaranteed by "that Synod held from all Eternity":

Before Abraham was, I am, is the saying of Christ, yet is it true in some sense if I say it of my selfe, for I was not onely before my selfe, but *Adam*, that is, in the Idea of God, and the decree of that Synod held from Eternity. And in this sense, I say, the world was before the Creation, and at an end before it had a beginning; and thus was I dead before I was alive, though my grave be *England*, my dying place was Paradise, and *Eve* miscarried of mee before she conceiv'd of *Cain*. (*RM* 132)

In *Pseudodoxia Epidemica* Browne discusses the nature of the blessed who – by virtue of the Eternal Present available to them – occupy a similar position *within* eternity: "so is it the happinesse of the blessed, who having their expectations present, are not distracted with futurities. So is it also their felicity to have no faith, for enjoying the beatifical vision there is nothing unto them inevident, and in the fruition of the object of faith, they have received the full evacuation of it" (*PE* 13). For Browne, true Christian faith self-destructs on its own principles, and at the instant of its fulfillment. Like time itself, which Browne claims both destroys and perfects, faith's fulfillment is its simultaneous and identical annihilation.[36]

But this still leaves the matter of time, and the question of how to "fill up" the time of the hundred years of the ideal life Browne imagines. How can we construe time so as to avoid its devastating negative effects and preserve the idea of time as distinct from both God's eternity, on the one hand, and simple human or temporal duration ("diuturnity"), on the other? The answer for Browne seems to reside in his thorough deconstruction of time as an absolute.

One of the primary questions of Browne's inquiry into time concerns time's status *vis-à-vis* sense perception. If Browne's scientific project in the *Pseudodoxia* is to some extent the production of an experimentalist discourse, then he necessarily must rely on the senses *at virtually every point along the interpretive chain*: the experiment is nothing other than an artificial and controlled gathering of sense data – whether or not the carbuncle emits light in darkness, for example, or if an elephant has joints, if the Red Sea is indeed red, and if it is true that a salamander can live in fire or that a beaver pursued by a hunter will bite off its testicles. This is not to say, of course, that in Browne's "Encyclopaedie and round of knowledge" *all* knowledge is perceptual. A great deal of the work in the *Pseudodoxia*, and in Browne's *œuvre* more generally, concerns conceptual knowledge: whether Adam and Eve had navels; or whether if children were taught no language, they would naturally speak Hebrew; or whether time can be said to exist or not.

Browne begins to answer this last question on the nature of time by first appealing to the notion of time as a perceptual phenomenon. Conventional understandings of time are essentially predicated upon sense-perception – from the quotidian motion of celestial bodies (particularly, of course, the sun and the moon) to feelings of fatigue and sleepiness, to longer-period recognition of time's evident progress, such as growth and aging. Time itself can be said to be available to perception by virtue of its *motion* – the passing of a moment in the future to a "place" in the past. Strictly speaking, then, one can never inhabit the present moment precisely because there is no one moment that is not either about to happen or has not already taken place. This is the dilemma of theorizing time. The present is only ever available to God, who is outside time altogether. This is the effect (or the cost) of narrative time; once submitted to a system of analysis and interpretation (such as language, itself governed by a kind of syntactical time) the present eludes us, fades into the oblivion that is time itself.[37]

Book IV, chapter 12 of *Pseudodoxia Epidemica*, "Of the great

Climactericall yeare, that is, sixty three," offers a discussion and evaluation of the notion that certain numbers have special (or hermetic) significance; in this instance, it is the number 63 (the product of two other significant numbers, 7 and 9), thought to be particularly ominous, especially in the context of age, hence, our "Climactericall yeare." But significantly, Browne's discussion of the ancient belief in the dangerous nature of the sixty-third year of one's life – which will range from a short treatment of numerology, to a discussion of the technology of timepieces, to a vision of the perpetual-motion machine – not only includes but is in part predicated upon a statement on the senses and their operation:

Certainly the eyes of the understanding, and those of the senses are differently deceived in their greatest objects; the sense apprehending them in lesser magnitudes then their dimensions require; so it beholdeth the Sunne, the Starres, and the Earth it selfe; but the understanding quite otherwise, for that ascribeth unto many things far larger horizons then their due circumscriptions require, and receiveth them with amplifications which their reallity will not admit. (*PE* 334)

If it is true that the understanding frequently engrosses its object – its tendency, for example, to transform heroes into legends – perhaps the same has happened, Browne suggests, to numbers, here the idea of the "Climactericall yeare." Browne proceeds to discredit philosophical or Pythagorian "Astrologicall considerations" (*PE* 335) that are sometimes invoked to support the notion of the "Climactericall yeare." He dismisses as well both the various hermetic accounts of the significance of 63 (standard numerological theories such as the occult significance of the number 10 "as containing even, odde, long, plaine, quadrate and cubicall numbers" [*PE* 335]), and accounts had from nature (the seven stars of Ursa minor, the seven "heads of Nyle," the seven circles of Philo's cosmography, or that "women are menstruant and men pubescent at the year of twice seven" [*PE* 336–37]). All of these, Browne asserts, are specious, and there are competing analytical versions of reality that could claim an equal or greater veracity – the testimony of geographers, for instance, that the number of Nile outlets fluctuates above and below seven, or current medical theory on relative moments of sexual maturation ("having observed a variation and latitude in most, agreeable unto the heat of clime or temper; men arising variously unto virility, according to the activity of causes that promote it" [*PE* 336]).

The number seven has also been accorded an occult value, Browne notes, because it has been related to the motions of the moon, "supposed to bee measured by sevens; and the criticall or decretory dayes dependent on that number" (*PE* 338) – and it is this turn that serves to link Browne's discussion of numbers and their nature to a consideration of time, and a consideration of motion, which is itself in some complicated way linked to time.

Browne understands that time is conventionally understood as (1) an experience that is undeniably true, but that cannot be theorized, and (2) a calculation of the passage of moments, articulated in terms of days, months and years. But what Browne refers to as our "compute" of time is far from accurate, far from true: months are not "exactly divisible" into weeks, and while seven days times four repetitions equals 28, the number we associate with the time it takes the moon to complete one whole cycle of movement through the zodiac, its actual period "containeth but 27. dayes, and about 8. howres, which commeth short to compleat the septenary account" (*PE* 339). Moreover, other calculations of lunar periods (in its relation not to the zodiac, known as Peragration, but to, say, the sun, known as Consecution) are different, resulting in the latter instance in a 29 day 12 hour period "so that this month exceedeth the latitude of Septenaries, and the fourth part comprehendeth more then 7. dayes" (*PE* 339). Similar variations appear in two other lunar calculations: in the Apparition month there are only 26 days 12 hours, while in the Medial there are 26 days and 22 hours. The effects of this lunar variation (which all of us are content more or less to ignore, still thinking of months as stable and knowable periods) are serious – and potentially destructive – for any attempt at time-keeping:

the imperfect accounts that men have kept of time, and the difference thereof both in the same and divers common wealths, will much distract the certainty of this assertion [the theory of the "Climactericall yeare"]; for though there were a fatality in this yeare, yet divers were, and others might bee out in their account, aberring severall wayes from the true and just compute, and calling that one yeare, which perhaps might be another. (*PE* 346–47)

Browne concludes:

in regard of the measure of time by months and years, there will be no small difficulty, and if we shall strictly consider it, many have been and still may bee mistaken; for neither the motion of the Moone, whereby months are computed, nor of the Sunne whereby yeares are accounted, consisteth of whole numbers, but admits of fractions, and broken parts. (*PE* 347)

Browne adds to his consideration of time the differences in time-keeping from one nation to another, the ancient practices of the three-month year, and the so-called old style of dating the new year on March 25; taken together, these observations on the nature of the passing of successive moments add up to a misconstruction of time:

All which perpended, it may be easily perceived with what insecurity of truth we adhere unto this opinion [the "Climactericall yeare"], ascribing not only effects depending on the naturall period of time unto arbitrary calculations, and such as vary at pleasure, but confirming our tenents by the uncertaine account of others and our selves; there being no positive or indisputeable ground where to begin our compute. (*PE* 351)

With this Browne deconstructs the notion of time as an absolute, and re-creates it as a wholly human artifact of existence: time exists only to the extent that human existence and human knowledge structure it. And to structure time is to place it within a particular narrative – to place it within some understanding of history and the historical. This is another way of saying that time only signifies once it has been submitted to a series of coordinate (and coordinating) discourses – narrative, history, motion, and death. Once emplotted within this nexus of discourse, time, Browne argues, emerges as its own perfection and as its own destruction.

The artifaction of time is a process in which we have routinely been engaged historically. In particular, human efforts to quantify time are nothing other than instances of our historical and continuing efforts to maintain time as a *produced* artifact of human knowledge-in-time. Browne calls to our attention the theory and practice of the production of time-pieces. He begins this project in Book V, chapter 18 of the *Pseudodoxia* by way of a consideration of a painting of St. Jerome in which a clock anachronistically hangs on the wall behind the contemplative theologian (plate 23). The image to which Browne refers is almost certainly this Dutch painting by an unknown artist in the style of Joos van Cleve, who is believed himself to have executed a painting of St. Jerome from which the anonymous painting is derived.[38] The Dutch copy replaces the hourglass in the van Cleve painting (and which had become a virtually standard feature of iconography of St. Jerome) with a clock. Browne, in his pursuit of true knowledge in whatever form, no matter how particularized, objects to this anachronism, pointing to the rather recent invention of the clock.

This leads Browne to a meditation on ancient timepieces or "horologies" – "Clepsammia," or sand glasses; "Clepsydrae," or water glasses; and "Sciotericall" or sun dials – and the ancient theory and practice of "horometry" (*PE* 413) that are then compared unfavorably to their seventeenth-century counterparts. This, Browne argues, is first a function of technology and (in particular) the advent of "Trochilick," or the "Doctrine of circular motions" (*PE* 414), and secondly a function of time itself: "now as one age instructs another, and time that brings all things to ruine perfects also every thing, so are these indeed of more generall and ready use then any that went before them" (*PE* 414).

The technological superiority of contemporary culture over its ancient counterparts does not surprise Browne; indeed, Browne will comment on what seems the virtually limitless capability of contemporary inventiveness and genius: "surely as in many things, so in this particular, the present age hath farre surpassed Antiquity, whose ingenuity hath been so bold not only to proceed, below the account of minutes, but to attempt perpetuall motions, and engines whose revolutions (could their substance answer the

Plate 23 *St. Jerome in his Study*, *c.* 1530–40. Netherlandish, unknown
artist. John G. Johnson Collection, Philadelphia Museum of Art.

designe) might outlast the exemplary mobility, and outmeasure time it
selfe" (*PE* 414).[39] Browne concludes his discussion of clocks and time with
this image of the perpetual-motion machine – an apt image of time as the
ultimate production of human will fashioned in the image of God's created
universe. The perpetual motion machine functions, as well, as an image of

knowledge-in-time, created within time but, by virtue of its parallel relation to God's eternity, destined to outlive time itself.

The perpetual-motion machine, however, is fictive – or, at the very least, it is only *textual* in nature: if it exists at all it does so only in a textual fashion, a story – or an artifact – from the works of John Dee retold by Browne near the end of his scientific *magnum opus*. But the *ideal* (as opposed to actual) nature of this machine does not disable its function in Browne's discourse because what is most important in its occurrence within the *Pseudodoxia* is precisely its status as text. Elsewhere, in speaking of the antediluvian generations, Browne identifies the past's wealth of (historical) knowledge and its ability to educate us; but even the past (like the "Chaos of Futurity") is insufficiently available to us because it has left us no texts:

Their Impieties were surely of a deep dye, which required the whole Element of Water to wash them away, and overwhelmed their memories with themselves; and so shut up the first Windows of Time, leaving no Histories of those longevous generations, when Men might have been properly Historians, when *Adam* might have read long Lectures unto *Methuselah*, and *Methuselah* unto *Noah*. For had we been happy in just Historical accounts of that unparallel'd World, we might have been acquainted with Wonders, and have understood not a little of the Acts and undertakings of *Moses* his mighty Men, and Men of renown of old; which might have enlarged our Thoughts, and made the World older unto us. (*CM* 448–49)[40]

By these lights, Moses stands as the most "original" of writers, having composed the Pentateuch, the only texts that offer a view into the world before history, and Moses the only writer, Browne states in *Religio Medici*, to have outdone all who would write the "History of their owne lives . . . [having] left not onely the story of his life, but as some will have it of his death also" (*RM* 97). The reference here is to the final chapter of Deuteronomy that narrates the death of Moses after he has seen the Promised Land which he will never enter. Browne alludes to the ostensible curiosity of Moses narrating his own death and burial (at God's hands). Strictly speaking, this act of narration is impossible; it can only be an explicit fiction. Unless, of course, one understands that Moses's narrative of his own death, like Browne's own – "thus was I dead before I was alive, though my grave be *England*, my dying place was Paradise" – are both manifestations of the processes of artifaction described both in Browne's production of knowledge-in-time, and in this chapter. With his discussion of Moses, Browne effects an identification between himself and the great patriarch, and in so doing enacts the culminating maneuver in the practice of artifaction: in effectively narrating his own death, burial, and redemption in heaven Browne produces *himself* as the transcendent artifact of his own devotional texts.

Coda

Self as artifact. We return, here at the end, to the beginning – to Hamlet's emblematic self-artifaction: "I am dead." For all its deeply moving poetic quality (and, perhaps, its genius) the truth of Hamlet's pronouncement is promissory. Hamlet is not dead *in the moment of his utterance* so whatever value "I am dead" has is strictly as prophecy (like any prediction) and can only be considered true once it has already come to pass – and then only as a matter of history. "I am dead" illustrates the condition of narrationality: the attempt to negotiate the three "domains" of time – future, present, and past, which are always inaccessible – by the anachronistic imposition of the narrational. Any act, any utterance, any textual or cultural practice enacted narrationally can only be prophetic and can only be true theoretically. Let me be clear: to say that truth is only ever theoretical is not to abandon hope or to consign *all* cultural practices (such as cultural criticism) to a defeated nihilism nor an unrigorous relativism. I resist such a formulation precisely because I know that in our lives we do find theoretical truths sometimes sufficient and enabling of our dreams and ambitions. We have built worlds upon such theoretical truths. But it also happens that theoretical truths are sometimes destructive – such as the narrationalities of sexism, class bias, and racism – or appropriative and colonialist, or coercive and violent. To call attention to the operations of narrationality is to call for a dedicated self-conscious review of such worlds and such "truths" upon which they are constructed.

Notes

INTRODUCTION

1 William Shakespeare, *Hamlet*, Harold Jenkins, ed. (London and New York: Methuen, 1982), 5.2.338.

2 Jonathan Goldberg, *Voice Terminal Echo: Postmodernism and English Renaissance Texts* (London and New York: Methuen, 1986), p. 99. Goldberg considers Hamlet's "I am dead" as something of the culmination of Hamlet's gradual movement toward an *identification* with the father: "Finally, he can, entirely, voice his father's text, speak as a ghost. 'I am dead,' he re-iterates, the impossible sentence that inscribes his voice within the iterability of writing. Like the ghost, Hamlet cannot tell his story, and passes it on to be told, a text to be re-enacted. 'The rest is silence.' Hamlet's remains" (p. 100).

3 Jacques Derrida, *Specters of Marx: The State of the Debt, the Work of Mourning, and the New International*, Peggy Kamuf, tr. (New York and London: Routledge, 1994). Hereafter cited as *Specters*.

4 Derrida discusses the possibility of "I am dead," and its status as enabling enunciation: "'I am dead' has a meaning if it is obviously false. 'I am dead' is an intelligible sentence. Therefore, 'I am dead' is not only a possible proposition for one who is known to be living, but the very condition for the living person to speak is for him to be able to say, significantly, 'I am dead.'" Jacques Derrida in Richard Macksey and Eugenio Donato, eds., *The Structuralist Controversy: The Languages of Criticism and the Science of Man* (Baltimore: Johns Hopkins University Press, 1970), p. 156.

5 Derrida continues, "Consequently, if there is no pure present, as tense of the pure *énonciation*, then the distinction between discursive time and historical time becomes fragile, perhaps. Historical time is already implied in the discursive time of the *énonciation*" (*The Structuralist Controversy*, 155).

6 Derrida further describes "hauntology" thus:

Repetition *and* first time, but also repetition *and* last time, since the singularity of any *first time* makes of it also a *last time*. Each time it is the event itself, a first time is a last time. Altogether other. Staging for the end of history. Let us call it *hauntology*. This logic of haunting would not be merely larger and more powerful than an ontology or a thinking of Being . . . It would harbor within itself, but like circumscribed places or particular effects, eschatology and teleology themselves. It would *comprehend* them, but incomprehensibly.

(*Specters* 10)

7 I place "properties" in quotation marks because, as Derrida remarks, the very notion of property is specious for both the "bodiless body of money" that Marx critiques, and for the ghost: "the ghost is a 'who,' it is not of the simulacrum in general, it has a kind of body, but without property, without 'real' or 'personal' right of property" (*Specters* 41–42).

8 The specter, Derrida argues, is "difficult to name: neither soul nor body, and both one and the other":

> what distinguishes the specter of the *revenant* from the *spirit*, including the spirit in the sense of the ghost in general, is doubtless a supernatural and paradoxical phenomenality, the furtive and ungraspable visibility of the invisible, or an invisibility of a visible X, that *non-sensuous sensuous* of which *Capital* speaks . . . it is also, no doubt, the tangible intangibility of a proper body without flesh, but still the body of some*one* as some*one other*. (*Specters* 6–7)

9 Derrida writes, "This spectral *someone other looks at us*, we feel ourselves being looked at by it, outside of any synchrony, even before and beyond any look on our part, according to an absolute anteriority . . . and asymmetry, according to an absolutely unmasterable disproportion. Here anachrony makes the law (*Specters* 7).

10 In a brief look at a number of French translations of Hamlet's critical assertion, "The time is out of joint," Derrida discusses Gide's "surprising" version: "Cette époque est déshonorée" ("This age is dishonored") – a translation that "gives an apparently more *ethical* or *political* meaning to this expression" than do most other translations: Bonnefoy's "Le temps est hors de ses gonds," Malaplate's "Le temps est détraqué," and Derocquigny's "Le monde est à l'envers," for example. But this ethical reading – this shift from "disadjusted" to "unjust" – is entirely apt for accessing the distinction between a disadjustment "with its rather more technico-ontological value affecting a presence" and an injustice "that would no longer be ontological" (*Specters* 19).

11 Roland Barthes, "The Discourse of History," Stephen Bann, tr., in E.S. Shaffer, ed. *Comparative Criticism: A Yearbook* 3 (Cambridge University Press, 1981), p. 17.

12 Derrida continues:

> One has to know . . . Now, to know is to know *who* and *where*, to know whose body it really is and what place it occupies – for it must stay in its place . . . Nothing could be worse, for the work of mourning, than confusion or doubt: one *has to know* who is buried where – and *it is necessary* (to know – to make certain) that, in what remains of him, *he remain there*. Let him stay there and move no more! (*Specters* 9)

13 Jean-François Lyotard, *The Postmodern Condition: A Report on Knowledge*, Geoff Bennington and Brian Massumi trs. (Minneapolis: University of Minnesota Press, 1984), p. xxiv.

14 See Hayden White, "The Value of Narrativity in the Representation of Reality," in *The Content of the Form: Narrative Discourse and Historical Representation* (Baltimore: Johns Hopkins University Press, 1987), pp. 1–25. See also, more generally, White's *Tropics of Discourse: Essays in Cultural Criticism* (Baltimore: Johns Hopkins University Press, 1978).

1 SHAKESPEARE'S *OTHELLO* AND VESALIUS'S *FABRICA*: ANATOMY, GENDER, AND THE NARRATIVE PRODUCTION OF MEANING

1 Hamlet, playing on an air/heir pun, confounds Claudius:

KING: How fares our cousin Hamlet?
HAMLET: Excellent, i' faith, of the chameleon's dish. I eat the air, promise-crammed
        – you cannot feed capons so.
KING: I have nothing with this answer, Hamlet. These words are not mine.
HAMLET: No, nor mine now.

William Shakespeare, *Hamlet*, Harold Jenkins, ed. (London and New York: Methuen, 1982), 3.2.92–97.

2 Sir Thomas Browne, *Pseudodoxia Epidemica*, Robin Robbins, ed. (Oxford: Clarendon Press, 1981), vol. I, p. 242. Hereafter cited as *PE*.

3 Tzvetan Todorov, *On Human Diversity: Nationalism, Racism, and Exoticism in French Thought*, Catherine Porter, tr. (Cambridge MA: Harvard University Press, 1993), p. 114.

4 See Michel Foucault, *Discipline and Punish: The Birth of the Prison*, Alan Sheridan, tr. (New York: Vintage, 1979).

5 Stanley Cavell, *Disowning Knowledge in Six Plays by Shakespeare* (Cambridge University Press, 1987), p. 126. Hereafter cited as Cavell.

6 I am thinking here primarily of the works of Michel Foucault, which in some general way are dedicated to tracing this "re-discovery" of "man":

Strangely enough, man – the study of whom is supposed by the naive to be the oldest investigation since Socrates – is probably no more than a kind of rift in the order of things, or, in any case, a configuration whose outlines are determined by the new position he has so recently taken up in the field of knowledge . . . It is comforting, however, and a source of profound relief to think that man is only a recent invention, a figure not yet two centuries old, a new wrinkle in our knowledge, and that he will disappear again as soon as that knowledge has discovered a new form.

Michel Foucault, *The Order of Things: An Archaeology of the Human Sciences* (New York: Vintage, 1973), p. xxiii.

7 Patricia Parker, "*Othello* and *Hamlet*: Dilation, Spying, and the 'Secret Place' of Women," in Russ McDonald, ed. *Shakespeare Reread: The Texts in New Contexts* (Ithaca: Cornell University Press, 1994), p. 106.

8 For Othello, Cavell asserts, conjugal love is, in the end, a matter of culpability: "The torture of logic in his mind we might represent as follows: Either I shed her blood and scarred her or I did not. If I did not then she was not a virgin and this is a stain upon me. If I did then she is no longer a virgin and this is a stain upon me. Either way I am contaminated" (Cavell 135).

9 For a discussion of ocularity and Renaissance theater, see Katharine Eisaman Maus, "Horns of the Dilemma: Jealousy, Gender, and Spectatorship in English Renaissance Drama," *English Literary History* 54 (1987), pp. 561–83.

10 Valerie Wayne, in her essay "Historical Differences: Misogyny and *Othello*," in Valerie Wayne, ed., *The Matter of Difference: Materialist Feminist Criticism of Shakespeare* (Ithaca: Cornell University Press, 1991), pp. 153–79, speaks to the

ways in which literary criticism of Renaissance texts depends, in large part, upon those dominant discourses we choose to privilege:

> While my focus will be on the play's allusions to the writing of texts in the Renaissance debate about women, and on the historically specific ideological positions and gender differences arising from it and from discourses on marriage, I want also to comment on how the discourses we privilege in relation to Renaissance texts inscribe the criticism we produce about them. (p. 154)

11 William Shakespeare, *Othello*, M.R. Ridley, ed. (London: Methuen, 1958), 3.3.400–2.
12 See Stephen Greenblatt's discussion of *Othello*, "The Improvisation of Power," in *Renaissance Self-Fashioning: From More to Shakespeare* (University of Chicago Press, 1980), pp. 222–54. See also Edward A. Snow, "Sexual Anxiety and the Male Order of Things in *Othello*," *English Literary Renaissance* 10 (1980), pp. 384–412.
13 For a discussion of narrative in *Othello* see Patricia Parker, "Shakespeare and Rhetoric: 'Dilation' and 'Delation' in *Othello*," in Patricia Parker and Geoffrey Hartman, eds., *Shakespeare and the Question of Theory* (New York: Methuen, 1985), pp. 54–74.
14 For a discussion of dismemberment as defensive male response to what is perceived as a threatening female presence, see Nancy J. Vickers, "Diana Described: Scattered Women, Scattered Rhyme," *Critical Inquiry* 8 (1981), pp. 265–79.
15 Othello's epistemology, as the rest of the play makes clear, is flawed, though not because of Desdemona's "offense" (which remains entirely fictive), but rather because of his own vulnerability to narrative.
16 This destruction does not remain for Othello exclusively epistemological but in fact initiates a corresponding collapse of Othello's ontological certainty. The speech which begins "I had been happy if the general camp,/ Pioners, and all, had tasted her sweet body,/ So I had nothing known" (3.3.351–53) and marks for Othello the end of his happiness ("Farewell the tranquil mind, Farewell content"), concludes with Othello's suspicion that the failure of his knowledge will result in the loss of his identity:

> Farewell the plumed troop, and the big wars,
> That makes ambition virtue: O farewell,
> Farewell the neighing steed, and the shrill trump,
> The spirit-stirring drum, the ear-piercing fife;
> The royal banner, and all quality,
> Pride, pomp, and circumstance of glorious war!
> And, O ye mortal engines, whose wide throats
> The immortal Jove's dread clamour counterfeit;
> Farewell, Othello's occupation's gone!   (3.3.355–63)

For a discussion of this speech and Othello's lost profession, see Mark Rose, "Othello's Occupation: Shakespeare and the Romance of Chivalry," *English Literary Renaissance* 15 (1985), pp. 293–311.
17 Kathleen McLuskie, *Renaissance Dramatists* (Atlantic Highlands: Humanities Press International, 1989), p. 154.
18 In his essay "Patriarchal Territories: The Body Enclosed," in Margaret W.

Ferguson, Maureen Quilligan, and Nancy J. Vickers, eds., *Rewriting the Renaissance: The Discourses of Sexual Difference in Early Modern Europe* (University of Chicago Press, 1986), pp. 123–42, Peter Stallybrass discusses the surveillance of women as focused on "mouth, chastity [and] the threshold of the house": "These three areas were frequently collapsed into each other . . . Silence, the closed mouth, is made a sign of chastity. And silence and chastity are, in turn, homologous to woman's enclosure within the house" (pp. 126–27).

19 The military metaphor is appropriate for Othello who seeks dominion as an expression of power. Othello's ambition, however, is not limited by this metaphor of conquest, but this metaphor indicates rather its larger scope: domination. For a discussion of this issue in Renaissance theater, see my "Desire and Domination in *Volpone*," *Studies in English Literature* 31 (1991), pp. 287–308.

20 Jean Howard, "Scripts and/versus Playhouses: Ideological Production and the Renaissance Public Stage," in Valerie Wayne, ed., *The Matter of Difference: Materialist Feminist Criticism of Shakespeare* (Ithaca: Cornell University Press, 1991), p. 224. Hereafter cited as Howard.

21 In "*Othello* and *Hamlet*," Parker contextualizes the "ocular" desires of the theater within a network of related practices:

The obsessively staged desire to see or spy out secrets, or in the absence of the directly ocular, to extract a narrative that might provide a vicarious substitute . . . implicates both "show" and "tell," eye and ear, in the broader sixteenth- and early seventeenth-century problem of testimony and report, the complexities of the relation between "ocular proof" and what in *Lear* is termed "auricular assurance" (1.2.92), a theatrical problem shared by the law courts and other contestatory sites of epistemological certainty and "evidence," of what might be reliably substituted for what could not be directly witnessed. (p. 143)

22 Ben Jonson, *Volpone, or The Fox*, Alvin Kernan, ed. (New Haven: Yale University Press, 1962).

23 These represent only two examples from a startlingly extensive list of theatrical representations or enactments of gendered violence against female characters. One could easily add many other plays in which this violence is central, including Heywood's *A Woman Killed With Kindness*, Chapman's *Bussy D'Ambois*, Webster's *The Duchess of Malfi*, and Shakespeare's *The Taming of the Shrew*. This list leaves aside the myriad plays which figure occasional and gratuitous violence. What strikes one, finally, is not only that such violence occurs, but rather the virtually systematic way in which the violence is executed in what we can perhaps call the theater of male desire.

24 Whether Desdemona and Othello have consummated their marriage is an issue frequently debated. My argument suggests that they have not, and offers a particular reading of the status of the ocular in the play to support this position.

25 Katharine Eisaman Maus, "Proof and Consequences: Inwardness and its Exposure in the English Renaissance," *Representations* 34 (1991), p. 31.

26 Maus cites recent critical and theoretical discussions of questions of subjectivity, especially the contention that "the psychological category of the inward or private hardly existed at all in Renaissance England" ("Proof and Consequences" 29), and that what we now call subjectivity was purely a social effect. However, Maus contends:

the fact that notions of subjectivity are socially constituted neither limits the extent of, nor determines the nature of, the power such notions can possess once they are culturally available. The pressures on thought and behavior exerted by commonly held conceptions of subjectivity are interesting in their own right, regardless of whether it is possible to show that at some level the assumptions upon which they are based are inadequate or misleading. In other words, the effects of a particular set of beliefs are not simply reducible to its causes. (p. 31)

For a more extended discussion of these issues, see Maus's book, *Inwardness and Theater in the English Renaissance* (University of Chicago Press, 1995).

27 Maus refers here to the argument about Hamlet offered by Francis Barker in *The Tremulous Private Body: Essays in Subjection* (London: Methuen, 1984).

28 This is certainly the case in Cavell's discussion of Desdemona and "the central sacrifice of romance":

Her virginity, her intactness, her perfection, had been gladly forgone by her for him, for the sake of their union, for the seaming of it. It is the sacrifice he could not accept, for then he was not himself perfect. It must be displaced. The scar is the mark of finitude, of separateness; it must be borne whatever one's anatomical condition, or color. It is the sin or the sign of refusing imperfection that produces, or justifies, the visions and torments of devils that inhabit the region of this play. (Cavell 137)

29 Jonathan Sawday, *The Body Emblazoned: Dissection and the Human Body in Renaissance Culture* (New York: Routledge, 1995), pp. 2–3.

30 Sawday argues that the Cartesian conception of the mechanical body arises directly out of the (prior) geographical conception, and does so through the notion of property:

Intrinsic to [the geographical–anatomical] project was the creation of the body's interior as a form of property. Like property, the body's bounds needed to be fixed, its dimensions properly measured, its resources charted. Its "new" owner – which would eventually become the thinking process of the Cartesian *cogito* – had to know what it was that was owned before use could be made of it. (*Body Emblazoned* 26).

I return to this question of the Cartesian notion of one's *ownership* of one's body in the final chapter of this book.

31 For a discussion of Vesalius see (in addition to Sawday's book): Jonathan Sawday, "The Fate of Marsyas: Dissecting the Renaissance Body," in Lucy Gent and Nigel Llewellyn, eds., *Renaissance Bodies: The Human Figure in English Culture, c. 1540–1660* (London: Reakton, 1990), pp. 111–35; Thomas Laqueur, *Making Sex: Body and Gender from the Greeks to Freud* (Cambridge, MA: Harvard University Press, 1990); Glenn Harcourt, "Andreas Vesalius and the Anatomy of Antique Sculpture," *Representations* 17 (1987), pp. 28–61; Luke Wilson, "William Harvey's *Prelectiones*: The Performance of the Body in the Renaissance Theater of Anatomy," *Representations* 17 (1987), pp. 62–95; Devon Hodges, *Renaissance Fictions of Anatomy* (Amherst: University of Massachusetts Press, 1985).

32 Barker, *The Tremulous Private Body*, pp. 73–85.

33 For a discussion of Bacon and "scientific anatomy" see Hodges, *Fictions of Anatomy*, pp. 89–106.

34 C.D. O'Malley, *Andreas Vesalius of Brussels, 1514–1564* (Berkeley: University of California Press, 1964), p. 320. Hereafter cited as O'Malley.

35 The identity of the artist(s) responsible for the illustrations remains a mystery. For a discussion of possible candidates see J.B. de C.M. Saunders and C.D. O'Malley, *The Illustrations from the Works of Andreas Vesalius of Brussels* (Cleveland: World Publishing, 1950).

36 Emily Martin, "Science and Women's Bodies: Forms of Anthropological Knowledge," in Mary Jacobus, Evelyn Fox Keller, and Sally Shuttleworth, eds., *Body/Politics: Women and the Discourses of Science* (New York: Routledge, 1990), p. 69.

37 Johannes Fabian, *Time and the Other: How Anthropology Makes its Object* (New York: Columbia University Press, 1983), p. 106, quoted in Martin, "Science and Women's Bodies," p. 69.

38 Vesalius's anatomy is teleological not only in its narratological imperative, but in its emphasis upon the *purpose* of structure:

> In man . . . the entire eye of necessity had to be soft and could not be placed on a long process without danger. Therefore, since it was inappropriate to place the human eyes at a lower level because of their function, and not fitting to attach them by naked necks, because nature did not wish to prevent their use nor endanger their security she created an elevated position and so neatly protected them from danger . . . The nose was erected as a wall for the parts . . . the eyes are hedged about on all sides by raised and extruding parts and advantageously lie hidden in a depressed valley. (O'Malley 152)

O'Malley comments on the teleological nature of Vesalius's belief that "structure of man had been . . . fashioned for an ultimate purpose." O'Malley continues,

> [This] was by no means a new proposal since it is to be found in Aristotle, Galen and the medieval anatomists, but where Vesalius's predecessors might have been content with the final cause, illustrative of God's purpose, and from that deduced – or failed to deduce – the structure, Vesalius, on the other hand, began by studying the anatomical structure as the key to purpose. (O'Malley 150)

39 For a discussion of this image see Laqueur, *Making Sex*, pp. 70–88 and Sawday, *Body Emblazoned*, pp. 221–22.

40 The two statutes governing public anatomies that are reproduced in part in O'Malley (pp. 199 and 451) require that the subjects for dissection be obtained from the state in the form of executed criminals, though this stipulation, by Vesalius's own account, was not rigorously observed or enforced; Vesalius tells tales of the stealing of dead bodies from the gibbet, of rummaging through Paris's Cemetery of the Innocents, and of similar exploits asked of his students.

41 It is important to note that even as the actual anatomies existed exclusively within a male (scientific) community, Vesalius imagined his books to participate in an analogous male economy of influence. The *Epitome* was dedicated to Philip II of Spain and the *Fabrica* to Philip's father, Charles V. In his letter to Charles that prefaces the *Fabrica*, Vesalius alludes to this male economy that obtains among fathers, sons, and their books:

> I came to this conclusion [Charles's certain interest in anatomy and the *Fabrica*] for many reasons, but I first conjectured it because among the large number of books dedicated to

your grandfather of happy memory, the great Emperor of the Romans Maximilian, none was ever more pleasing than a little book on the present subject. Nor shall I ever forget with what pleasure you examined my *Tabulae anatomicae*, once presented for you inspection by my father Andreas, chief and most faithful apothecary of your Majesty, and how carefully you inquired about each thing. (O'Malley 323–24)

42 Vesalius's anatomies of male bodies were performed not only on the bodies of executed criminals, though this was largely the case, but they were also performed on the bodies of men from the opposite end of the social and political spectrum: various nobles, as well as Henry II. Vesalius was called to the side of the King after his jousting injury, which he did not survive, and upon his death performed (in some fashion) a pathological anatomy (O'Malley 396–98).

43 Freud's *Fragment of an Analysis of a Case of Hysteria* (*The Standard Edition of the Complete Psychological Works of Sigmund Freud*, James Strachey *et al*. ed. and tr., 24 vols. [London: Hogarth Press, 1953–74], vol. III) is the example *par excellence*.

44 John Ford, *'Tis Pity She's a Whore*, Brian Morris, ed. (London: Ernest Benn and New York: W.W. Norton, 1968), 4.3.53–58.

2 (DIS)EMBODIED LETTERS AND *THE MERCHANT OF VENICE*: WRITING, EDITING, HISTORY

1 McGann offers the following extended definition:

> Both the practice and the study of human culture comprise a network of symbolic exchanges. Because human beings are not angels, these exchanges always involve material negotiations. Even in their most complex and advanced forms – when the negotiations are carried out as textual events – the intercourse that is being human is materially executed: as spoken texts or scripted forms. To participate in these exchanges is to have entered what I wish to call here "the textual condition."

Jerome McGann, *The Textual Condition* (Princeton University Press, 1991), p. 3.

2 Jerome McGann, *A Critique of Modern Textual Criticism* (University of Chicago Press, 1983; rpt. Charlottesville: University of Virginia Press, 1992), p. 11.

3 The growing list of such works is extensive; what follows is not intended to be complete, but rather suggestive of the range and depth of this work: W. Speed Hill, ed., *New Ways of Looking at Old Texts: Papers of the Renaissance English Text Society, 1985–1991* (Binghamton: Medieval and Renaissance Texts and Studies, 1993); Margreta De Grazia and Peter Stallybrass, "The Materiality of the Shakespearean Text," *Shakespeare Quarterly* 44 (1993), pp. 255–83; Stephen Orgel, "The Poetics of Incomprehensibility," *Shakespeare Quarterly* 42 (1991), pp. 431–37; Leah S. Marcus, *Puzzling Shakespeare: Local Reading and its Discontents* (Berkeley: University of California Press, 1988); Paul Werstine, "Narratives About Printed Shakespearean Texts: 'Foul Papers' and 'Bad' Quartos," *Shakespeare Quarterly* 41 (1990), pp. 65–86; Marion Trousdale, "A Second Look at Critical Bibliography and the Acting of Plays," *Shakespeare Quarterly* 41 (1990), pp. 87–96; Randall McLeod (Random Cloud), "'The very names of the Persons': Editing and the Invention of Dramatik Character," in

David Scott Kastan and Peter Stallybrass, eds., *Staging the Renaissance: Reinterpretations of Elizabethan and Jacobean Drama* (New York: Routledge, 1991), pp. 88–96; Margreta De Grazia, *Shakespeare Verbatim: The Reproduction of Authenticity and the 1790 Apparatus* (Oxford: Clarendon Press, 1991). See also the important critical work by Steven Urkowitz, Michael Warren, Gary Taylor, and Stanley Wells.

4 For theoretical and practical discussions of "unediting," see Randall McLeod, "UnEditing Shakespeare," *Sub-Stance*, 33/34 (1982), pp. 26–55, and Leah S. Marcus, "Textual Indeterminacy and Ideological Difference: The Case of *Doctor Faustus*," *Renaissance Drama* n.s. 20 (1989), pp. 1–29. Hereafter cited as Marcus.

5 Marcus writes, "[T]he A text could be described as more nationalist and more Calvinist, Puritan, or ultra-Protestant, the B text as more internationalist, imperial, and Anglican, or Anglo-Catholic – but each version places the magician at the extreme edge of transgression in terms of its own implied system of values" (p. 5).

6 Marcus discusses these revisions:

> The 1602 revisions worked to keep *Doctor Faustus* on the thrilling/unnerving edge of transgression by inscribing the play with a new set of national priorities and anxieties. A theatrical company and its hired "hack" writers transformed what was then extant as "Marlowe" in order to keep the "Marlowe effect" alive, to keep Marlowe sounding like himself even decades after his physical demise. In the curious case of *Doctor Faustus*, non-authorial revision functioned to heighten, not to destroy, an aura of authorial "authenticity" in the theater. ("Textual Indeterminancy" 15)

7 Jonathan Goldberg, "Textual Properties," *Shakespeare Quarterly* 37 (1986), p. 214. Goldberg continues, "The historicity of the text means that there is no text itself; it means that a text cannot be fixed in terms of original or final intentions. At best, Shakespearean practice authorizes the dispersal of authorial intention" (p. 214). De Grazia and Stallybrass also discuss the illusory nature of the "original":

> Return to the early texts provides no access to a privileged "original"; on the contrary, for the modern reader it bars access. The features that modernization and emendation smooth away remain stubbornly in place to block the illusion of transparency – the impression that there is some ideal "original" behind the text. ("Materiality" 256)

8 Elizabeth Pittenger, "Dispatch Quickly: The Mechanical Reproduction of Pages," *Shakespeare Quarterly* 42 (1991), p. 399. Hereafter cited as Pittenger.

9 Goldberg discusses the Shakespearean text in which, now, "no word . . . is sacred." Moreover, he continues, with this "radical instability" of the Shakespearean text, "all criticism that has based itself on the text, all forms of formalism, all close reading, is given the lie" ("Textual Properties" 215).

10 One especially significant trend in traditional textual criticism that participates in the overall desire to elucidate texts – even, and perhaps, especially – in their moments of obscurity is the desire to offer (editorially constructed) clarity. In "The Poetics of Incomprehensibility" Stephen Orgel cautions against the allegedly "common sense" of such intervention:

> What does it mean that a drama speaks incomprehensibly? Even if we were persuaded that we had successfully elucidated all the play's obscurities, no actor can speak meaning rather

than words, and no audience, least of all Shakespeare's . . . comes supplied with the necessary glosses. Of course, we assume we are, by elucidating, recovering meaning, not imposing it; but is this assumption really defensible? How do we know that the obscurity of the text was not in fact precisely what it expressed to the Renaissance audience? Is meaning, in any case, a transhistorical phenomenon?. . . there is nothing common about common sense; it is as culturally specific as anything else in our intellectual lives. Renaissance strategies of interpretation call into question our axiomatic assumption that a plain prose paraphrase is the bottom line in unlocking the mysteries of the occluded text. ("Incomprehensibility" 434)

11 William Shakespeare, *The Merchant of Venice*, John Russell Brown, ed. (London: Methuen, 1955).

12 Jonathan Goldberg, *Writing Matter: From the Hands of the English Renaissance* (Stanford University Press, 1990), p. 78.

13 The phrase "Hayes Quarto" refers to the earliest text of *Merchant*, dated 1600. This quarto was printed by James Robert, who two years previously had entered the play under his name in the Stationers' Register. Roberts evidently transferred his rights to the play to Thomas Hayes in 1600 and printed the quarto for him. For further discussion of Roberts and Hayes and the 1600 printing of *Merchant*, see John Russell Brown's discussion in his Arden edition of the play.

14 William Shakespeare, *The Merchant of Venice*, John Dover Wilson, ed. (Cambridge University Press, 1926), p. 97. Subsequent references to Wilson appear parenthetically.

15 William Shakespeare, *The Merchant of Venice, 1600*, Shakespeare Quarto Facsimiles, vol. II (Oxford: Clarendon Press, 1957), 3.2.316–25.

16 There are two further differences between the modern and the Quarto versions of the letter and its physical/material presentation: in our modern editions we are accustomed to the addition of two linguistic items not found in the Quarto text: the parentheses around "since in paying it, it is impossible I should live," and the insertion of a comma after the phrase "all debts are cleared between you and I." In the first instance, the addition of the parentheses serves to make Antonio's recognition of the cost of the forfeiture subordinate to the act of forgiveness within which it occurs, a highly intrusive editorial decision that alters the sense of the passage. As punctuated in the Quarto, the passage makes perfect sense, though not the sense we have ascribed to it (or to Antonio, for that matter) in our modern editions. The letter may well want to register linguistically the equivalence of Antonio's death and Bassanio's debts; the subordinating effect of the parentheses suppresses such a reading. In the second instance – the instance of the comma – the Quarto's syntax makes rather explicit that there is a causal relationship between the forgiveness of the debt and Bassanio's appearance at Antonio's death: the former is more explicitly conditional upon the latter. The editorial addition of the comma serves to mitigate the force of Antonio's determination. Again, such an editorial decision is intrusive and revises the sense of the letter.

17 Jonathan Goldberg, "Hamlet's Hand," *Shakespeare Quarterly* 39 (1988), p. 324.

18 This is the same sort of faith in (bodily) immanence I traced in the anatomical works of Andreas Vesalius in chapter 1. In addition to the present chapter's discussion of immanence and textual production, I turn in chapter 5 to considerations of this idea in both *Hamlet* and Sir Thomas Browne's *Hydriotaphia*.

19 This is the same faith that can be said to under-write drama as a genre: a belief in presence-in-writing is given the extraordinary dimension and expression in the representational embodiments of characters in the figures of the actors who portray them on stage before our very eyes. Drama is, perhaps, the expression of the metaphysics of writing *par excellence.*

20 Freud's essay begins by reading the caskets as symbols for women: if the scene of the three caskets from *Merchant* appeared in a dream, Freud says, "it would at once occur to us that caskets are also women, symbols of the essential thing in woman, and therefore of a woman herself, like boxes, large or small, baskets, and so on" ("The Theme of the Three Caskets," in *Sigmund Freud: The Collected Papers* 4 vols., Joan Riviere, tr., Ernst Jones, ed. [New York: Basic Books, 1959], vol. IV, pp. 245–46). Then, by way of a circuitous path through various national mythologies, folk-tales, and *King Lear*, Freud arrives at his perhaps predictable conclusion that the theme of the three caskets allegorically represents "the three inevitable relations man has with woman": "that with the mother who bears him, with the companion of his bed and board, and with the destroyer. Or it is the three forms taken on by the figure of the mother as life proceeds: the mother herself, the beloved who is chosen after her pattern, and finally the Mother Earth who receives him again" (p. 256).

21 In a discussion of letters and their circulation in Shakespearean texts, "Shakespearean Inscriptions: The Voicing of Power," in Patricia Parker and Geoffrey Hartman, eds., *Shakespeare and the Question of Theory* (New York and London: Methuen, 1985), pp. 116–37, Jonathan Goldberg argues that Portia's position in court and her ultimate success there – and in the fifth-act drama of the ring – depend upon the sheer impossibility of the "self-sameness" of the letter:

> The "turn" that Portia takes calls into question the differences upon which the play rests, male and female, Jew and Christian, letter and spirit, for the lewdness of the play that she initiates – sending the letter and donning the disguise (the device) – rests upon equivocations within the letter, differences within the self-same. Portia's "whole device" involves filling a place – the place of Bellario, the place of the law – through an act of replacement that calls into question the possibility of duplication (the repeatability and self-sameness upon which the law rests). (p. 122)

22 This reversal also manifests the play's fundamental dependence upon Christian historiography that posits two related phases of post-lapsarian history – the Mosaic or Old Testament articulation of life under the law, and the New Testament life of the spirit. In this processive vision of history, the Christian progresses from the first phase to the second in a movement that is suggested by Christ's example and guaranteed by virtue of the spirit's redemption of the law and its letter. Portia leads the Christians of the play in this progress toward redemption and salvation while Shylock, on the other hand, is its clear victim.

23 Portia's and Nerissa's taunting of Bassanio and Gratiano over the matter of the rings has special significance as well, in part because their laughter – and their husbands' initial consternation – are explicitly linked to the politics of embodiment and textuality. Portia can assure Bassanio that she will welcome the doctor to her bed ("Know him I shall, I am well sure of it" [5.1.229]) because of her embodiment as both "herself" and as "the doctor." In fact, the moment Portia

produces the ring – "I had it of him: pardon me Bassanio,/ For by this ring the doctor lay with me" (5.1.258–59) – she stands, as it were, as both herself and the doctor. This "crisis" is averted not simply with Portia's announcement that she was the doctor and Nerissa the clerk, but only when she produces the letter as evidence:

> you are all amazed;
> Here is a letter, read it at your leisure, –
> It comes from Padua from Bellario, –
> There you shall find that Portia was the doctor,
> Nerissa there the clerk.   (5.1.266–70)

24 William Shakespeare, *The Merchant of Venice*, M.M. Mahood, ed. (Cambridge University Press, 1987), p. 56. Hereafter cited as Mahood.

25 Jonathan Goldberg discusses a similar manifestation of logocentrism in Shakespeare's second tetralogy: "the subsequent plays are haunted too by what is put on deposit in the deposition scene [of *Richard II*]: the alliance of kingship with the repression of textuality, and the ways in which the play both supports that logocentrism and undermines it" ("Rebel Letters: Postal Effects from *Richard II* to *Henry IV*," *Renaissance Drama* n.s. 19 [1988], p. 10).

26 It is worthwhile noting that in the 1939 Clark Lectures at Trinity College, Cambridge (later published as *The Editorial Problem in Shakespeare: A Survey of the Foundations of the Text*, 2nd edn. [Oxford: Clarendon Press, 1951]), Greg rejects both the conclusions drawn by Dover Wilson on the textual genealogy of *Merchant* and its production from assembled prompt-book, and his own evident participation in the argument:

I do not regard the presentation of the prompt-book for registration [in the Stationers' Register] as involving its use as copy. Like Chambers "I see no clear reason why the copy used . . . should not have been in Shakespeare's hand" – and foul papers at that, at least in the technical sense, for the text is remarkably good . . . A prompt copy would surely have straightened out the tangle of ambiguous prefixes that according to Wilson led to the creation of a ghost character in Salarino. *It appears that I once argued that a passage at the foot of sig. I2 was an insertion probably written on a separate piece of paper.* Wilson and Chambers allow the possibility: but the addition might have been made in foul papers as easily as in the prompt-book. (p. 123, my emphasis)

27 In Goldberg's discussion of the important textual crux in *1 Henry IV* regarding the identity of the character that actually reads aloud the paper taken from the sleeping Falstaff's pocket, he discerns a similar class-based agenda on the part of traditional textual critics:

Dover Wilson and Bowers indulge fantasies about restoring Shakespeare's lost original text . . . Bower's elaborate argument about stage history and its role in shaping Q1 is quite clearly bent on saving Hal from being sullied with low companions like Peto . . . The Petos of the world, Bowers insists, cannot read without being risible. Shakespeare cannot originally have wanted the Prince to have ended the scene in his company. Modern editors, on the whole, are willing enough to leave Peto there, and reading, as he does in F1; but they, too, share similar suppositions. The Prince must not read. And perhaps the editorial emendation in F1 is the result of the ideological construction of scenes of reading in the play; rebels read, but royalty do not. ("Rebel Letters" 23)

28 Terence Hawkes, "Telmah," in Patricia Parker and Geoffrey Hartman, eds., *Shakespeare and the Question of Theory* (New York and London: Methuen, 1985). Hereafter cited as Hawkes. Hawkes identifies Dover Wilson's political conservatism in his renunciation of the Bolsheviks and his explicit endorsement of Tsarism in the article, "Russia and Her Ideals":

> [Autocracy] still has a long life before it and much work to perform in Russia. It is therefore wiser to face the facts and to recognize that the Tsardom is after all Russia's form of democracy . . . it is the kind of government the people understand and reverence, and it is their only protection against the tyranny of an aristocratic clique . . . when the will of the autocrat is clearly and unmistakably expressed, it has always been found to correspond with the needs of the people.

John Dover Wilson, "Russia and Her Ideals," *The Round Table* 5. 17 (1914), pp. 103–35, quoted in Hawkes, 323.

29 Hawkes offers the curtain call – "that complex of revisionary ironies" – as yet another theatrical practice that marks the emergence of the counter-current of recursive movement:

> Here [in the curtain call] . . . any apparent movement in one direction of the play halts, and it begins to roll decisively in the opposite direction (if only towards the next performance, when its "beginning" will emerge from these smiling actors). In short, the sense of straight, purposive, linear motion forward through the play – the sense required by most "interpretations" of it – evaporates at the curtain call, and we sense an opposing current.
>
> (p. 313)

30 Jacques Derrida, *Specters of Marx: The State of the Debt, the Work of Mourning, and the New International*, Peggy Kamuf, tr. (New York and London: Routledge, 1994), p. 28.

3 POLITICAL MAPS: THE PRODUCTION OF CARTOGRAPHY IN EARLY MODERN ENGLAND

1 For an insightful and thorough discussion of the history of the study of cartography, see J.B. Harley, "The Map and the Development of the History of Cartography," in J.B. Harley and David Woodward, eds., *The History of Cartography*, vol. I: *Cartography in Prehistoric, Ancient, and Medieval Europe and the Mediterranean* (University of Chicago Press, 1987), pp. 1–42.

2 J.B. Harley, "*Imago Mundi*: The First Fifty Years and the Next Ten," *Cartographica* 23.3 (1986), p. 1.

3 Denis Wood and John Fels, "Designs on Signs: Myth and Meaning in Maps," *Cartographica* 23.3 (1986), p. 65.

4 Denis Wood, with John Fels, *The Power of Maps* (New York: Guilford Press, 1992), p. 19.

5 J.B. Harley, "Silences and Secrecy: The Hidden Agenda of Cartography in Early Modern Europe," *Imago Mundi* 40 (1988), p. 57.

6 The interpretive model Harley suggests is of course a familiar one in a number of disciplines, particularly in literary and cultural criticism. What Harley proposes we do for maps – read them, finally, as texts and as artifacts of cultural practices – is precisely the "innovation" we find in new historicist, cultural

materialist, and feminist–materialist criticism of rich varieties of cultural practices. I want to stress that by identifying these critical and theoretical discourses
as similarly constituted *vis-à-vis* cultural practices and cultural artifacts I am
certainly not suggesting that they are in any way necessarily monological in their
philosophical or political approaches, nor that there are not frequently extreme
differences either in approach or objective or both. Such assertions are not only
insensitive, but misconstrue divergent practices as inevitably identical.

7 John Donne, "Hymn to God my God, in my sickness," in *John Donne*, John
Carey, ed. (Oxford University Press, 1990), pp. 332–33.

8 The microcosm/macrocosm conceit is integral to a wide range of Donne's poetry
and prose. See, for example, the fourth Meditation from his *Devotions Upon
Emergent Occasions* (Anthony Raspa, ed. [Oxford University Press, 1987]):

> It is too little to call *Man a little World*; Except *God*, Man is a *diminutive* to nothing. Man
> consistes of more pieces, more parts, then the world; then the world doeth, nay then the
> world is. And if those pieces were extended, and stretched out in Man, as they are in the
> world, Man would bee the *Gyant*, and the world the *Dwarfe*, the world but the *Map*, and
> the Man the *World*. (p. 19)

For an influential study of this issue in the tradition of Renaissance philosophy,
see Ernst Cassirer, *The Individual and the Cosmos in Renaissance Philosophy*,
Mario Domandi, ed. and tr. (New York: Barnes and Noble, 1963). See also
Leonard Barkan, *Nature's Work of Art: The Human Body as Image of the World*
(New Haven: Yale University Press, 1975).

9 For discussions of early Christian allegorical maps, see Arno Peters, *The New
Cartography*, Ward Kaiser, D.G. Smith, and Heinz Wohlers, trs. (New York:
Friendship Press, 1983), pp. 9–49; and David Woodward, "Medieval
Mappaemundi," in Harley and Woodward eds., *History of Cartography*, pp.
286–370. For detailed discussions of the science and mathematics of projection,
see Peters, *New Cartography* pp. 20–27, and pp. 105–48.

10 Peters discusses the heliocentric universe as well as the spherical earth theories
of the ancient Greeks, pp. 16–24.

11 For studies of Donne and his relationship to astronomy see A.J. Meadows, *The
High Firmament: A Survey of Astronomy in English Literature* (University of
Leicester Press, 1969) and R. Chris Hassel, Jr., "Donne's *Ignatius His Conclave*
and the New Astronomy," *Modern Philology* 68 (1971), pp. 329–37.

12 John Donne, *Ignatius His Conclave*, T.S. Healy, ed. (Oxford University Press,
1969), p. 9.

13 Donne concludes *Ignatius* by having Lucifer decide that Ignatius is indeed
nearest him in evil, but that Hell cannot be shared. Lucifer strikes upon an alternative resolution: he will enlist the Pope's aid in causing "*Galilaeo* the
Florentine" to "draw the *Moone*, like a boate floating upon the water, as neere
the earth as he will." Once near enough

> thither (because they ever claime that those imployments of discovery belong to them)
> shall all the Jesuites bee transferred, and easily unite and reconcile the *Lunatique Church*
> to the *Romane Church*; without doubt, after the Jesuites have been there a little while, there
> will soone grow naturally a *Hell* in that world also: over which, you *Ignatius* shall have
> dominion. (*Ignatius* 81)

14 Donne's references to and use of cosmology and cartography are numerous; see, for example, "The Good Morrow," "Good Friday, 1613. Riding Westward," "An Anatomy of the World: The First Anniversary," and "Of the Progress of the Soul: The Second Anniversary."

15 Frank Lestringant, *Mapping the Renaissance World: The Geographical Imagination in the Age of Discovery*, David Fausett tr. (Berkeley: University of California Press, 1994), p. 12. Hereafter cited as Lestringant.

16 André Thevet. *Cosmographie universelle* (Paris, 1584); quoted in Lestringant, p. 29.

17 In "Deconstructing the Map" (*Cartographica* 26 [1989], pp. 1–20) Harley describes the nature of the "scientific nature" of the cartographic enterprise and the cartographic epistemology:

From at least the seventeenth century onward, European mapmakers and map users have increasingly promoted a standard scientific model of knowledge and cognition. The object of mapping is to produce a "correct" relational model of the terrain. Its assumptions are that the objects in the world to be mapped are real and objective, and that they enjoy an existence independent of the cartographer; that their reality can be expressed in mathematical terms; that systematic observation and measurement offer the only route to cartographic truth; and that this truth can be independently verified. The procedures of both surveying and map construction came to share strategies similar to those in science in general: cartography also documents a history of more precise instrumentation and measurement; increasingly complex classifications of its knowledge and a proliferation of signs for its representation. ("Deconstructing the Map" 4)

18 Jean Baudrillard, *Simulations*, Paul Foss, Paul Patton, and Philip Beitchman, trs. (New York: Semiotext(e), 1983), p. 2.

19 For another discussion of Donne's poem and its relation to cosmography/cartography, see John Gillies, *Shakespeare and the Geography of Difference* (Cambridge University Press, 1994), pp. 182–88. This poem, Gillies argues, offers compelling proof that the New Geography was entirely receptive to a kind of poetic figurative play available to cartographers and poets alike:

The role of the engraver of this map [Claes Janszoon Visscher's world map of 1617] is far more than that of a mere transcriber or copyist of established formulae. It is closer to the role of the Renaissance artist who creates surprise out of stereotype and new architectures from available repertoires. Ultimately, the difference between the poetic map-maker and the cartographic poet is less important than their similarity. (p. 182)

20 Victor Morgan, "The Cartographic Image of 'The Country' in Early Modern England," *Transactions of the Royal Historical Society*, 5th ser., 29 (1979), p. 138.

21 Denis Wood, "Pleasure in the Idea: The Atlas as Narrative Form," *Cartographica* 24.1 (1987), p. 29.

22 The first chapter of *The Power of Maps*, titled "Maps Work by Serving Interests," is dedicated to the careful articulation of the ways in which all maps – in part, by virtue of being embedded within semiotic systems, which (following Barthes) are always at the same time *value* systems – are by their very nature in the service of a particular set (or of particular sets) of interests.

23 For important studies of chorography, see Lesley B. Cormack, "'Good Fences

Make Good Neighbors': Geography as Self-Definition in Early Modern England," *Isis* 82 (1991), pp. 639–61; Stan A.E. Mendyk, *"Speculum Britanniae": Regional Study, Antiquarianism, and Science in Britain to 1700* (University of Toronto Press, 1989); Stuart Piggott, *Ancient Britons and the Antiquarian Imagination: Ideas from the Renaissance to the Regency* (New York: Thames and Hudson, 1989); Stuart Piggott, *Ruins in a Landscape: Essays in Antiquarianism* (Edinburgh University Press, 1976). See also Joseph M. Levine, "The Antiquarian Enterprise, 1500–1800," in his study, *Humanism and History: Origins of Modern English Historiography* (Ithaca: Cornell University Press, 1987). For an insightful discussion of "conceptual cartography" and colonialism in early modern English attempts to subjugate Ireland, see David J. Baker, "Off the Map: Charting Uncertainty in Renaissance Ireland," in Brendan Bradshaw, Andrew Hadfield and Willy Maley eds., *Representing Ireland: Literature and the Origins of Conflict, 1534–1660* (Cambridge University Press, 1993), pp. 76–92.

24 Cormack ("Fences" 656).

25 *Leland's Itinerary in England and Wales*, Lucy Toulmin Smith, ed., 3 vols. (London: George Bell, 1907), vol. I, p. xxxvii. Hereafter cited as Leland.

26 Camden's *Britannia* went through seven editions in his lifetime, the first (in Latin) in 1586, the last (and the first in English) in 1610, and was republished (much enlarged) by Edmund Gibson in 1695. For this discussion I use the last edition, *Camden's Britannia, 1695* (New York and London: Johnson Reprint, 1971).

27 For a discussion of Christopher Saxton and the production of his atlas, see Ifor M. Evans and Heather Lawrence, eds., *Christopher Saxton: Elizabethan Map-Maker* (Wakefield and London: Wakefield Historical Publications and the Holland Press, 1979).

28 Richard Helgerson, "The Land Speaks: Cartography, Chorography, and Subversion in Renaissance England," in Stephen Greenblatt, ed., *Representing the English Renaissance* (Berkeley: University of California Press, 1988), pp. 327–61. Helgerson offers a brilliant discussion of the complicated ways in which cartography and chorography initially participate in the monarchical attempts to centralize governmental authority, but subsequently subvert these attempts. He focuses on a number of instances of this change, including the eventual disappearance of signs of the monarchy and the patron printed on Saxton's map, and their replacement by Saxton's own name: "In these small changes we can . . . discern the trace of a momentous transfer of cultural authority from the patron and the royal system of government of which patronage was an integral part to the individual maker" (p. 330). Helgerson reprints this article as a chapter in his book, *Forms of Nationhood: The Elizabethan Writing of England* (University of Chicago Press, 1992).

29 For Drayton, one of the most significant historical tales he wishes to tell is the history of the figure of Brutus – the (legendary) ancient figure, descendent of Aeneas, whose story serves to establish an ancient heritage for Britons.

30 *Britannia* (1695 edn.), D2ᵛ.

31 Helgerson comments on Camden's sense of *personal* accomplishment and – even more importantly – personal authority ("The Land Speaks" 343–44).

32 In *Portrait of the King* (Martha M. Houle, tr. [Minneapolis: University of

Minnesota Press, 1988]), Louis Marin discusses another of the central operations of cartography: the production of the point of view from which the land is seen and the map thus produced:

Henceforth, on [the] outspread map, truth *reigns* and, with it, the real, suddenly . . . clear and distinct in its representation: the truth of rational knowledge and the whims and fantasies of the imaginary. All the singular routes, their stages and stopping points and crossing points, and all the particular places and the relationships that link them to one another – fortuitous and accidental when a concrete individual occupies, traverses, and traces them – find their ordered arrangement and their true marks through the art and usage of the instrument of science. And what the theoretical eye contemplates is none other than reality itself, which the sensory eye has never seen. (p. 172)

33 John Norden, *Surveiors Dialogue* (London, 1618, rpt. Amsterdam: Theatrum Orbis Terrarum, 1979), pp. 2–3.

34 In this regard, Norden's book is similar to an earlier text to which Norden acknowledges an indebtedness: Valentine Leigh, *The Moste Profitable and Commendable Science, of Surveying of Lands, Tenementes, and Hereditamentes* (London, 1577).

35 For a discussion of Norden's *Speculum Britanniae* see Mendyk (*Regional Study* 57–81).

36 Helgerson prints a transcription of a letter from Norden to Elizabeth, written on the flyleaf of his presentation copy of the second installment of his *Speculum Britanniae*, requesting her support for his research ("The Land Speaks" 341–42).

37 Johannes Fabian, *Time and the Other: How Anthropology Makes its Object* (New York: Columbia University Press, 1983), p. 106.

38 Harley relates this notion of cartographic progression to an underlying faith in science, even though, he suggests, in "'plain' scientific maps, science itself becomes the metaphor":

Such maps contain a dimension of "symbolic realism" which is no less a statement of political authority and control than a coat-of-arms or a portrait of a queen . . . The metaphor has changed. The map has attempted to purge itself of ambiguity and alternative possibility. Accuracy and austerity of design are now the new talismans of authority culminating in our own age with computer mapping. ("Deconstructing the Map" 10)

39 This is not to suggest that Camden's and Drayton's historical ambitions or sentiments were identical; Drayton was heavily invested in the story of Brutus, for example, while Camden rejected the story out of hand as purely mythological.

40 One of the most striking instances of the narratological nature of cartography is Norden's *England: An Intended Guyde For English Travailers* (London, 1625; Johnson Reprint, Amsterdam: Theatrum Orbis Terrarum, 1979). While from the title one may well expect a prototypic "travel book," what the book offers instead is an extended series of mileage tables showing the distances between cities and towns within a given shire. The entire book is made up of these charts; the only prose that appears in the book (in addition to a prefatory letter and a brief note appended to the pages devoted to Lancashire and Lincolnshire explaining the effects of water-travel on the calculation of distances) is the "legend" explaining "the use of this table" which is in fact reproduced verbatim

on every page of the book (and only slightly expanded in the instance of Yorkshire, again due to inaccuracies in distance calculations occasioned by water-travel).

41 In his chorographical–philosophical travel book *America* (Chris Turner, tr. [London and New York: Verso, 1988]), Jean Baudrillard discusses the American freeway system and its effects:

> Gigantic, spontaneous spectacle of automotive traffic. A total collective act, staged by the entire population, twenty-four hours a day . . . Unlike our European motorways, which are unique, directional axes, and are therefore still places of expulsion (Virilio), the freeway system is a place of integration . . . their signs read like a litany. "Right lane must exit." This "must exit" has always struck me as a sign of destiny. I have got to go, to expel myself from this paradise, leave this providential highway which leads nowhere, but keeps me in touch with everyone. This is the only real society or warmth here, this collective propulsion, this compulsion – a compulsion of lemmings plunging suicidally together . . . At every hour of the day approximately the same number split off towards Hollywood or towards Santa Monica. Pure, statistical energy, a ritual being acted out – the regularity of the flows cancels out individual destinations. What you have here is the charm of ceremonies: you have the whole of space before you, just as ceremonies have the whole of time before them. (pp. 52–54)

42 The opening sections of Wood and Fels's "Designs on Signs" is, in fact, a sustained reading of the *Official State Highway Map of North Carolina*, especially the ways in which the highway map in particular is dedicated to the naturalization of the cultural and *political*:

> A state highway map . . . is unavoidably a map *of the state*: that is, an instrument of state polity, an assertion of sovereignty . . . Not only has effective territorial control long been dependent on effective mapping, but it is among other things the repetitive impact of the image of the territory mapped that lends credence to the claims of control (and hence the extensive logogrammatical application of the state's outline to seals, badges and emblems). Who would question the pretensions, the right to existence, the reality of North Carolina? Look! There it is on the map! The 1.6 million copies . . . constitute 1.6 million assertions of the state's sovereignty, assertions which, however, at the moment of being noticed have the ability to fade back into the map where their appearance is taken entirely for granted, overlooked because expected, naturally a part of the surface. (pp. 63–64)

43 The particular narratives that finally are told, however, are preselected by social, political, and economic forces. Harley discusses the strict class-exclusivity of early modern maps:

> For map makers, their patrons, and their readers, the underclass did not exist and had no geography, still less was it composed of individuals. Instead, what we see singled out on these maps are people privileged by the right to wear a crown or a mitre or to bear a coat of arms or a crozier. The peasantry, the landless labourers, or the urban poor had no place in the social hierarchy and, equally, as a cartographically disenfranchised group, they had no right to representation on the map. ("Silences and Secrecy" 68)

It would be comforting indeed to suppose that such gross class-based prejudice no longer informs our production of maps and various other cartographic or demographic texts. Yet one need only look as far as the debate concerning the numbers of so-called illegal aliens living in the United States and whether or not they were entitled to representation in the 1990 US Census to see that in many ways we remain committed to a cartography of privilege.

44 Arno Peters identifies the ideological significance of Mercator's projection and its legacy:

> It is appropriate at this time to examine our own global concept critically. This is based directly upon our global maps and the maps of our own country but these are still rooted in the work of cartographers of a bygone age – the age of European world domination and exploitation. These concepts must be discarded in this era of the realization of the basic equality of all the nations on earth.
>
> The new cartography, based on and dedicated to objectivity alone, must promote and accompany this breakthrough into the new age of human solidarity. New scales must be applied in many fields. The revolutionary ingredient of this new cartography lies in its conception, based on the learning of the current technological revolution, the world revolution and the end of the era of colonial exploitation. With a great leap forward it takes its place in the forefront of the general development. (*New Cartography* 7)

Peters's book stands as a sustained critique of Mercator's projection, to which Peters poses his own antidote by way of a new projection (the Peters projection).

4 POSSESSING THE NEW WORLD: HISTORICISM AND THE STORY OF THE ANECDOTE

1 J.B. Harley, "Rereading the Maps of the Columbian Encounter," *Annals of the Association of American Geographers* 82.3 (1992), p. 532. For a discussion of cartography and the New World, see J.B. Harley, *Maps and the Columbian Encounter: An Interpretive Guide to the Travelling Exhibition* (Milwaukee: the Golda Meir Library and the University of Wisconsin Press, 1990).

2 In his recent study, *Marvelous Possessions: The Wonder of the New World* (University of Chicago Press, 1991), Stephen Greenblatt discusses Columbus and the complex European systems dedicated to the legalization of New World possession; see especially pp. 52–85.

3 Tzvetan Todorov, *The Conquest of America: The Question of the Other*, Richard Howard, tr. (New York: Harper and Row, 1984).

4 I am indebted in this discussion to the works of Emmanuel Levinas, especially *Totality and Infinity: An Essay on Exteriority*, Alphonso Lingis, tr. (Pittsburgh: Dusquesne University Press, 1969). Levinas remains today one of the most important theorists of alterity. Among his many important works, see also *Existence and Existents* (1978), *Otherwise Than Being or Beyond Essence* (1981), and *Time and the Other* (1987).

5 Walter Benjamin, "The Storyteller" in *Illuminations*, Harry Zohn, tr. and Hannah Arendt, ed. (New York: Schocken, 1969), pp. 83–109.

6 Richard Hakluyt, *The Principal Navigations, Voyages, Traffiques & Discoveries of the English Nation*, 12 vols. (Glasgow and New York: MacLehose and Macmillan, 1903), vol. I, pp. xvii–xviii.

7 It is also clear that the inverse of this is true – Hakluyt also understands writing and its rigors as a form of daring, exhausting, and heroic travel. He writes in his dedicatory epistle to Lord Charles Howard, High Admiral of England, that introduces the first volume of the second edition of *Principal Navigations* (1598):

the ardent love of my countrey devoured all difficulties, and as it were with a sharpe goad provoked me and thrust me forward into the most troublesome and painfull action. And after great charges and infinite cares, after many watchings, toiles, and travels, and wearying out of my weake body; at length I have collected three severall Volumes of the English Navigations, Traffiques, and Discoveries, to strange, remote, and farre distant countreys. (Hakluyt I, pp. xxxi–xxxii)

Similarly, in the Preface to the Reader of the same volume, Hakluyt continues to characterize this relation between travel and writing:

what painefull dayes, what heat, what cold I have indured; how many long & chargeable journeys I have traveiled; how many famous libraries I have searched into; what varietie of ancient and moderne writers I have perused; what a number of old records, patents, privileges, letters, &c. I have redeemed from obscuritie and perishing; into how manifold acquaintances I have entred; what expenses I have not spared; and yet what faire opportunities of private gaine, preferment, and ease I have neglected . . . Howbeit . . . the honour and benefit of this Common weale wherein I live and breathe, hath made all difficulties seeme easie, all paines and industrie pleasant, and all expenses of light value and moment unto me. (Hakluyt I, pp. xxxix–xl)

8 Mary C. Fuller, *Voyages in Print: English Travel to America, 1576–1624* (Cambridge University Press, 1995), p. 156.
9 Fuller argues a similar point: "Hakluyt's excitement was kindled not so much by the prospect of visiting far-away places as by the hope of knowing about them, of pursuing 'that knowledge and kind of literature'; his commitment was not to travel but to information" (*Voyages in Print* 145).
10 Hakluyt was not the only – nor, perhaps, the most ardent – apologist for his nationalist project. James Froude, a nineteenth century historian, regarded *Principal Navigations* as "the Prose Epic of the modern English nation" ("England's Forgotten Worthies," in *Short Studies of Great Subjects* [London 1867]). Fuller offers an extended discussion of the nineteenth-century recuperation of Hakluyt expressly for nationalistic purposes – an enterprise in which Froude figures significantly (*Voyages in Print* 156–74).
11 There are numerous examples of narratives collected by Hakluyt that serve to illustrate the commodity nature of global travel and the merchant nature of *Principal Navigations*. I will quote from only one: "Notes given in 1580: to Mr Arthur Pet, and to Mr Charles Jackman, sent by the merchants of the Moscovy Company for the discovery of the Northeast Strait":

Things to be carried with you: kerseys of all orient colours, frizadoes, motleys, bristow friezes, Spanish blankets, bays of all colours, felts of divers colours. Taffeta hats. Deep caps for mariners, whereof if ample vent may be found, it would turn to an infinite commodity of the common poor people by knitting.

Quilted caps of Levant taffeta of divers colours, for the night.
Knit stocks of silk of orient colours.
. . .
Gloves of all sorts knit, and of leather.
Gloves perfumed.
Shoes of Spanish leather.
Shoes of other leather.

Velvet shoes and pantoufles.
Purses knit, and of leather.
. . .
Glasses of English making.
Looking glasses for women, great and fair.
Spectacles of the common sort.
Hour glasses.
. . .
Buttons.
. . .

Take with you the map of England set out in fair colours, one of the biggest sort I mean, to make show of your country from whence you come. And also the large map of London to make show of your city. And let the river be drawn full of ships of all sorts, to make the more show of your great trade and traffic in trade of merchandise.

Richard Hakluyt, *Voyages and Discoveries*, Jack Beeching, ed. (Harmondsworth: Penguin, 1972), pp. 210–23.

12 For a sophisticated discussion of chronology, see Michel de Certeau, *The Writing of History*, Tom Conley, tr. (New York: Columbia University Press, 1988), especially pp. 88–92.

13 For a new historicist discussion of the cabinet of curiosities see Steven Mullaney, "The Rehearsal of Cultures," in his book *The Place of the Stage: License, Play, and Power in Renaissance England* (University of Chicago Press, 1988), pp. 60–87. See also Jody Greene's critical discussion of Mullaney's chapter in "New Historicism and its New World Discoveries," *Yale Journal of Criticism* 4.2 (1991), pp. 163–98.

14 Sir Walter Ralegh, *Discovery of Guiana*, in *Hakluyt's Voyages* Richard David, ed. (Boston: Houghton Mifflin, 1981), p. 492.

15 For a discussion of the profoundly gendered relation to Guiana that Ralegh constructs in his travel narrative, see Louis Montrose, "The Work of Gender in the Discourse of Discovery," *Representations* 33 (1991), pp. 1–41.

16 In an apt characterization of Ralegh's acquisitive and (after Todorov) "transitive" notion of discovery, Fuller argues that "Ralegh's expedition is literally a search for the referent" (*Voyages in Print* 66).

17 Mary B. Campbell, *The Witness and the Other World: Exotic European Travel Writing, 400–1600* (Ithaca: Cornell University Press, 1988), p. 231. Hereafter cited as Campbell.

18 Campbell discusses what she theorizes as the confusion caused by the "alien" objects confronting the traveler – the "nothing" identified by Humphrey Gilbert in his communication to Richard Hakluyt: "But what shall I say, my good Hakluyt, when I see nothing but a very wilderness?" (*Witness and the Other World* 222).

19 Campbell offers a further discussion of Ralegh's use of narrativity, rather than the "interpretive description" employed by Columbus (*Witness and the Other World* 228–33).

20 Sir Walter Ralegh, *The Discovery of Guiana*, in *The History of the World*, 6 vols. (Edinburgh: Archibald Constable, 1820), vol. VI, p. 8.

21 Fuller offers a compelling reading of the issue of proof as it relates to the

aftermath of Ralegh's voyages, particularly Francis Bacon's discussion of the evidential in his *Declaration of the Demeanor and Cariage of Sir Walter Raleigh* (*Voyages in Print* 60–65).

22 On morality and narrative see Hayden White, "The Value of Narrativity in the Representation of Reality," in his *The Content of the Form: Narrative Discourse and Historical Representation* (Baltimore: Johns Hopkins University Press, 1987), pp. 1–25.

23 Roland Barthes, "The Discourse of History," Stephen Bann, tr. in E.S. Shaffer, ed., *Comparative Criticism: A Yearbook* 3 (Cambridge University Press, 1981), p. 17.

24 Greenblatt takes issue with Todorov's assertion, arguing that while there was a "demonstrable linguistic element" to the Spanish conquest of Mexico, "that element is the possession not of writing but of competent translators" (*Marvelous Possessions* 12). Neither writer sees non-alphabetic writing as a form of written language. See also David E. Johnson's discussion of non-alphabetic writing in his essay "Voice, the New Historicism, and the Americas," *Arizona Quarterly* 48.2 (1992), especially pp. 82–83.

25 For an important discussion of European conceptions of New World language, see Gordon Brotherston, "Towards a Grammatology of America: Levi-Strauss, Derrida, and the Native New World Text," in Francis Barker, Peter Hulme, Margaret Iversen, and Diana Loxley eds., *Literature, Politics, and Theory: Papers from the Essex Conference, 1976–1984* (London and New York: Methuen, 1986), pp. 190–209.

26 See Andrew P. Norman, "Telling It Like It Was: Historical Narratives on Their Own Terms," *History and Theory: Studies in the Philosophy of History* 30.2 (1991), pp. 119–35.

27 Louis A. Montrose, "Professing the Renaissance: The Poetics and Politics of Culture," in H. Aram Veeser, ed., *The New Historicism* (New York: Routledge, 1989), p. 20.

28 For a detailed and rigorous discussion of the place of *voice* in new historicism see Johnson, "Voice, the New Historicism, and the Americas."

29 Jean-François Lyotard, *The Postmodern Condition: A Report on Knowledge*, Geoff Bennington and Brian Massumi, trs. (Minneapolis: University of Minnesota Press, 1984), p. xxiv.

30 Joel Fineman, "The History of the Anecdote: Fiction and Fiction," in Veeser, ed., *The New Historicism*, p. 50. Hereafter cited as Fineman.

31 At the very center of this collapse, Benjamin suggests, lies the vulnerable and helpless human body:

> With the [First] World War a process began to become apparent which has not halted since then. Was it not noticeable at the end of the war that men returned from the battlefield grown silent – not richer, but poorer in communicable experience? . . . For never has experience been contradicted more thoroughly than strategic experience by tactical warfare, economic experience by inflation, bodily experience by mechanical warfare, moral experience by those in power. A generation that had gone to school on a horse-drawn streetcar now stood under the open sky in a countryside in which nothing remained unchanged but the clouds, and beneath these clouds, in a field of force of destructive torrents and explosions, was the tiny, fragile human body. (Benjamin, p. 84)

32 Benjamin writes: "Counsel woven into the fabric of real life is wisdom," and it is this wisdom – "the epic side of truth" – that is dying out (Benjamin 86–87).

33 Benjamin also links the rise of the novel to the eventual emergence of the middle class:

> It took the novel, whose beginnings go back to antiquity, hundreds of years before it encountered in the evolving middle class those elements which were favorable to its flowering. With the appearance of these elements, storytelling began quite slowly to recede into the archaic; in many ways, it is true, it took hold of the new material, but it was not really determined by it. On the other hand, we recognize with the full control of the middle class, which has the press as one of its most important instruments in fully developed capitalism, there emerges a form of communication which, no matter how far back its origins may lie, never before influenced the epic form in a decisive way. (Benjamin 88)

34 In the final chapter of *Marvelous Possessions*, Greenblatt, drawing in part from the work of François Hartog, takes up the issue of nomadism in terms of Herodotus (whom Greenblatt's discussion celebrates as an exemplar of the cultural "go-between"), and his attempt to calculate the population of the nomadic Scythians. The Scythians were to the Athenians "people who had absolutely no attachment to any place," and for the Athenians "nomadism was the indelible mark of the Scythians' distance from civility, the sign and substance of an alien existence, the quintessence of otherness" (*Marvelous Possessions* 124). And yet it is precisely the fact of their nomadism that Herodotus finds "the Scythians' uniquely admirable positive accomplishment" (*Marvelous Possessions* 126).

Nomadism begins to emerge – in recent philosophical thought (and perhaps covertly in this chapter, too) – as an alternate discursive form. In *Totality and Infinity* – the same passage, in fact, from which I borrowed this chapter's opening epigram – Levinas discusses nomadism's opposite – sedentarism – and Heidegger's "'egoism' of ontology":

> Ontology as first philosophy is a philosophy of power. It issues in the State and in the non-violence of the totality, without securing itself against the violence from which this non-violence lives, and which appears in the tyranny of the State ... The "egoism" of ontology is maintained even when, denouncing Socratic philosophy as already forgetful of Being and already on the way to the notion of the "subject" and technological power, Heidegger finds in Presocratism thought as obedience to the truth of Being. This obedience would be accomplished in existing as builder and cultivator, effecting the unity of the site which sustains space. In bringing together presence on the earth and under the firmament of the heavens, the waiting for the gods and the company of mortals in the presence to the things – which is to build and to cultivate – Heidegger, with the whole of Western history, conceives of the relation with the Other as enacted in the destiny of sedentary peoples, the possessors and builders of the earth. Possession is preeminently the form in which the other becomes the same, by becoming mine. (*Totality and Infinity* 46)

See also the work of Gilles Deleuze, especially "Nomad Thought," and his use of the figure of the nomad in his philosophical writings.

5 BROWNE'S SKULL

1 Sir Thomas Browne, *Hydriotaphia*, in *Sir Thomas Browne: Major Works*, C.A. Patrides, ed. (Harmondsworth: Penguin, 1977). References to Browne's work –

with the exception of "The Prophecy" and *Pseudodoxia Epidemica* (*PE*) – are to this edition and will be cited parenthetically either by short title or by the following abbreviations: *Christian Morals* as *CM*, *Religio Medici* as *RM*, "Letter to a Friend" as Letter. References to "The Prophecy" and Browne's commentary on it are to *The Works of Sir Thomas Browne* Geoffrey Keynes, ed., 4 vols. (London: Faber and Faber, 1964). References to the *Pseudodoxia* are to *Pseudodoxia Epidemica* Robin Robbins, ed., 2 vols. (Oxford: Clarendon, 1981).

2 The United Press International carried this story on the wire service on August 13, 1982. Two slightly different versions of the story were carried under two slightly different headlines: "A fellow of infinite jest" and "Ahead of his time." I would like to thank my colleagues Harrison Meserole and James Harner for bringing this news story to my attention.

3 For an important contribution to the theorization of "race" see Henry Louis Gates, Jr., ed., *"Race," Writing, and Difference* (University of Chicago Press, 1986).

4 William Shakespeare, *Hamlet*, Harold Jenkins, ed. (London and New York: Methuen, 1982), 5.1.166–77.

5 In some ways Hamlet never recovers from the disgust he feels for the death-image. This disgust contrasts sharply with Sir Thomas Browne's sense of shame over death:

> I am not so much afraid of death, as ashamed thereof; tis the very disgrace and ignominy of our natures, that in a moment can so disfigure us that our nearest friends, Wife, and Children stand afraid and start at us. The Birds and Beasts of the field that before in naturall feare obeyed us, forgetting all allegiance begin to prey upon us. This very conceite hath in a tempest disposed and left me willing to be swallowed up in the abysse of waters; wherein I had perished, unseene, unpitied, without wondring eyes, teares of pity, Lectures of mortality, and none had said, *quantum mutatus ab illo*! (*RM* 111)

6 Bacon's letter to Hawthorne is in the Folger Shakespeare Library, MS YC 2599 no. 99.

7 Delia Bacon, "William Shakespeare and his Plays: An Inquiry Concerning Them," *Putnam's Monthly Magazine* 7 (1856), p. 102. Hereafter cited as Bacon.

8 Bacon continues her celebratory (and perhaps in *our* cyber-age, her *prophetic*) praise:

> The plough and the loom are in magnetic communication with the loftiest social centres. The last results of the most exquisite culture of the world . . . are within reach of the lowest haunt, where latent genius and refinement await their summons . . . The Englishman who but reads "The Times," to-day, puts himself into a connection with his age, and attains thereby a means of enlargement of character and elevation of thought and aims, which in the age of Elizabeth was only possible to men occupying the highest official and social position. ("An Inquiry" 130–31)

9 C.M. Ingleby, *Shakespeare's Bones: The Proposal to Disinter Them* (London: Trübner, 1883; rpt. Norwood: Norwood Editions, 1976), p. 2. Hereafter cited as Ingleby. Ingleby appends an annotated bibliography of sorts to his study, in which he quotes (among numerous writers) J. Parker Norris, an American who wrote in the April 1876 issue (vol. 8, p. 38) of the *American Bibliopolist* in favor of disinterment of Shakespeare's remains, asking, "Is it not worth making an effort to secure 'the counterfeit presentment' of him who wrote 'for all time'? If

we could even get a photograph of Shakespeare's skull it would be a great thing, and would help us to make a better portrait of him than we now possess" (qtd. in Ingleby, 41). Ingleby then adds his own voice in support: "[Norris's] courageous article is particularly useful for the adduction of cases in which corpses have lain in the grave far longer than that of Shakespeare, and been discovered in a state of comparative perfection. What would one not give to look upon Shakespeare's dead face!" (Ingleby 41).

10 For an interesting discussion of the figure of the Norman in *Hamlet*, see Margaret W. Ferguson, "*Hamlet*: Letters and Spirits," in Patricia Parker and Geoffrey Hartman, eds., *Shakespeare and the Question of Theory* (London and New York: Methuen 1985), especially pp. 301–3.

11 Freud offers this hope at numerous moments in his career. See, for example, *The Interpretation of Dreams* and *Mourning and Melancholia*.

12 Miriam L. Tildesley, "Sir Thomas Browne: His Skull, Portraits and Ancestry," *Biometrika: A Journal for the Statistical Study of Biological Problems* 15 (1923), pp. 1–76. Hereafter cited as Tildesley.

13 Peter Brooks, *Body Work: Objects of Desire in Modern Narrative* (Cambridge, MA: Harvard University Press, 1993), p. 1.

14 René Descartes, *Meditations Concerning First Philosophy* in *Philosophical Essays*, Laurence J. Lafleur, ed. and tr. (Indianapolis: Bobbs-Merrill, 1951), p. 130.

In *The Tremulous Private Body: Essays on Subjection* (London and New York: Methuen, 1984) Francis Barker discusses this moment in Descartes *Meditations*:

The *problem* of the body is signalled in the attention this text [*Meditations*] must pay to it, but the recuperation of that problem consists not in a full reinstatement of the body in its old splendour: the "unity" of I with it that Descartes posits is only maintained across a mutual, although not symmetrical, distinctness – a non-identity which is defined at last, significantly and *reasonably* enough under the historical circumstances, as a property relation. (p. 98)

15 We find another instance of the prejudice associated with the notion of "lowbrow" in *The Tempest* in Caliban's fear of Prospero's transformative vengeance: "I will have none on't: we shall lose our time,/ And all be turn'd to barnacles, or to apes/ With foreheads villainous low" (William Shakespeare, *The Tempest*, Frank Kermode, ed. [New York: Routledge, 1954], 4.1.247–49).

16 This desire is mirrored in – or perhaps displaced onto – the antiquarian interest manifest in the *Chronicle* narrative:

The coffin-plate was of brass, in the form of a shield, and bore the following inscription:

AMPLISSIMUS VIR
DNS. THOMAS BROWNE, MILES, MED-
ICINAE DR. ANNOS NATUS 77
DENATUS 12 DIE MENSIS OCTOBRIS,
ANNO DNJ. 1682. HOC LOCULO
INDORMIENS, CORPORIS SPAGY-
RICI PULVERE PLUMBUM IN AURUM
CONVERTIT.

[MOST HONORABLE MAN. SIR THOMAS BROWNE, KNIGHT, DOCTOR OF MEDICINE. SEVENTY-SEVEN YEARS OLD. DIED ON THE TWELFTH DAY OF OCTOBER 1682. SLEEPING IN THIS LITTLE PLACE, IN THE DUST OF THE BODY OF THE SPAGYRIC, HE CONVERTED LEAD INTO GOLD.]

> For the accuracy, in every respect, of the above copy we can safely vouch, since it is carefully taken from an actual impression of the engraving on the plate. Not so, however, as to the "doing into English," which is here subjoined merely for the use of "readers in general." – Whether the last two lines of the original latinity were meant to predict an alchemic transmutation, or to express a hyperbolic compliment, we leave to the learned, with this remark that the coffin is *still a leaden one.* (qtd. in Tildesley 34–35)

17 Tildesley points out – and laments over – the flawed and sometimes unreliable system of authentication and attribution that remains susceptible to abuses:

> The cheerful self-confidence with which people will assign a portrait to a certain artist, and name the person it represents – and affix labels accordingly, without finding it at all necessary to state whether what they record is mere opinion or a historical fact – is unfortunately far too familiar to us. Possibly "T. Wright Covent Garden" was a sinner in this respect; possibly Simon himself was. Therefore we are quite prepared to believe that Zoust (if he was the artist) was not attempting Shakespeare at all, but was painting the portrait of a contemporary, its identity being forgotten later. (Tildesley 24)

18 Keith construes the disinterment as motivated by phrenological desire: "In 1840, the crypt was opened, the skull extracted so that a phrenological study might be made of it." (Sir Arthur Keith, *Phrenological Studies of the Skull and Brain Cast of Sir Thomas Browne of Norwich*, Henderson Trust Lectures, no. 3 [Edinburgh: Oliver and Boyd, 1924], p. 1. Hereafter cited as Keith.)

19 Keith writes, "The brain itself in which this strange mosaic of faculties was built up, has long since gone the way of all flesh, but from its bony husk we may yet learn much concerning its architecture and its configuration – and, incidentally, something of its owner" (Keith 7).

20 Elsewhere in his study Keith demonstrates a true propensity toward teleological argumentation:

> Thus it comes about that the part of the base of the skull which lies behind the ears – the post-auricular base – has a double role to play – it has to serve for the leverage of the head, and it has to protect the underlying part of the brain – the cerebellum and medulla oblongata, and will therefore undergo modification as one function or the other takes the upper hand. In bull-necked men this part of the base of the skull is moulded to serve the purposes of the muscles of the neck; the underlying parts of the brain are moulded in conformity to the need of these muscles. (Keith 8)

21 These are called "mental" tendencies, when in fact they are physiological (chemical) and not structural in nature.

22 In "The Storyteller" (in *Illuminations* Harry Zohn, tr.. and Hannah Arendt, ed. [New York: Shocken, 1969]), Walter Benjamin discusses the transformation of the "face of death . . . identical with the one that has diminished the communicability of experience to the same extent as the art of storytelling has declined":

> It has been observable for a number of centuries how in the general consciousness the thought of death has declined in omnipresence and vividness. In its last stages this process is accelerated. And in the course of the nineteenth century bourgeois society has,

by means of hygienic and social, private and public institutions, realized a secondary effect which may have been its subconscious main purpose: to make it possible for people to avoid the sight of dying. Dying was once a public process in the life of the individual and a most exemplary one . . . In the course of modern times dying has been pushed further and further out of the perceptual world of the living. There used to be no house, hardly a room, in which someone had not once died . . . Today people live in rooms that have never been touched by death, dry dwellers of eternity, and when their end approaches they are stowed away in sanatoria in hospitals by their heirs. ("The Storyteller" 93–94)

23 In a similar passage from *Religio Medici*, Browne discusses "Platoes yeare," which he glosses in a marginal note as "A revolution of certaine thousand yeares when all things should returne unto their former estate and he be teaching againe in his schoole as when he delivered this opinion":

for as though there were a *Metempsuchosis*, and the soule of one man passed into another opiniones doe finde after certaine revolutions, men and mindes like those that first begat them. To see our selves againe wee neede not looke for *Platoes* yeare; every man is not onely himselfe; there have beene many *Diogenes*, and as many *Timons*, though but few of that name; men are lived over againe, the world is now as it was in ages past, there was none then, but there hath been some one since that parallels him, and is as it were his revived selfe. (*RM* 66–67)

24 In *Pseudodoxia Epidemica*, Browne offers a similar discussion of God's informing causality: "as he created all things, so is he beyond and in them all, not onely in power, as under his subjection, or in his presence, as being in his cognition, but in his very Essence, as being the soule of their causalities, and the essentiall cause of their existences" (*PE* 10).

25 Browne further describes the mechanisms of this error – "transferring the speciall consideration of things unto their generall acceptions, or concluding from their strict acception, unto that without all limitation" (*PE* 25).

26 In chapter 10, "Of the last and common promoter of false Opinions, the endeavours of Satan," Browne focuses further attention on Satan's role as "the first contriver of Error, and professed opposer of Truth" (*PE* 58). While Satan's sinfulness and evil is beyond human comprehension ("To attempt a particular of all his wiles, is too bold an Arithmetick for man" [*PE* 58]), Browne can discuss the five Satanic strategies: "That there is no God. That there are many. That he himselfe is God. That he is lesse then Angels or Men. That he is nothing at all" (*PE* 65).

27 In chapter 10 Browne furthers this notion of the *textual* nature of Satan's sin and his agenda:

Now to induce and bring about these falsities he hath laboured to destroy the evidence of truth, that is the revealed verity and written word of God. To which intent he hath obtained with some to repudiate the books of Moses, others those of the Prophets, and some both: to deny the Gospell and authentick histories of Christ, to reject that of John, and receive that of Judas, to disallow all and erect another of Thomas. And when neither their corruption by Valentinus and Arrius, their mutilation by Marcion, Manes and Ebion could satisfie his designe, he attempted the ruine and totall destruction thereof, as he sedulously endeavoured, by the power and subtilty of Julian, Maximinus and Dioclesian.
(*PE* 65)

28 For John Donne, the question of the proper relation between the sign and the thing signified is most crucially at stake in the ritual of Christian communion. In the seventh Expostulation of the *Devotions* (*Devotions Upon Emergent Occasions*, Anthony Raspa, ed. [Oxford University Press, 1987]), Donne calls upon God to secure for his devout followers a coherence between sign and signified:

> And that I may associate thy *Word*, with thy *Sacrament*, the *Seale* with thy *Patent*; and in that *Sacrament* associate *the signe* with the *thing signified*, the *Bread* with the *Body* of thy *Sonne*, so, as I may be sure to have received both, and to bee made thereby, (as thy blessed servant *Augustine* sayes) the *Arke*, and the *Monument*, & the *Tombe* of thy most blessed *Sonne*, that *hee*, and all the *merits* of his death, may, by that receiving, bee buried in me, to my quickning in this world, and my immortall establishing in the next. (*Devotions* 39)

29 Satan's corruption of the relationship between sign and signified on the macro level has its micro-level counterpart in his invention of superstitious and prophetic interpretations:

> But above all he deceiveth us when wee ascribe effects of things unto evident and seeming causalities which arise from the secret and undiscerned action of himself. Thus hath he deluded many Nations in his Auguriall and Extispicious inventions, from casuall and uncontrived contingencies divining events succeeding . . . Now these divinations concerning events being in his power, to force, contrive, prevent or further, they must generally fall out conformably unto his predictions . . . So was there no naturall dependance of the event upon the signe, but an artificiall contrivance of the signe unto the event. (*PE* 68)

30 Browne writes, "No man knows the end of the world, nor assuredly of any thing in it: God sees it because unto his Eternity it is present, hee knoweth the ends of us, but not himself, and because hee knowes not this, he knoweth all things, and his knowledge is endlesse, even in the object of himselfe" (*PE* 452).

31 In a section of *Religio Medici* in which Browne discusses various heresies, he mentions "a Divine and man of singular parts" who on his inability to believe in the immortality of the soul, "was so plunged and gravelled with three lines of *Seneca*, that all our Antidotes, drawne from both Scripture and Philosophy, could not expell the poyson of his errour – 'There is nothing after death, and death itself is nothing. Death is indivisible, destructive to the body, and unsparing of the soul . . . We die wholly, and no part of us remains'" (*RM* 87). Also, "It is the heaviest stone that melancholy can throw at a man, to tell him he is at the end of his nature; or that there is no further state to come, unto which this seemes progressionall, and otherwise made in vaine" (*Hydriotaphia* 305).

32 In *Religio Medici*, Browne comments on the "slender and doubtfull respect I have alwayes held unto Antiquities," and the greater admiration he has for that which is above all antiquity:

> for that indeed which I admire is farre before antiquity, that is Eternity, and that is God himselfe; who though hee be stiled the Antient of dayes, cannot receive the adjunct of antiquity, who was before the world, and shall be after it, yet is not older then it: for in his yeares there is no Climacter, his duration is eternity, and farre more venerable then antiquitie. (*RM* 96–97)

It is interesting to note that this renunciation of antiquities (and with them, antiquarianism more generally) occurs just as Browne repudiates relics. Perhaps

Browne's announced slight regard for antiquarianism (and its objects) arises in part from his Protestant sensibility which would of course reject the object turned relic. But there is nevertheless a fine distinction at play here between the relic (in Browne's pejorative sense) and the artifact, as I invoke that term here; the artifact is the relic extricated – by Browne, by science – from its religious over-determination.

33 Browne offers the following marginal note: "θ The character of death" (*Hydriotaphia* 309).

34 In *Religio Medici* Browne discusses the nature of the soul in time: "Thus we are men, and we know not how, there is something in us, that can be without us, and will be after us, though it is strange that it hath no history, what it was before us, nor cannot tell how it entred in us" (*RM* 107).

35 Cf. Patrides's Introduction (*Major Works* 29–30).

36 In *A Letter to a Friend, upon the occasion of the Death of his Intimate Friend*, Browne offers the following advice meant to move his friend (and his readers) to a closer approximation of the Eternal Present: "Time past is gone like a shadow; make Times to come, present; conceive that near which may be far off; approximate thy last Times by present Apprehensions of them: live like a Neighbour unto Death, and think there is but little to come" (*Major Works* 413).

37 In the fourteenth Meditation of his *Devotions*, Donne, too, considers the virtu-ally inexpressible nature of time:

What poore *Elements* are our *happinesses* made off, if *Tyme*, *Tyme* which wee can scarce consider to be *any thing*, be an essential part of our hapines?. . . All things are done in *time* too; but if we consider *Tyme* to be but the *Measure of Motion*, and howesoever it may seeme to have three *stations*, *past*, *present*, and *future*, yet the *first* and *last* of these *are* not (one is not, now, & the other is not yet) And that which you call *present*, is not *now* the same that it was, when you began to call it so in the *Line*, (before you found that word, *present*, or that *Monosyllable*, *now*, the present, & the *Now* is past), if this *Imaginary halfe-nothing*, *Tyme*, be of the Essence of our *Happinesses*, how can they be thought *durable*?

(*Devotions* 71)

Donne then (like Browne) will attempt to situate this ineffable non-entity "Time" within its true context, which is God's Eternity:

If we consider *Eternity*, into that, *Tyme* never Entred; *Eternity* is not an everlasting flux of *Tyme*; but Tyme is as a short *parenthesis* in a longe *period*; and *Eternity* had bin the same, as it is, though time had never beene; If we consider, not *Eternity*, but *Perpetuity*, not that which had no *tyme* to beginne in, but which shall out-live *Tyme* and be, when *Tyme shall bee no more*, what A *Minute* is the life of the Durablest *Creature*, compared to that? (*Devotions* 71–72)

38 For a discussion of these images and the relationships between them, see Max J. Friedländer, *Early Netherlandish Painting*, vol. I: *Joos van Cleve, Jan Provost, Joachim Patenier* (New York: Praeger, 1972). Friedländer considers the painting with the clock an "imitation leaning strongly towards caricature" (p. 58).

39 As supporting evidence Browne offers an account from the writings of John Dee – in "Mathematicall Preface" to Euclid, *Elements of Geometrie* (1570) – in which he describes a perpetual motion machine presented to Charles V that contained

"one wheele that moved at such a rate, that in seven thousand yeares onely his owne period should be finished; a thing almost incredible" (*PE* 414).

40 Browne writes:

> Amuse not thy self about Riddles of future things. Study Prophecies when they are become Histories, and past hovering in their causes. Eye well things past and present, and let conjectural sagacity suffise for things to come . . . But a Retrograde cognition of times past, and things which have already been, is more satisfactory than a suspended Knowledge of what is yet unexistent. And the Greatest part of time being already wrapt up in things behind us; it's now somewhat late to bait after things before us; for futurity still shortens, and time present sucks in time to come (*CM* 458–59).

Bibliography

Bacon, Delia, "William Shakespeare and his Plays: An Inquiry Concerning Them," *Putnam's Monthly Magazine* 7 (1856), pp. 98–155.

Baker, David J., "Off the Map: Charting Uncertainty in Renaissance Ireland," in Brendan Bradshaw, Andrew Hadfield, and Willy Maley (eds.), *Representing Ireland: Literature and the Origins of Conflict, 1534–1660*, Cambridge University Press, 1993, pp. 76–92.

Barkan, Leonard, *Nature's Work of Art: The Human Body as Image of the World*, New Haven: Yale University Press, 1975.

Barker, Francis, *The Tremulous Private Body: Essays on Subjection*, London and New York: Methuen, 1984.

Barthes, Roland, "The Discourse of History," Stephen Bann (tr.) in E.S. Shaffer (ed.), *Comparative Criticism: A Yearbook*, Cambridge University Press, 1981, pp. 3–20.

Baudrillard, Jean, *America*, Chris Turner (tr.), London and New York: Verso, 1988.

  Simulations, Paul Foss, Paul Patton, and Philip Beitchman (trs.), New York: Semiotext(e), 1983.

Benjamin, Walter, *Illuminations*, Hannah Arendt (ed.), Harry Zohn (tr.), New York: Schoken, 1969.

Brooks, Peter, *Body Work: Objects of Desire in Modern Narrative*, Cambridge, MA: Harvard University Press, 1993.

Brotherston, Gordon, "Towards a Grammatology of America: Lévi-Strauss, Derrida, and the Native New World Text," in Francis Barker, Peter Hulme, Margaret Iverson, and Diana Loxley (eds.), *Literature, Politics, and Theory: Papers from the Essex Conference, 1976–1984*, London and New York: Methuen, 1986.

Browne, Sir Thomas, *Sir Thomas Browne: Major Works*, C.A. Patrides (ed.), Harmondsworth: Penguin, 1977.

  Pseudodoxia Epidemica, Robin Robbins (ed.), 2 vols., Oxford: Clarendon Press, 1981.

  The Works of Sir Thomas Browne, Geoffrey Keynes (ed.), 4 vols., London: Faber and Faber, 1964.

Camden, William, *Camden's Britannia, 1695*, New York and London: Johnson Reprint, 1971.

Campbell, Mary B., *The Witness and the Other World: Exotic European Travel Writing, 400–1600*, Ithaca: Cornell University Press, 1988.

Cassirer, Ernst, *The Individual and the Cosmos in Renaissance Philosophy*, Mario Domandi (ed. and tr.), New York: Barnes and Noble, 1963.

Cavell, Stanley, *Disowning Knowledge in Six Plays by Shakespeare*, Cambridge University Press, 1987.

Cormack, Leslie, "'Good Fences Make Good Neighbors': Geography as Self-Definition in Early Modern England," *Isis* 82 (1991), pp. 639–61.

De Certeau, Michel, *The Writing of History*, Tom Conley (tr.), New York: Columbia University Press, 1988.

De Grazia, Margreta and Peter Stallybrass, "The Materiality of the Shakespearean Text," *Shakespeare Quarterly* 44 (1993), pp. 255–83.

Deleuze, Gilles, "Nomad Thought," Jacqueline Wallace (tr.), *Semiotext(e)*, *Nietzsche's Return* 3. 1 (1978), pp. 12–20.

Derrida, Jacques, *Specters of Marx: The State of the Debt, the Work of Mourning, and the New International*, Peggy Kamuf (tr.), New York and London: Routledge, 1994.

Descartes, René, *Meditations Concerning First Philosophy* in Laurence J. Lafleur (ed. and tr.), *Philosophical Essays*, Indianapolis: Bobbs-Merrill, 1951, pp. 67–143.

Donne, John, *Devotions Upon Emergent Occasions*, Anthony Raspa (ed.), Oxford University Press, 1987.

Ignatius His Conclave, T.S. Healy (ed.), Oxford University Press, 1969.

John Donne, The Oxford Authors, John Carey (ed.), Oxford University Press, 1990.

Drayton, Michael, *Poly-Olbion*, London, 1612; rpt. New York: Burt Franklin, 1970.

Evans, Ifor M. and Heather Lawrence (eds.), *Christopher Saxton: Elizabethan Map-Maker*, Wakefield and London: Wakefield Historical Publications and the Holland Press, 1979.

Fabian, Johannes, *Time and the Other: How Anthropology Makes its Object*, New York: Columbia University Press, 1983.

Ferguson, Margaret, "*Hamlet*: Letters and Spirits," in Patricia Parker and Geoffrey Hartmen (eds.), *Shakespeare and the Question of Theory*, London and New York: Methuen, 1985, pp. 292–309.

Fineman, Joel, "The History of the Anecdote: Fiction and Fiction," in H. Aram Veeser (ed.), *The New Historicism*, New York: Routledge, 1989, pp. 49–76.

Ford, John, *'Tis Pity She's a Whore*, Brian Morris (ed.), London: Ernst Benn and New York: W.W. Norton, 1968.

Foucault, Michel, *Discipline and Punish: The Birth of the Prison*, Alan Sheridan (tr.), New York: Vintage, 1979.

The Order of Things: An Archaeology of the Human Sciences, New York: Vintage, 1973.

Freud, Sigmund, *Fragment of an Analysis of a Case of Hysteria*, in James Strachey, Anna Freud, Alix Strachey, and Ann Tyson (eds. and trs.), *The Standard Edition of the Complete Psychological Works of Sigmund Freud*, 24 vols., London: Hogarth Press, 1953–74, vol. III.

"The Theme of the Three Caskets," Joan Riviere (tr.), in Ernst Jones (ed.), *Sigmund Freud: The Collected Papers*, 4 vols., New York: Basic Books, 1959, vol. IV, pp. 245–56.

Friedländer, Max J., *Early Netherlandish Painting*, vol. I: *Joos van Cleve, Jan Provost, Joachim Patenier*, New York: Praeger, 1972.

Froude, James Anthony, "England's Forgotten Worthies," *Short Studies of Great Subjects*, 1 (1867): 443–501. Reprint, London, 1988

Fuller, Mary C., *Voyages in Print: English Travel to America, 1576–1624*, Cambridge University Press, 1995.

Gates, Henry Louis, Jr., *"Race," Writing and Difference*, University of Chicago Press, 1986.

Gillies, John, *Shakespeare and the Geography of Difference*, Cambridge University Press, 1994.

Goldberg, Jonathan, "Hamlet's Hand," *Shakespeare Quarterly* 39 (1988), pp. 307–27.

"Rebel Letters: Postal Effects from *Richard II* to *Henry IV*," *Renaissance Drama* n.s. 19 (1988), pp. 3–28.

"Shakespearean Inscriptions: The Voicing of Power," in Patricia Parker and Geoffrey Hartman (eds.), *Shakespeare and the Question of Theory*, New York and London: Methuen, 1985, pp. 116–37.

"Textual Properties," *Shakespeare Quarterly* 37 (1986), pp. 213–17.

Voice Terminal Echo: Postmodernism and English Renaissance Texts, London and New York: Methuen, 1986.

Writing Matter: From the Hands of the English Renaissance, Stanford University Press, 1990.

Greenblatt, Stephen, *Marvelous Possessions: The Wonder of the New World*, University of Chicago Press, 1991.

Renaissance Self-Fashioning: From More to Shakespeare, University of Chicago Press, 1980.

Greene, Jody, "New Historicism and its New World Discoveries," *Yale Journal of Criticism* 4.2 (1991), pp. 163–98.

Greg, W.W., *The Editorial Problem in Shakespeare: A Survey of the Foundations of the Text*, 2nd edn., Oxford: Clarendon Press, 1951.

Hakluyt, Richard, *The Principal Navigations, Voyages, Traffiques & Discoveries of the English Nation*, 12 vols., Glasgow and New York: MacLehose and Macmillan, 1903.

Voyages and Discoveries, Jack Beeching (ed.), Harmondsworth: Penguin, 1972.

Harcourt, Glenn, "Andreas Vesalius and the Anatomy of Antique Sculpture," *Representations* 17 (1987), pp. 28–61.

Harley, J.B., "Deconstructing the Map," *Cartographica* 26 (1989), pp. 1–20.

"*Imago Mundi*: The First Fifty Years and the Next Ten," *Cartographica* 23.3 (1986), pp. 1–15.

"The Map and the Development of the History of Cartography," in J.B. Harley and David Woodward (eds.), *The History of Cartography*; vol. I: *Cartography in Prehistoric, Ancient, and Medieval Europe and the Mediterranean*, University of Chicago Press, 1987, pp. 1–42.

Maps and the Columbian Encounter: An Interpretive Guide to the Travelling Exhibition, Milwaukee: the Golda Meir Library and the University of Wisconsin Press, 1990.

"Maps, Knowledge, and Power," in Denis Cosgrove and Stephen Daniels (eds.), *The Iconography of Landscape: Essays on the Symbolic Representation, Design, and Use of Past Environments*, New York: Cambridge University Press, 1988, pp. 227–312.

"Rereading the Maps of the Columbian Encounter," *Annals of the Association of American Geographers* 82.3 (1992), pp. 522–42.

"Silences and Secrecy: The Hidden Agenda of Cartography in Early Modern Europe," *Imago Mundi* 40 (1988), pp. 57–76.

Hassel, R. Chris, Jr., "Donne's *Ignatius His Conclave* and the New Astronomy," *Modern Philology* 68 (1971), pp. 329–37.

Hawkes, Terence, "Telmah," in Patricia Parker and Geoffrey Hartman (eds.), *Shakespeare and the Question of Theory*, New York and London: Methuen, 1985, pp. 310–32.

Helgerson, Richard, *Forms of Nationhood: The Elizabethan Writing of England*, University of Chicago Press, 1992.

"The Land Speaks: Cartography, Chorography, and Subversion in Renaissance England," in Stephen Greenblatt (ed.), *Representing the English Renaissance*, Berkeley: University of California Press, 1988, pp. 327–61.

Hill, W. Speed (ed.) *New Ways of Looking at Old Texts: Papers of the Renaissance Text Society, 1985–1991*, Binghamton: Medieval and Renaissance Texts and Studies, 1993.

Hodges, Devon, *Fictions of Anatomy*, Amherst: University of Massachusetts Press, 1985.

Howard, Jean, "Scripts and/versus Playhouses: Ideological Production and the Renaissance Public Stage," in Valerie Wayne (ed.), *The Matter of Difference: Materialist Feminist Criticism of Shakespeare*, Ithaca: Cornell University Press, 1991, pp. 221–36.

Ingleby, C.M., *Shakespeare's Bones: The Proposal to Disinter Them*, London: Trübner, 1883; rpt. Norwood: Norwood Editions, 1976.

Johnson, David E., "Voice, the New Historicism, and the Americas," *Arizona Quarterly* 48.2 (1992), pp. 81–116.

Jonson, Ben, *Volpone, or The Fox*, Alvin Kernan (ed.), New Haven: Yale University Press, 1962.

Keith, Sir Arthur, *Phrenological Studies of the Skull and Brain Cast of Sir Thomas Browne of Norwich*, Henderson Trust Lectures, no. 3, Edinburgh: Oliver and Boyd, 1924.

Laqueur, Thomas, *Making Sex: Body and Gender from the Greeks to Freud*, Cambridge, MA: Harvard University Press, 1990.

Leigh, Valentine, *The Moste Profitable and Comendable Science, of Surveying of Lands, Tenementes, and Hereditamentes*, London, 1577.

Leland, John, *Leland's Itinerary in England and Wales*, Lucy Toulmin Smith (ed.), 3 vols., London: George Bell, 1907.

Lestringant, Frank, *Mapping the Renaissance World: The Geographical Imagination in the Age of Discovery*, David Fausett (tr.), Berkeley: University of California Press, 1994.

Levinas, Emmanuel, *Totality and Infinity: An Essay on Exteriority*, Alphonso Lingis (tr.), Pittsburgh: Dusquesne University Press, 1969.

Levine, Joseph M., *Humanism and History: Origins of Modern English Historiography*, Ithaca: Cornell University Press, 1987.

Lyotard, Jean-François, *The Postmodern Condition: A Report on Knowledge*, Geoff

Bennington and Brian Massumi (trs.), Minneapolis: University of Minnesota Press, 1984.

Macksey, Richard and Eugenio Donato (eds.), *The Structuralist Controversy: The Languages of Criticism and the Sciences of Man*, Baltimore: Johns Hopkins University Press, 1970.

Mandeville, Sir John, *The Travels of Sir John Mandeville*, C.W.R.D. Moseley (ed. and tr.), Harmondsworth: Penguin, 1983.

Marchitello, Howard, "Desire and Domination in *Volpone*," *Studies in English Literature* 31 (1991), pp. 287–308.

Marcus, Leah S., "Textual Indeterminacy and Ideological Difference: The Case of *Doctor Faustus*," *Renaissance Drama* n.s. 20 (1989), 1–29.

Marin, Louis, *Portrait of the King*, Martha M. Houle (tr.), Minneapolis: University of Minnesota Press,1988.

Martin, Emily, "Science and Women's Bodies: Forms of Anthropological Knowledge" in Mary Jacobus, Evelyn Fox Keller, and Sally Shuttleworth (eds.), *Body/Politics: Women and the Discourses of Science*, New York: Routledge, 1990, pp. 69–82.

Maus, Katharine Eisaman, "Horns of the Dilemma: Jealousy, Gender, and Spectatorship in English Renaissance Drama," *English Literary History* 54 (1987), pp. 561–83.

Inwardness and Theater in the English Renaissance, University of Chicago Press, 1995.

"Proof and Consequences: Inwardness and its Exposure in the English Renaissance," *Representations* 34 (1991), pp. 29–52.

McGann, Jerome, *A Critique of Modern Textual Criticism*, University of Chicago Press, 1983; rpt. Charlottesville: University of Virginia Press, 1992.

The Textual Condition, Princeton University Press, 1991.

The Romantic Ideology: A Critical Investigation, University of Chicago Press, 1983.

McLeod, Randall, "UnEditing Shakespeare," *Sub-Stance* 33/34 (1982), pp. 26–55.

McLuskie, Kathleen, *Renaissance Dramatists*, Atlantic Highlands: Humanities Press International, 1989.

Meadows, A.J., *The High Firmament: A Survey of Astronomy in English Literature*, University of Leicester Press, 1969.

Mendyk, Stan A.E., *"Speculum Britanniae": Regional Study, Antiquarianism, and Science in Britain to 1700*, University of Toronto Press, 1989.

Montrose, Louis A., "Professing the Renaissance: The Poetics and Politics of Culture," in H. Aram Veeser (ed.), *The New Historicism*, New York: Routledge, 1989, pp. 15–36.

"The Work of Gender in the Discourse of Discovery," *Representations* 33 (1991), pp. 1–41.

Morgan, Victor, "The Cartographic Image of 'The Country' in Early Modern England," *Transactions of the Royal Historical Society* 5th ser., 29 (1979), pp. 129–54.

Mullaney, Steven, *The Place of the Stage: License, Play, and Power in Renaissance England*, University of Chicago Press, 1988.

Norden, John, *England: An Intended Guyde For English Travailers*, London, 1625; rpt. Amsterdam: Theatrum Orbis Terrarum, 1979.

Surveiors Dialogue, London, 1618, rpt. Amsterdam: Theatrum Orbis Terrarum, 1979.

Norman, Andrew P., "Telling It Like It Was: Historical Narratives on Their Own Terms," *History and Theory: Studies in the Philosophy of History* 30.2 (1991), pp. 119–35.

O'Malley, C.D., *Andreas Vesalius of Brussels, 1514–1565*, Berkeley: University of California Press, 1964.

Orgel, Stephen, "The Poetics of Incomprehensibility," *Shakespeare Quarterly* 42 (1991), pp. 431–37.

Parker, Patricia, "*Othello* and *Hamlet*: Dilation, Spying, and the 'Secret Place' of Women," in Russ McDonald (ed.), *Shakespeare Reread: The Texts in New Contexts*, Ithaca: Cornell University Press, 1994, pp. 105–46.

"Shakespeare and Rhetoric: 'Dilation' and 'Delation' in *Othello*," in Patricia Parker and Geoffrey Hartman (eds.), *Shakespeare and the Question of Theory*, New York: Methuen, 1985, pp. 54–74.

Peters, Arno, *The New Cartography*, Ward Kaiser, D.G. Smith and Heinz Wohlers (trs.), New York: Friendship Press, 1983.

Piggott, Stuart, *Ancient Britons and the Antiquarian Imagination: Ideas from the Renaissance to the Regency*, New York: Thames and Hudson, 1989.

Ruins in a Landscape: Essays in Antiquarianism, Edinburgh University Press, 1976.

Pittenger, Elizabeth, "Dispatch Quickly: The Mechanical Reproduction of Pages," *Shakespeare Quarterly* 42 (1991), pp. 389–408.

Ralegh, Sir Walter, *Discovery of Guiana*, in Richard David (ed.), *Hakluyt's Voyages*, Boston: Houghton Mifflin, 1981.

History of the World, 6 vols., Edinburgh: Archibald Constable, 1820.

Rose, Mark, "Othello's Occupation: Shakespeare and the Romance of Chivalry," *English Literary Renaissance* 15 (1985), pp. 293–311.

Saunders, J.B. de C.M., and C.D. O'Malley, *The Illustrations from the Works of Andreas Vesalius of Brussels*, Cleveland: World Publishing, 1950.

Sawday, Jonathan, *The Body Emblazoned: Dissection and the Human Body in Renaissance Culture*, New York: Routledge, 1995.

"The Fate of Marsyas: Dissecting the Renaissance Body," in Lucy Gent and Nigel Llewellyn (eds.), *Renaissance Bodies: The Human Figure in English Culture, c. 1540–1660*, London: Reakton Books, 1990, pp. 111–35.

Shakespeare, William, *Hamlet*, Harold Jenkins (ed.), London and New York: Methuen, 1982.

Othello, M.R. Ridley (ed.), London: Methuen, 1958.

The Merchant of Venice, 1600, Shakespeare Quarto Facsimiles, vol. II, Oxford: Clarendon Press, 1957.

The Merchant of Venice, John Russell Brown (ed.), London: Methuen, 1955.

The Merchant of Venice, M.M. Mahood (ed.), Cambridge University Press, 1987.

The Merchant of Venice, John Dover Wilson (ed.), Cambridge University Press, 1926; rpt. 1968.

The Tempest, Frank Kermode (ed.), New York: Routledge, 1954.

Snow, Edward A., "Sexual Anxiety and the Male Order of Things in *Othello*," *English Literary Renaissance* 10 (1980), pp. 384–412.

Stallybrass, Peter, "Patriarchal Territories: The Body Enclosed," in Margaret W. Ferguson, Maureen Quilligan, and Nancy J. Vickers (eds.), *Rewriting the*

Renaissance: The Discourses of Sexual Difference in Early Modern Europe, University of Chicago Press, 1986, pp. 123–42.

Tildesley, Miriam L., "Sir Thomas Browne: His Skull, Portraits and Ancestry," *Biometrika: A Journal for the Statistical Study of Biological Problems* 15 (1923), pp. 1–76.

Todorov, Tzvetan, *The Conquest of America: The Question of the Other*, Richard Howard (tr.), New York: Harper and Row, 1984.

On Human Diversity: Nationalism, Racism, and Exoticism in French Thought, Catherine Porter (tr.), Cambridge, MA: Harvard University Press, 1993.

Vickers, Nancy J., "Diana Described: Scattered Women, Scattered Rhyme," *Critical Inquiry* 8 (1981), pp. 265–79.

Wayne, Valerie, "Historical Differences: Misogyny and *Othello*," in Valerie Wayne (ed.), *The Matter of Difference: Materialist Feminist Criticism of Shakespeare*, Ithaca: Cornell University Press, 1991, pp. 153–79.

White, Hayden, *The Content of the Form: Narrative Discourse and Historical Representation*, Baltimore: Johns Hopkins University Press, 1987.

Tropics of Discourse: Essays in Cultural Criticism, Baltimore: Johns Hopkins University Press, 1978.

Wilson, Luke, "William Harvey's *Prelectiones*: The Performance of the Body in the Renaissance Theater of Anatomy," *Representations* 17 (1987), pp. 62–95.

Wood, Denis, "Pleasure in the Idea: The Atlas as Narrative Form," *Cartographica* 24.1 (1987), pp. 24–45.

Wood, Denis and John Fels, "Designs on Signs: Myth and Meaning in Maps," *Cartographica* 23.3 (1986), pp. 54–103.

The Power of Maps, New York: Guilford Press, 1992.

Woodward, David, "Medieval *Mappaemundi*" in J.B. Harley and David Woodward (eds.), *The History of Cartography*, vol. I: *Cartography in Prehistoric, Ancient, and Medieval Europe and the Mediterranean*, University of Chicago Press, 1987, pp. 286–370.

Index

Cambridge Studies in Renaissance Literature and Culture

DATE DUE

NOV 10 2001			